HUMAN FREEDOM AND ENVIRONMENT
(Contemporary Paradigms and Moral Strategies)

HUMAN FREEDOM AND ENVIRONMENT

(Contemporary Paradigms and Moral Strategies)

Edited by

Indoo Pandey Khanduri

KALPAZ

Human Freedom and Environment

Rs. 750

ISBN: 978-81-7835-814-7

Published in 2010 in India by
Kalpaz Publications
C-30, Satyawati Nagar,
Delhi-110052
E-mail: kalpaz@hotmail.com
Phone : 9212729499

Lasser Type Setting by: Quick Media, Delhi
Printed at : Chawla Offset Printers, Delhi

Contents

Preface

The contemporary scenario of environmental crisis has attracted the attention of moral philosophers to review the notion of freedom of man in terms of actions those are detrimental to environment as a whole. The conscious man, being the only rational being in the entire cosmos, has the freedom to choose the action. The Nature as a whole has its own course of Rules to direct the functioning of the entire cosmos and it determines the physical nature of environment. Since Human being is only rational creature thus he can think, he can choose and act accordingly. This constitutes the crux of his freedom. But being a rational being, he may act according to laws of nature and establish a harmony and coordination or he may exercise his rational power to change the course of Nature in his favor. The kind of environmental crisis, we are encountered with today exhibits man's freedom to think, to choose and to act has been guided by his attempts to mold nature by violating its laws.

The ground reality of environmental crisis has threatened not only freedom of man rather the existence itself. The ancient Greek theory of Socrates' *the virtue is single, the virtue is knowledge and no one does wrong deliberately* has been challenged by the man's exercise of his freedom to interfere and distort the nature and environment and face the threat. This is so because one can clearly see that during last several decades the environmental issue is being addressed through policy formulation, awareness and extension programs but deterioration speed has not been checked and controlled. This is evident through the launching of programs like Kyoto Protocol and declaration of International Year of Planet Earth. All the programs, launched to save the environment, accept in one voice that it is undue interference of human beings which has led to this piquant problem but studies on humans' detrimental actions and root causes in terms of the analysis of his nature has been hardly taken up. Thus, the root of problems is yet to be addressed. This requires the understanding of human nature, his freedom and attitude towards the environment. This is necessary because the understanding of human nature is vital for molding the human nature to develop a care, concern coordination and harmony with environment.

Here come some of the prominent questions. A balance moral theory of assessing the causes and implications of human actions presupposes that human beings have and use both rationality and emotions for taking a decision for particular actions and an imposed situation of care and concern may curtail his emotional freedom to fulfil his desires. The pertinent questions are: is there any moral conflict in maintaining and accepting the law of nature willingly or unwillingly? If human being is the integral part of the entire cosmos and in the condition of imposed proposition to abide by the laws of nature, how far is he free? What is the difference between impulsive and motivated anarchism and real human freedom clubbed with responsibility? Is respecting the laws of nature a curve and curtail of human freedom in essence or is the harmony, sustainability, concern and care are the real strengthening value to realize the essence of freedom? The important role of philosophy in general and ethics in particular lies in clarifying the concepts like development, sustainability, harmony and relating it to the freedom and responsibility. The interpretation of the terms needs a paradigm shift in approach and attitude for the concentrations is not focused on describing the relation between two conscious being but it is more focused on discussing the relation between Man and Nature, in other words between conscious living being and living but non-rational being as well as non-living beings. It invited the attention of thinkers to have innovative vision for interpreting eco-values like sustainability, development, harmony, care and concern from moral perspectives. The concepts are widely available in Indian texts for example- Veda, Upnishad, Samkhy-Yoga, Vaiseshika and Budhism- Jaininsm; in western tradition- sustainability- in Plato –Aristotle, durability in rationalist thinkers, moral imperatives in Kant's philosophy may provide the guiding lines.

It must be made clear that there are some problems which cannot be addressed by a single traditional subject but require interdisciplinary approaches for a better understanding and solutions. Environmental crisis is one of such critical problems which though involves the knowledge of scientific and technical aspects but cannot be addressed without involving society, its socio-economic conditions and guiding moral principles. Actually the environmental degradation in terms of pollution, deforestations, and natural resource exploitations cannot be resolved without molding the attitude and behavior of human beings. This is important for the reason because all the environmental havocs are the result of misuse of techno-scientific knowledge and unrestricted exploitation of resources by the human beings. The increasing greed for instant prosperity and self-centered dominating attitude of human is also responsible for this problem. Since the root of the problems lies in human behavior, thus the solution could also be sought through rectifying the human behavior in which environmental ethics has to play a vital role by reformulating its ideals and value- oriented understanding of environmental issues to mold human behavior in favor of environment in terms of respect, protect and conserve the environment. As India has a rich tradition of respecting nature and environment which is depicted through its philosophy, religious scripture, cultural traditions and thoughts, there is a need to understand the Indian values and reformulate it to address environmental problems and compare it with western theories of environmental ethics. So that it becomes easier to evolve some strategies for promoting moral conscience for environment. It is with this end in the mind that the present book is being designed. It has focused attention on addressing the problems and strategic solution which could be provided by the philosophical discourse.

It is the most appropriate opportunity for me to records my deep sense of gratitude to Indian Council of Philosophical Research, New Delhi for providing the financial assistance to organize the seminar which enabled me to collect the quality research papers by the eminent scholars. I also wish to express my thanks to the HNB Garhwal University cell of University Grants Commission, New Delhi for contributing its share of financial assistance for the seminar. But my task of recording thanks and gratitude would remain incomplete, unless and until I thank and express my deep sense of gratitude to Uttarakhand State Council for Science and Technology, Dehradun, for providing assistance for the seminar in general and for providing fund for the publication of this book.

It is the most appropriate place to record my deep respect to Professor JP Shukla, the Ex- Vice-chancellor of RDVV University, Jabalpur, Professor Sabhajeet Mishra, the ex- pro-vice-chancellor of DDU University, Gorakhpur and Prof. RL Singh for their movtivation to go further in the academic analysis and developing a sense of evalution and critical assessment. Besides, I wish to express my heartfelt thanks to the teachers of Philosophy from various Universities in general and contributors in particular, who inculcated interest and understanding of philosophical arguments and implications of arguments. I would also like to express my deep sense of thanks and gratitude to Prof. SK Singh, the Vice-chancellor, of the University for encouragement and support to take up the academic activities. I also wish to record my thanks to my colleagues, research scholars and students for their co-operation for this work.

The individual authors of the research papers will be responsible for the view expressed and the reference cited. But I owe the responsibility of the unnoticed errors, if it is left in the editing work.

I also wish to express my thanks and gratitude to the Kalpaz Publication for the timely publication of this book.

Indoo Pandey Khanduri
Department of Philosophy
HNB Garhwal University
Srinagar (Garhwal)
Uttarakhand.

Introduction

In view of the grim scenario of environmental crisis, the debate on how to promote an awareness and sensitized the moral concerns through environmental ethics has become a global concern. The recent report by UN Commission for Environment and The World Commission on the Ethics of Scientific Knowledge and Technology (COMEST) have indicated that if serious steps are not taken immediately, the humanity is going to suffer immensely. No doubt, the efforts for the moral provocation started back in 1960 with publication of *The Silent Spring,* and sound theoretical formulations in the field of environmental ethics such as anthropocentric, bio-centric and eco-centric approaches and shallow ecology, deep ecology and ecological humanism kept on going on. But there has been a gap between theoretical deliberations for the purpose of analysis and formulating strategies in terms of understanding how the theoretical ideologies are applicable on the ground level for harmony, sustainability and conservation of environmental entities through recognizing its intrinsic value. Philosophy requires formulating strategies to bridge the gap between theory and practice. The contributors of the research papers, in this book, have attempted to explore the strategies to explicate the meaning of human freedom with reference to environmental issues. It is meant to provide moral ways to mold human behavior in favor of natural entities. The strategies have been explored from moral, social, economic, scientific, and technical perspectives to address the environmental crisis faced by human race.

Prof. Ashok Vohra, in his paper, **has** explained the meaning of environment in its **multiple** uses and explored that the best could be understood in three dimensions *i.e.* we live *from* it; we live *in* it; and we live *with* it. While carrying on the discussion on the instrumental and intrinsic value of natural entities, he exposed the culture of consumerism and contradiction of Dam construction. In his view environmental tragedies like the species loss cannot be measured in monetary terms. "You can't put a price on the environment. You can't put a price on what you are going to leave for your children's children . . . It's a heritage. It's not an open cattle market." The way we treat the natural world reveals our attitude to those from whom we inherited it as well as towards those who will follow us. We have a spiritual bondage with them. This relationship is incompatible and incommensurable with the market relations. To confuse them would be making a category mistake. In such a relationship the guiding maxim is not cost benefit perspective, or trade-off, rather it is an attitude of reverence. As a strategy, he has suggested to overcome the greed and fulfil the need. For this purpose, he gives the reference of Gandhi, Gita and time tested suggestion of Yoga Darshan.

Prof. YV Satyanarayna, in his research paper, focuses his attention on environmental issues and stated that these issues are closely connected to man's relation to nature, especially man's relation with the environment. Unless we understand clearly the relation between man and nature, it may not be possible to find a plausible solution to environmental issues confronting man, or threatening the human survival. He explained the relation of Man with nature, under Nature and over Nature. He raised several questions regarding controlling pollution, moral obligation, right and responsibility. He explained the contemporary problem, attitude and approach. While discussing the impact of religious commitment and development of scientific temperament, he highlighted the fundamental content of anthropocentric and eco-centric moral theories and suggested that just as a bee extracts honey from a flower without causing harm to the fragrance, or to the beauty of that flower, so also humans must learn to extract things from nature, without inflicting damage, or causing harm to the natural world.

Prof. Dilipkumar Mohanta has asserted that the Ethical approach of Buddhism towards Nature is similar to the **Deep Ecological Concern** of the Environmental Philosophy of today. The ethical teachings of Buddhism ask us to purify the mind to control our desire. It observes that being greedy human beings want to take as much as they can from the earth and from others to satisfy their immediate wants without consideration for the future. **Any kind of devaluation of other creatures and rating them in lower levels than human beings, empathetically disconnect us from the harmonious principle of nature and lead us to do harm to others as well as to ourselves.** It is this moral dimension of ecological problems which may be addressed from the ethical perspective of Buddhism. This paper is a thorough investgation in this direction.

Prof. SE Bhelke starts his paper with assertion that most of the problems before man are rooted either in his understanding or in his action. He himself has solutions to them. When he knows himself and the world in a right way, he does not face problems. But what is meant by a right way? Is it a fact that man is free, but in what way does he understand his freedom and exercises it when he interacts with others and the world? The reason, he goes astray from the right way, again, is located in his nature. Where he has to regulate and moderate the way in which his freedom will neither turn off to be self-annihilating nor destroying the nature. The present crisis of environmental issues needs to be understood in the right way of his freedom and natural inclinations which tend to make any directions due to freedom. If there are problems before men, he is responsible to them and he has to solve them by himself. If man is cause of the problems, he has a capacity to solve them whether it is an epistemological problem or an axiological problem or a logical problem or a scientific problem. Protagoras placed man at the centre of the world as the knower and as a moral agent. Does this doctrine issue unrestricted licences to interact with nature? The freedom of man is to be understood in the light of his nature on the one hand and his place in the cosmos on the other hand. Secondly, is freedom a condition of morality of a license to be immoral? All these questions need to be answered philosophically. The present paper is discussing some of these issues to get a fresh outlook in the matters of environmental crisis of which man is the responsible agent.

Tarique Islam viewed the problems from the theoretical perspective of dualism. He asserts that the ecological crisis and the ensuing debate is the result of what has been lucidly and aptly portrayed by Carson as "The 'control of nature' is a phrase conceived in arrogance, born of the Neanderthal age of biology and philosophy, when it was supposed that nature existed for the convenience of man". The notion of nature revolves around the 'philosophy of man' in Western thought. The Cartesian dualism of the physical and the non-physical, with emphasis on the latter sealed the fate of nature. The question of identity in the Cartesian framework depended entirely on non-physical aspects of man. This brought the great divide between nature and man, with man being very different from nature and nature being the 'other'. This reflected the broad Judeo-Christian view of the great 'Chain of Being' with its emphasis on a hierarchy within nature with man at the top with the privilege of using nature, the 'other', to its advantage, which became the predominant 'philosophy of man' in Western thought. Nature then, as part of the 'Chain of Being', appeared in Western thought as the 'other' to be dominated. The will to overpower or tame nature became urgent and more emphatic with the fast growing capitalist society structured around the general dual principle of exploitation and domination.

The non-Western thought was not quite as impacting on environment as the Western with its advances in

Sciences and development of technology, which became primarily the tool to dominate physical nature. Most of the non-Western thought was more integrated with nature and its 'philosophy of man' did not galvanize around the hierarchical structures of being. However, the most commonly held views, now-a-days; whether one likes it or not, are those arising out of Western metaphysics and these form the contemporary thought on environment. By this the author does not deny the importance of non-Western thought but simply suggest that environment has been brought into focus by two different principles operating simultaneously. The domination of nature and thereby deep exploratory concern with it, both are the products of Western Judeo-Christian outlook. The paper will be a modest attempt to historically trace out the treatment of nature as the 'other' and attempt an analysis of the result of such a treatment. The paper will conclude by attempting an alternative that may go some way towards achieving an understanding.

Prof. Mridula Ravi Prakash reflected in her paper that the present modern society whether national or international has enough resources and technology to ensure for every human being on earth. The physical, intellectual, material, and spiritual inputs are necessary for full and healthy life but on the other hand surely the poison is also spread upon us. It is in this chilling context that the necessity for an alternative philosophy of life becomes so intense and because of the universal values that it enshrines, the Vedanta represents precisely such an integrated and universal philosophy. Vedanta is basically based upon the great source of knowledge the Upnishads and the Bhagvatgita, a testimony to the magnificent spiritual endeavour to solve the problems of present society. It provides insights which can have crucial value for the survival of humanity in this nuclear age. The basic principles of Vedanta provide the framework for a Philosophy to sustain the emerging global consciousness on our planet.

Prof. Asha Mudgil focuses her attention on elaborating the fact that pollution and the depletion of natural resources have not been the only environmental concerns since long time: dwindling plant and animal biodiversity, the loss of wilderness, the degradation of ecosystems, and climate change are all part of a raft of "green" issues that have implanted themselves into both public consciousness and public policy over subsequent years. The job of environmental ethics is to outline our moral obligations in the face of such concerns. In a nutshell, the two fundamental questions that environmental ethics must address are: what duties do humans have with respect to the environment, and why? The latter question usually needs to be considered prior to the former. In order to tackle just what our obligations are, it is usually thought necessary to consider first *why* we have them. For example, do we have environmental obligations for the sake of human beings living in the world today, for humans living in the future, or for the sake of entities within the environment itself, irrespective of any human benefits? Different philosophers have given quite different answers to this fundamental question which, as we shall see, has led to the emergence of quite different environmental ethics.

Prof. DN Yadav finds that there is a spectrum of perceived proceedings from that we have two main types of concepts in Environmental Ethics: (1) Anthropocentric-which is entirely restricted to humanity meaning thereby human centered value, thoroughly (2) Ecocentric -meaning thereby earth-centered value. It follows then, that we must concentrate increasingly on the latter as we proceed through that spectrum, looking at the strengths of each major position on it, but also with limitations that point to the need for a more eco-centric alternative. However, let it be made clear that ecological ethics is not intended to replace traditional human centered ethics- which has a perfectly legitimate and important role in intra-human relationships or its extension to say, animals and other non-human living beings. Therefore, we cannot prefer either of the value to other; rather we should have to deal with both the nature of value i.e. eco-centric through the anthropocentric and the vice-versa or anthropocentric cum eco-centric nature of value.

Bharat Jhunjhunwala's paper starts with presupposition that man has higher degree of freedom than other living beings. It is man's solemn responsibility to exercise his freedom in a way that leads to evolution of his consciousness. Man is part of Brahman, hence evolution of his consciousness spontaneously becomes evolution of Brahman. There is a caveat, however. Man's consciousness can evolve in two ways: Evolution: While helping others in raising of their consciousness. Devolution: While hitting at others and reducing their level of consciousness. Apart from this, he opines that there seems to be a difference between Asuras and Devtas. Both are *bhogi.* But Asuras undertake bhoga while hitting at others while devtas undertake bhoga by helping others evolve along with. Cutting of a forest for making charcoal may be done both by Asuras and Devtas. The Asuras will cut the forest and leave the land barren. Devtas will cultivate the land and grow wheat and paddy. Thus, Rig Veda mentions cutting of forests in a positive sense: The author explains his thesis of decreasing or increasing level of conscious through an empirical study on the water flow used for the project of Hydro-electric power.

According to **Sanjay Singh Mahar & Prof. SC Bagri** mass tourism has been widely exploited as a development tool, resulting in numerous negative impacts. Present study area is an example of many ecotourism destinations in Uttarakhand where community development is strongly empowered and action-oriented, an allevation of mass tourism. Local people have started banking upon the rich reservoir of Dodital Lake, where hundreds of thousands of tourists throng every year. Village Development Committees have been formed and a best route is charted out to sell Dodital on a sustainable basis. Various settlements of villagers' en route Dodital have been entrusted with a separated task to educate tourists' on environmental issues besides letting them feel the serenity of Dodital and surrounding area. Main components of ecotourism like nature-based, education, and sustainability, includes ethical and conservation principles where guest-host relationship needs to be trustworthy lest it reaches the zenith of extinction. Thus, it also investigates the importance of local population to preserve the natural resources having positive views.

Dr. RK Maikhur et al reflect the fact that when the Man and Biosphere (MAB) program was launched in 1971 by UNESCO, a natural consequence of it was to have Biosphere reserves which can preserve and generate natural and cultural values, through management that is scientifically correct, culturally creative and operationally sustainable. The biosphere reserves were established and developed to fulfill the objectives such as a) conservation of biodiversity, b) research, monitoring, training and education, and c) socio-economic development of local communities living in and around reserve. These objectives are associated together through a some degree of zonation system consisting of a core zone, buffer zone and transition zone. Though, ideally, the core zone is left free of human influence, in reality in India and many Asian regions, even the core zone may not be free from human interaction, though at a reduced level. The buffer zone and a transition zone surrounded by the human population usually involved in conservation linked with sustainable development. The world network of biosphere reserves, as implemented through the Seville Strategy, is thus an integrating tool which can help to create greater solidarity among peoples and nations of the world (UNESCO, 1995) for linking conservation with sustainable development.

According to **Dr. Kanchan Saxena** environment decay poses serious problems for contemporary society– problem, which did not arise for our ancestors. Before the advent of industrial technology and its mixed blessings, drinkable water and breathable air were thought to be virtually limitless. Before the consumption habits underlying our standard of living had taken root such natural resources as coal and oil were thought to be inexhaustible. It is now widely accepted that such beliefs, however defensible in their own time, are no longer defensible in the contemporary world. As a result, we find ourselves confronted with ethical questions in regard to environmental conservation.

The central ethical question with regard to ecological concern might be phrased as follows "To what extent, if at all, are we normally obliged to end present practices which in effect serve to pollute the environment and /or to decimate its resources?" In attempting to answer this question, we will have to take note not only of the needs and interests of the presently existing human community but also of the needs and interests of the posterity

Dr. Indoo Pandey Khanduri, in her paper, attempts to search some moral ways to maintain the balance between the economic growth and environmental protection through the guidelines of environmental ethics. For the above purpose, this paper has been divided in three parts. The first part will try to answer the question whether economic growth is detrimental to environmental cause? It will also try to present the brief description of environmental deterioration, attempts to check it, obstruction seems to be grasped at the fronts of economic growth and the connections and relations between the two have been underlined. In the second part it will try to see consequences of economic values preference with reference to environmental cause and in third part of the present paper the author tries to discuss the Indian and Western ways of sustainable development to maintain a balance between the two. In the concluding remarks it attempts to examine the moral strategies meant for maintaining balance between the economic growth and environmental protection which are suitable for the present scenario.

Dr. Beena Sakalani in her paper states that environmental crisis is a serious issue for Uttarakhand Himalayas and more so for its most primitive indigenous community like Bhuksas. This tribe is showing signs of deep distress and panic in a fast changing world where they feel incapable of coping with changing times and insecure to survive and protect their identity and culture. Their fear is that 'we will not last long as a tribe and be lost for ever by next generation'. Land alienation in the hands of new migrants after Indian independence and now due to the pressures of new industrial economy, growing urbanization, has increased and compounded new stresses related to their survival, growth and development. Identity crisis has generated feeling of self depreciation and low self esteem due to their feelings of failing, and incapability to adjust with the fast changing times . Sense of dejection and apathy towards manual work has accentuated habits of drinking, which has emerged as a major cause of degeneration of the tribe as a whole .Low self confidence in their capacity and culture has become real cause of concern. There is a sense of panic looming in their eyes as they find themselves helpless and incapable in coping with dominant culture and new economy which is engulfing and riding rough shod over their traditional modes of subsistence and way of life. Once upon a time (pun intended), primary aim and objective of our intellectual life was Brahma- Gyana and today Profit-Gyana is the Vedanta of our times. Dilemma generated by demands of materialism and sustainability of human civilization and its ultimate destiny is one of the basic intellectual poser and challenge before the civil society, today.

Dr. Nitish Dubey raised the question whether Indian religious and philosophical traditions embody an ancient environmental ethic has been debated by environmental philosophers. From the time environmental ethics was becoming established as an academic discipline. The present paper is an attempt to look at Indian tradition not as a resource for western environmental philosophy, but to appreciate the manner in which environmental sensibilities and consciousness is found in the Indian tradition. The concern for the environment is grounded in the value that human beings ascribe to nature itself. In our Indian philosophical tradition, we treat Nature not as inanimate and dead matter, but as animate and living capable of sentience and consciousness. Nature is perceived as a manifestation of the same Divine Spirit which manifests itself as man. *SarvaÆ Khalu IdaÆ Brahma* (All is Brahman). All existence – earth, heavens, planets, gods, living and non-living objects – is conceived here as the parts of One Great Person (*Puru¿a*) Who pervades the world, but also remains beyond it. Man and Nature (in fact, all living and non-living beings) are parts of the Divine Spirit and they remain inseparable *(aveda)* from It.

Dr. DC Srivastva in his paper finds that while responding to the growing global environmental crisis, scholars have begun to interrogate religious traditions as a possible resource for the development of an environmental ethic. At one end of the spectrum are apologists who see the world's religions as a key resource in addressing the environmental crisis; at the other, critics point to religion as redounding to the crisis. In his controversial 1967 article on Christianity and the environment, Lynn White commends Buddhism for its holistic, egalitarian worldview, and an environmentally friendly style of life in contrast to the Biblical worldview and mainstream Christianity that White sees as promoting human dominance over nature and, hence, contributing to the environmental crisis. White's positive evaluation of Buddhism's eco-friendly worldview has been promoted by Buddhists and scholars of Buddhism in Asia and the West. My purpose in this paper is to assess and evaluate a selection of contributions to the field of Buddhism and ecology. My analysis here is intended to highlight what I construe as four sometimes overlapping positions regarding Buddhism and the environment. I have labeled this four-fold taxonomy: *eco-apologists, eco-critics, eco-constructivists, and eco-ethicists.* I hasten to add that these categories are intended to be suggestive rather than definitive, and that I intend them primarily for heuristic purposes.

Dr. Shiva Bhanu Singh in his discussion opines, besides display of marvelous remarkable technological knowledge and spectacular changes in our living environment in the last century, the whole world is presently facing ecological imbalance and environmental degradation, the rising awareness and movement of environmentalism and eco-friendliness are direct reflection of our candid confession of our folly and insensitivity. It is very unfortunate that the most rational and intelligent species on earth lives such an eco-unfriendly life on it. Contemporary western ecologists have made a distinction between surface ecology and deep ecology and have pleaded for accepting the intrinsic value of even non-human beings and the whole natural world. Norwegian philosopher Arne Naess and Aldo Leopold have developed an environmental ethics that shows the inter-dependence of the whole system of biosphere and ecosphere. Here we are reminded of the classical Indian philosophical vision of the ultimate unity of each thing as propounded in Sankhya, Advaita Vedanta and Buddhism. In this paper an interesting comparison has been made between Indian Cosmo centric view and Western deep ecological viewpoint.The paper attempts to analyze the different views regarding environment and the attitudinal problems pertaining to the same. The man-environment partite is questioned and the requirement for inculcating an integral view about man-nature relation is emphasized. In the present paper, the main consideration is laid upon understanding human quest for freedom. The Indian views on liberation are emulated so as to better depict the integrity of man-nature relation. It is also advocated that liberation is neither a myth nor a hypothetical state of existence. The quest for liberation effectively transforms man's attitude towards nature and the entire conflict between human freedom and environment vanishes.

Dr. Kiran Dangwal, in her the research paper, gives the picture of women participation for saving the environment in Himalyan region. The paper narrates the mesmerizing beauty and its vital importance in determining the entire climatic conditions of the Globe. Since, women in Himalyan region are directly related to forest and other entities of environment like water and hills; they have natural affinity to the entire environment. The paper provides women role and active participation in internationally acknowledge Cipako Movement of Raini, and Gopeshwar to save trees.. Further, they saved the trees in Bhyundar valley in January 1978 which was to be felling for Badrinath temple. On February 25th , 1978, the auction of the trees of Damargarh was stopped due to the threat of Chipko by women. Similarly, the marking of the trees in three places of the Chamoli district was stopped on 25th January, 1979. It was 12 th August, 1979 the Bhotiyas of Parsari village saved the trees of their village from felling by taking the help of Chipako movement. After this Chipako movements or threat of such movement saved the trees. Women of Dungari –Paintoli threatened Horticulture department to launch Chipako movement to save their forest and were successful. The Government in March, 1980 in view of the recommendations of the high power committee put the ban on cutting the forests. Later on; the Chipako movement also covered other aspects related to forest conservation. The women have also shown their active participation in other environmental movement like Maiti, Save the Seeds, Save the Ganga, Anti Dams and other movements. Mahila Mangal Dal has also been actively participating in the movements related to the issues of environmental conservation and awareness. The hill women also have taken up the issues related to make a healthy social environment. They have been actively not only participating but also leading such movements.

Dr. Abha Singh has discussed in her research paper that the man, in his endeavour enjoys unbridled freedom, and has reached to somewhat perverse state of mind. His consciousness and action have been shaped by the commands and imperatives of how to manipulate nature to his advantage, often with disastrous consequences. Action without reflection is blind, while reflection without action is impotent. Unguided and un-illumined action frequently leads to destruction. On the other hand, one should also be aware that so much abstract thought consists of merely scholastic exercises, which help nobody and only exhaust the mind. What is needed today is to make a balance in thought and deed. Such balance one finds in the philosophy of ecology. A deep study of the philosophy of ecology shows that it is reverence in action. It is a deep identification with the beauty of life pulsating through the universe until we become part of it. Its central spiritual tenet is that the human species is a part of the Earth and not separate from it. A process of self-realization would help an individual to intuitively gain an eco-centric perspective. The notion is based on the idea that the more we *expand the self* to identify with "others" (people, animals, ecosystems), the more we realize ourselves.

Dr. Suraj Bahadur Thapa in his paper discusses the strategies from the literary work in general and Hindi poetry in particular. He states that the desire to have a very fast rate of economic growth in the developing economies, as well as, the concerns of the developed nations to keep maintained their status quo, have eventually shown a sheer lack of prudence and profligacy in the use of natural resources of the world. As a result the earth which is the only habitat of human being in the universe is facing the menace of its existence. In order to save the earth, the developed countries want to impose several precautionary measures in the form of different restrictions on the industrialization of the developing economies and on the other hand, the developing economies have argued in favour of their right to economic growth. According to them, the turn to sacrifice now comes in part of developed countries because the people of other countries have yet to grow up to the required level of life and from this point of view they need development in true sense. This world wide debate has divided the world and has shown the self centered hunger for growth of the human being it self. No doubt this clash of opinions has weakened the united efforts of the whole world to control the unbalanced exploitation of the natural resources. Here one may ask on what cost we want development. The time has come when we shall have to retrace the meaning of development. Only material prosperity or gain will not work. Along with economic development we need to preserve and develop human values and sensibility to our eco-system too. Matthew Arnold had severely criticized the most prosperous and rich English Society of the Victorian Age in his famous book **'Culture and Anarchy'** (1869) because it lacked **'sweetness'** (sensitivity and love for morality) and **'light'** (The real understanding of life). In the field of Hindi literature a lot of poets, fiction writers, and critics have shown utmost emphasis on the very close relationship between man and nature because nature has the unique power of keeping human being in its non-artificial natural form of life. Hence man will be safe if the earth and its environment remain safe. Hindi literature depicts the several ways with the help of which we can develop many moral and ethical values inside our soul for the nature and our environment. Having left the notion of aggression towards nature, man will have to grow eco-friendly attitude for it in order to save his existence. Man must get rid off its arbitrary kind of freedom. He should keep faith on the principle of 'live and let live'.

Dr. Seema Srivastava and **Dr. Ambuj Srivastava** have analyzed the problem of environmental crisis from the historical point of view from the 20th century. The paper deals with the different dimensions environmental problems like; global warming, Acid Rain, Ozone Depletion, Extinct of Different Species of Plants & Animals, Climatic Change. After explaining the different dimensions of environmental crisis, the researchers put a list of programs taken up to address the environmental problems during the twentieth and twenty first century at national and International fronts. The paper deals with the notion of sustainability and tries to explore the strategies to address environmental crisis from the instructions available in Vedas and indigenous day to day practice of people in India, be it religious practice or social. The paper gets concluded with assertion that concentration, self control, patience, middle path, purgation of consciousness under which education is given to win over kama, krodh and lobh-moh hinsha and to ensure pity, generosity, non-violence, sacrifice, non-stealing (asteya) not being greedy (aprigraha). These qualities are developed among the Human Beings. These qualities teach us to behave equally with nature and to all creatures as well as Human Beings. This means as violence against human being is considered to be a sin. Similarly, violence against Humanism can ensure the protection and preservation of environmental pollution or Ecosystem or else we are facing mass destruction.

Dr. Varun Tripathi in his paper attempts to analyze the different views regarding environment and the attitudinal problems pertaining to the same. The man-environment partite is questioned and the requirement for inculcating an integral view about man-nature relation is emphasized. The attitudinal difficulties arise precisely because of the segmented view regarding man and nature. Nature is treated as 'other'. The segmentation in views is an off-shoot of the constricted understanding of freedom i.e. when we take up human freedom in terms of individual freedom. Freedom is evaluated in terms of fulfillment of our needs, our rights and sometime our lusts. This results into treating nature as an object. At conceptual level, the treatment of nature as non-rational or non-living being is also a kind of attitudinal problem. The classification into rational and non-rational produces 'othernesses and a gap between human reality and what is taken as external-material reality. The contemporary eco-values like sustainability, development etc. are apparent values which are founded in presupposing a division between man and nature.

In the present paper, the main consideration is laid upon understanding human quest for freedom. The Indian views on liberation are emulated so as to better depict the integrity of man-nature relation. It is also advocated that liberation is neither a myth nor a hypothetical state of existence. The quest for liberation effectively transforms man's attitude towards nature and the entire conflict between human freedom and environment vanishes.

Dr. Alok Tondan in his paper states that too often, the compatibility of sustainability and economic growth is taken for granted and the issue of sustainable development is perceived as seeking a compromise with being natural environment and pursuit of economic growth. This perception of the problem as mere technical, prevent critical reflection on the frame of reference in which the problem formulation originates. But, if the notion of subtlety, is to be taken seriously, the conflict of conceptual and normative orientations between the two concepts require the consideration of our frame of reference. An analysis of both, the versions of sustainability, conservative and radical, suggests that only a radical approach can relieve the acute tension between Individual autonomy and wider social ecological good. This calls for rethinking about human well being and poses a strong challenge to the market ethics, dominant in modern liberal democracy. The challenge can be met only while addressing to radical social transformation.

In the view of **Kavita Bhatt,** the present crisis of environmental degradation is the result of greedy nature of Man and consequently high level of exploitation of nature. The greedy tendency of human being leads towards undue damage to the natural entities and the degradation of the biodiversity- created by various species. Our anarchist activities and high consumption of nature are the root causes of the imbalance of eco-system, which resulted as the destruction of whole organism. The eco-system imbalance has reached up to the point that one should be careful not only for oneself but whole bio-diversity to maintain eco-system for universal balance of environment. The present paper is an attempt to review the fundamental cause of the degradation of biodiversity with reference to human greed which leads him towards the exploitation of Nature and creating violence to the species other than human being. Violence could be countered only by inculcation of the moral values based on the theory of non-violence. In the present scenario, the writer reflects the need of a strong strategy for the protection and balance of bio-diversity for prosperous eco-system; definitely it will be an essential step towards healthy environment. From this point of view Jain Model of *Ahimsa* is the most ideal model and thus she focuses her attention on describing the importance of *Ahimsa* with reference to the conservation of biodiversity.

But, before taking up the strategy to protect bio-diversity, it is necessary to know the concept of bio-diversity in its technical sense and then, understand the concept of *Ahimsa* for the conservation of it. To know the role of Ahimsa in field of the conservation of bio-diversity it is essential to know what bio-diversity is. And, what are the root causes of degradation? It tries to answer the above questions in the first part of the present paper. After that the author attempts try to examine the *Ahimsa* (non-violence) according to Jainism, in the second part of the paper. Then, it has attempted to ascertain a strategy for the conservation of bio-diversity.

List of Contributors

1. *Prof. Ashok Vohra,* Head, Department of Philosophy, University of Delhi, Delhi.
2. *Prof. YV Satyanarayana*, Department of Philosophy, Andhra University, Vishakhapatnam, A.P.
3. *Prof. Dilipkumar Mohanta,* Department of Philosophy, University of Calacatta, Kolkata.
4. *Tarique Islam,* Department of Philosophy, Aligarh Muslim University, Aligarh, UP.
5. *Prof. SE Bhelke,* Department of Philosophy, University of Pune, Pune.
6. *Prof. Mridula Ravi Prakash,* Department of Philosophy, University of Allahabad, Allahabad, U.P.
7. *Prof. Asha Mudgil,* Department of philosophy, Panjab University, Chandigarh.
8. *Prof. DN Yadav,* Department of Philosophy, University of Gorakhapur, U.P.
9. *Bharat Jhunjhunwal*, Freelance Journalist, Maletha, Tehri, Uttarakhand.
10. *Sanjay Singh Mahar* and *Prof. SC Bagri,* Centre of Mountain Tourism, HNB Garhwal University, Srinagar (Garhwal) Uttarakhand.
11. *Dr. RK Maikhuri,* G.B. Pant Institute of Himalayan Environment and Development, Garhwal Unit, Srinagar (Garhwal), Uttarakhand.
12. *Dr. Kanchan Saxena,* Department of Philosophy, University of Lucknow, Lucknow, U.P.
13. *Dr. Indoo Pandey Khanduri,* Department of Philosophy, HNB Garhwal University, Srinagar (Garhwal) Uttarakhand.

14. *Dr. Beena Sakalani,* Department of Anthropology, HNB Garhwal University, Srinagar (Garhwal) Uttarakhand.
15. *Dr. Nitish Dubey,* PG & Research Department of Philosophy, DAV College, C.S.J.M. University, Kanpur, U.P.
16. *Dr. DC Srivastva,* Head, Department of Philosophy, Christ Church College, C.S.J.M. University, Kanpur, U.P.
17. *Dr. Shiva Bhanu Singh,* Head, Philosophy Department, Ewing Christian College, Allahabad (An Autonomous Constituent College of Allahabad University), U.P.
18. *Dr. Kiran Dangwal,* Department of Sociology, HNB Garhwal University, Srinagar (Garhwal) Uttarakhand.
19. *Dr. Abha Singh,* Head, Department of Philosophy, B.S. College, Danapur, Patna, Bihar.
20. *Dr. Suraj Bahadur Thapa,* Department of Hindi, University of Lucknow, Lucknow, U.P.
21. *Dr. Seema Srivastava,* Agastyamuni PG College, Agastyamuni, Rudraprayag, Uttarakhand and Dr. Ambuj Srivastava.
22. *Dr. Varun Tripathi,* School of Philosophy and Culture, Shri Mata Vaishno Devi University, Katra, J&K.
23. *Dr. Alok Tondan*, 53, Asharaf Tola, Hardoi, U.P.
24. *Ms. Kavita Bhatt,* Project Fellow, Department of Philosophy, HNB Garhwal University, Srinagar (Garhwal) Uttarakhand.

1

MAN AND ENVIRONMENT

Prof. Ashok Vohra

The word 'environment' is a noun and is used in two senses. In the first sense, it means 'the natural world', 'nature', 'the earth, 'the ecosystem', 'and the biosphere'. In this sense, it refers to rivers and forests, mountains and hills, seas, vallies wastelands, deserts, wilderness and wildlife, flora and fauna, man and the Mother Nature, cities and villages etc. In this sense it is something *given* to us. In the second sense it means 'situation', 'setting', 'milieu', 'background', 'backdrop', 'context', 'conditions', 'ambience', 'atmosphere'. The usage of the term environment in this sense refers to a variety of places, processes and things. In this sense, it is something which may be *given* to us but which we may manipulate or control either to our advantage or to our disadvantage.

A concern with the environment is imperative for us because we live *from* it; we live *in* it; and we live *with* it. By saying that we live *from* it we mean that it is a means to our existence in the sense that "we mine its resources; cultivate and harvest its fruits; shape the contours of the land for human habitation, roads, minerals and agriculture; dredge rivers for transport"[1]. By providing the raw material for all our economic and productive activities, the environment becomes the foundation of our economic life. Any change in the ecosystem directly effects "the health and the life chances of citizens and (has a bearing on) the productivity of agriculture, forests, and fisheries" By saying 'we live *in* it' is meant that "the environment is not just a physical precondition for human life and productive activity; it is where humans (and other species) lead their lives. Environment matters to us for social, aesthetic and cultural reasons"[2]. It is where our working life takes place and derives its significance. It is where our individual and collective histories are made and embodied. It is where besides work we indulge in leisure walking, fishing climbing, swimming, playing etc. The environment – forests, beaches, rivers, seas and mountains – provide us the backdrop for each of these activities. In this sense, it has what economists call 'recreation value'.

We live *with* the environment in the sense that the environment existed prior to our arrival and shall outlast the last man on earth. It is given to us. We can only respond to it by expressing a feeling of awe and wonder towards it. It has an inherent value and any 'loss of bio-diversity, the disappearance of particular habitat and the extinction, local and global, of particular species of flora and fauna' is mourned for its own sake. The economists however term it as 'existence value'.

Even if one agrees with the economists in assigning asset or instrumental value to nature and environment, that is one regards them as goods and services, one has to take into account just and equitable distribution of the natural resources. Developmental activities like building of roads, laying of railway lines, construction of dams, power stations, dumps for toxic wastes etc. damages the quality of life of particular individual and community. The elites of the first and third world countries may benefit from an increase in the production of green house gases but the lives of the marginalised and the poor are adversely affected by the costs involved. In the case of renewable resources one may find a method to compensate the affected parties and take steps to adequately replenish the resources. However, in the case of non-renewable resources such a compensation and renewal is not only impossible for the present generation but is more so for the future generations. The present generation will have exploited and consumed the non-renewable resources to the disadvantage of the future generations. Do we own no responsibility for the future generations?

The chief objection to economists' treating nature as a commodity or a consumer item– goods and/or services – to put a price on is that much social meaning, social relations and evaluative commitments are invested in our environment. These cannot be measured in monetary terms. This is illustrated by an actual reply to the letter written by the Chief Minister addressed to the inhabitants of the Narmada Valley facing eviction due to the construction of Sardar Sarovar Dam. The letter asked them for the quantum of compensation which they would consider adequate for vacating their lands, dwellings and villages. The reply goes as under:

You tell us to take compensation. What is the state compensating us for? For our land, for our fields, for the trees along the fields. But we don't live only by this. Are you going to compensate us for our forest? . . .Or are you going to compensate us for our great river – for her fish, for water, for vegetables that grow along her banks, for the joy of living beside her? What is the price of this? . . . How are you compensating us for fields either – we didn't buy this land; our forefathers cleared it and settled here. What price this land? Our gods, the support of those who are our kin – what price do you have for these? Our *adivasi* (tribal) life – what price do you put on it?[3]

One of the ways to express that we care for, cherish, or treasure, or are committed to a value is to refuse to put a price on it. In fact the whole idea of measuring the value of environment in material terms or in terms of satisfaction of preferences is a disgusting idea. Environmental tragedies like the species loss cannot be measured in monetary terms. "You can't put a price on the environment. You can't put a price on what you are going to leave for your children's children . . . It's a heritage. It's not an open cattle market"[4]. The way we treat the natural world reveals our attitude to those from whom we inherited it as well as towards those who will follow us. We have a spiritual bondage with them. This relationship is incompatible and incommensurable with the market relations. To confuse them would be making a category mistake.

In such a relationship the guiding maxim is not the cost benefit perspective, or trade-off, rather it is an attitude of reverence. Trade-off implies that we have lost the goods in question. Environment is not 'goods'. It is only in the case of goods or services that we talk of calculations and trade-offs. "Trade-off suggests that we compute the value of the alternative goods on whatever scale is at hand, whether cardinal or ordinal, precise or rough and ready. Sacrifice suggests precisely that we abstain from doing so. Devotion to the one exacts an uncalculated loss of the other"[5].

From the above discussion, we can conclude that environment does not have an extrinsic or instrumental value but has an intrinsic value in the sense that it has objective value as contrasted with subjective value. It has intrinsic value in the sense employed by Moore when he says, "To say a kind of value is 'intrinsic' means merely that a question whether a thing possesses it, and to what degree it possesses it, depends solely on the intrinsic nature of the thing in question"[6]. Stevenson[7] explains the notion of 'intrinsic value' thus: 'X is intrinsically good' asserts that the speaker approves of X intrinsically, and acts emotively to make the hearer or hearers likewise approve of X intrinsically. Environment or non-human world is not of value as a means to some human end. It is an end in itself. Arne Naess the founder of the notion of 'deep ecology' puts it thus: "The well being of non-human life on Earth has value in itself. This value is independent of any instrumental usefulness for limited human purposes"[8]. The implication of treating the environment as an end in itself is that it changes the focus of attention from an anthropocentric, egoist, purely humanist view of the world to a much broader 'biocentric' view which includes all living things. Flourishing and growth of the non-human things is good for the flourishing of the human beings themselves. The two cannot be separated. The two are identical. One cannot look at the non-human things as things made solely for his pleasures or profits or enjoyment. Our relationship with the non-human world is one of friendship. In friendship, which is a paradigm of meaningful relationship, we do not care for our friends or love them for the profits that we may draw from our association with them. Rather we care for them for their own sake. We should do the same with the non-human world we live in. Just as the spirit of friendship is humility and co-operation and not conquering, our relationships with the nature is also one of co-existence and not plunder. On this view "A thing is right when it tends to preserve the integrity, stability, and beauty of the biotic community. It is wrong when it tends otherwise"[9].

In fact the relationship between man and nature is as old as man. Man has always been concerned and thinking about nature. According to JS Mill, "'nature', and 'natural' and the group of words derived from them, or allied to them in etymology, have at all times filled a great place in the thoughts and taken a strong hold on the feelings of mankind"[10]. These feelings and attitude of mankind towards nature can be of two types. One, he can either be subservient to nature; two, he can reign nature. According to JS Mill though nature is both impressive and awe inspiring, yet its powers are hurtful, cruel, severe and at the most indifferent. He thinks that "The doctrine that the man ought to follow nature, or, in other words, ought to make the spontaneous course of things the model of his voluntary actions, is equally irrational and immoral"[11]. He therefore, pleads that 'man must wrest by force and ingenuity what little he can for his own use' to improve his own and humankind's condition and employ all his physical and intellectual powers to ward off natural calamities.

JS Mill's call for overcoming, conquering, overpowering, winning nature to man's advantage has, as we all know lead to the present dismal scenario in which not only is the environment but our own very existence is endangered. It has lead to a situation in which we have by our act of releasing carbon monoxide and other gasses in the atmosphere depleted the ozone layer and managed to alter the power of the sun, have increased its heat. "And that increase" according to Bill McKibben "could change the pattern of moisture and dryness, breed storms in new places, breed deserts. Those things may not have yet begun to happen, but it is too late to prevent them from happening. We have produced the carbon dioxide – we have ended nature. We have not ended rainfall or sunlight . . . But the *meaning* of the wind, the sun, the rain – of nature – has already changed". We have so to say 'instrumentalised' nature and in the process converted it into our hand maiden and destroyed its pristine glory. We have ruined the relationship of friendship and turned it into our foe. It is only after the nature has begun to strike back that we have realised our folly. We have started taking steps to protect nature from human incursion; make attempts to restore and tried our hand at restitution of natural features and enhancing biodiversity wherever possible.

Our existential situation vis-a-vis nature and environment has forced us to talk in terms of sustainability. The notion of sustainability has embedded in it three questions. These are: What is to be sustained? For whom, it is to be sustained and why? The answer to the former is that a certain level of human welfare is to be sustained. The answer to the second is that the aim of sustainability is the benefit of the present and future generations of human beings and to maximise welfare over time and to meet the demands of distributional justice between generations. From this it is clear that 'Sustainability' "implies something about maintaining the level of human well-being so that it might improve but at least never decline (or, not more than temporarily, anyway)"[12].

The question that arises now is: Why have we reached a situation where our very existence is in peril and we are forced to talk about sustainability and adopt sustainable models of development alone? Mahatma Gandhi traces it to the human greed. Making a distinction between greed and need he maintained that there is enough in nature to meet the needs of the humankind but not enough for the greed of anyone. It is because human greed has no end. The more we have the more we want. The desire to possess more, more and even more is a never ending desire. The economists make the distinction between need and greed in terms of 'needs' and 'preferences' or 'desire satisfaction'.

The distinction between 'preference' and 'need' is that the former is an intentional concept while the later is an extensional concept. "Whether or not a person needs something depends on the objective condition of the person and the nature of the object – specifically, its capacities to contribute to the flourishing of a person. Whether a person prefers one object to another depends rather upon the nature of the person's beliefs about the objects. It is in part for this reason that the need can be understood as part of an objectivist account of well-being"[13]. Moreover while the concept of need is a threshold concept but the concept of preference is not. Need is a threshold concept because having more or less than one's needs would harm his well-being. Need is that without which the individual cannot survive. For example, a person needs certain amount of water, food or shelter to lead his life and maintain social relations. Moreover while the objects required for 'preference' or 'desire satisfaction' may have several alternative substitutes, the needs are objective and specific and do not admit of any substitutes. For example, it is admitted by everyone that there is no substitute for good health, good friends and good environment. They are specific to the needs for the well-being of individuals. "A loss in one dimension can only be properly addressed by the provision of goods in that dimension. A person who suffers from malnutrition requires specific objects of nutrition: more entertainment or better housing will not do. A person who has had no chance to develop basic capacities for literacy requires an education; offering more food will not do. To say this is not to deny that there are causal relations between different dimensions of well-being. Deficiencies in one dimension of well-being are likely to reinforce and be reinforced by those in others. However, remedies in the end must address deficiencies in each dimension"[14].

Desires and preferences can be artificial or superfluous. For example, the desires for accessories are artificial. They are market governed and even market determined. Desires can be natural or non-natural. Let me explain the distinction between needs and preferences or desires by narrating the conversation, as reported by Palladius and translated into Latin by St. Ambrose in the Fourth century AD, between Alexander and an Indian thinker Dandamis. "Alexander was greatly struck by the austerity of life and majesty of the Indian thinker. The Indian told Alexander that natural desires are quenched easily: thirst by water, hunger by food. But the craving for possession is an artificial one; it goes on unceasingly and is never fully satisfied"[15]. To prove his point the Indian sage explained the criterion for making a distinction between a natural or real and a non-natural, artificial, or contrived desire. A natural desire according to him is fulfilled or satisfied the moment one gets what he sought. For example "if you drink the water you thirst for, your desire ceases. Similarly, if feeling hungry, you receive the food you seek;

your hunger comes to an end. If, then, man's appetite for gold were on the same natural level, no doubt his cupidity would cease as soon as he obtained what he wished for. But this is not the case. On the contrary, it always comes back, a passion never satiated, and so man's craving goes on without an end, because it does not proceed from an inclination implanted by nature"[16].

We may use nature to meet the needs for the development of the well-being of the present generation without compromising the ability of future generations to meet their own needs. We have to have an attitude of care for the future generations.

If man by nature, as the Indian thinkers have time and again asserted, is *nitya-shuddha-buddha-mukta-svabhaava- parmaatman* – the eternally pure, awakened and free self then the question that naturally arises is: Why does he become selfish, greedy and non-caring and exploit and plunder nature to the disadvantage of all? The most satisfying answer is given in Gita 2.62 and 63. It says that man has to live in the world of objects. While being with them it is but natural for him to be attracted by them, 'to think about' them. "In the case of a person who dwells on objects, there arises attachment for them. From attachment grows hankering . . .". This hankering is nothing but desire – a non-natural desire, or what modern Economists call preferences. This hankering leads to loss of equanimity, sense of balance of mind and propriety. The Man with an imbalanced mind constantly strives to fulfil his desires in any possible – right or wrong manner. He has no care for even his fellow beings, what to talk of his future generations. He loses the sense of what he ought to do and what he ought not to do. He loses his rational powers, sense of discrimination and consequently he loses his personhood that is his true nature. Patanjali in his *Yoga-Sutra* II.5 traces this loss of true personhood which is *nitya-shuddha-buddha-mukta-svabhaava-parmaatman* to *avidya* – nescience. "Nescience is the seeing of [that which is] eternal, pure, joyful and the Self in [that which is] ephemeral, impure, sorrowful and the non-self"[17]. Once we remove this *avidya* man sees the difference between *nihsreyas* and *preyas*, the ephemeral and the eternal, recognises the nature of his true self and stops exploiting nature which makes the whole environment around him conducive to his own and his fellow beings – present and future – welfare.

References

1. John O'Neill, Alan Holland, and Andrew Light, *Environmental Values,* Rutledge, London and New York, 2008, pp. 1-2.
2. *Ibid.,* p. 2.
3. *Ibid.,* p. 2.
4. Mahalia, B. "Letter from a Tribal Village", *Lokayan Bulletin,* September-December, 1994.
5. Burgess, J., et al, *Valuing Nature: what lies Behind Responses to Contingent Valuation Surveys?, London: UCL,* 1995, quoted in John O'Neill et al, *op.cit.*, p. 78.
6. Sreven Lukes, "Comparing the Incomparable: Trade-offs and Sacrifices", *Incommensurability, Incompatibility and Practical Reason,* ed. R. Chang, Harvard University Press, 1997 p. 188.
7. GE Moore, "The Conception of Intrinsic Value", *Philosophical Studies,* 1922, p. 260.
8. CL Stevenson, *Ethics and Language,* Yale University Press, 1944, p. 178.
9. Arne Naess, "*A Defence of the deep Ecology Movement*", *Environmental Ethics,* 1984, p. 266.

10 Arnold Leopold, *A sand Country Almanac,* Oxford University Press, 1949, pp. 224-225.

11. "On Nature", *Three Essays on Religion, Harper,* 1884, p. 8.

12 Ibid. p. 64.

13 *The End of Nature, Viking, 1990,* p. 44.

14 David Pearce, *Economic Values and Natural World*, Earthscan, 1993, p. 48.

15. John O'Neil et. al, Op. Cit., pp. 192-93.
16. *Ibid.,* p. 194.
17. Quoted in S. Radhakrishnan, *Our Heritage*, Orient Paperbacks, Delhi, 1984, p. 14.
18. *Ibid.,* p. 151.
19. *The Yoga Sutra of Patanjali,* translated by George Feuerstein, Inner Traditions, 1989, p. 63.

2

A PLAUSIBLE APPROACH TO MAN—NATURE RELATION

Prof. Y.V. Satyanarayana

Environmental issues are closely connected to man's relation to nature, especially man's relation with the environment. Unless we understand clearly the relation between man and nature, it may not be possible to find a plausible solution to environmental issues confronting man, or threatening the human survival.

Human beings are not alone living on the planet Earth. We live among a multitude of plants, animals and inanimate natural objects. Our interaction with the nonhuman forms of life, and with the environment as a whole raise a variety of moral questions such as:

- Is it not morally wrong to pollute soil, water, and air?
- What kind of moral obligations do humans have to the non-human forms of life?
- Are humans morally obliged to preserve the natural environment, endangered plant and animal species, and wilderness areas?
- Do the beings and things of nonhuman world have intrinsic value, or worth?
- What rights, if any, do the beings and objects of the nonhuman world have?
- Do humans have moral duties to future generations to conserve natural resources?

- Can we extend the boundaries of the moral community to the entire natural world?

Man-Nature Relation

From historical and evolutionary standpoints, we can identify three different patterns of human attitudes in relation to nature.

*1. **Man-under-Nature:*** This attitude is prevalent among the prehistoric and primitive tribes. The primitive man identified himself as a part of nature; dependant on nature for his survival; lived like a slave of nature; subservient to the domineering forces of nature; survived at the mercy of hidden and immutable laws of nature, accompanied by a general inability to transform nature with the simple and rudimentary tools and technology available to him.

*2. **Man-over-Nature:*** This attitude is evolved gradually from its previous stage. As a result of rapid growth in man's knowledge of science and technology, he conceived nature as something to be conquered and exploited for his own benefit. He forced the nature to work for himself, and exploited it to an unprecedented extent to fulfil his ever-expanding desires and needs. As a consequence of man's mastery over nature, he no longer regards himself as a slave of nature, rather master of nature.

*3. **Man-with-Nature:*** This attitude is evolved as a reaction to the disastrous consequences of the exploitation of nature, whereby man realised himself as an integral part of nature, or a member of the biotic community, which includes all animate and inanimate things of the ecological system, including water, air and earth. Hence he felt that any irresponsible damage done to the biotic community has its disastrous consequences to the survival of his own existence.

Why and under what circumstances the idea of man against nature has grown up and prospered in the West? The Judo-Christian tradition, the age of Reason, and the advent of technology are all responsible for the development of man-over-nature attitude in the West.

The Impact of Judo-Christian Tradition

Western conception of the natural world grew out of a blend of Hebrew and Greek traditions, especially that of Aristotle. These traditions gave religious sanction to the human-centred morality, and considered humans alone as morally significant beings of the world. The biblical theory of creation, the Genesis, establishes the Hebrew perspective of the special place given to humans in the divine plan. The Genesis says:

> "And God said, let us make man in our image, after our likeness: and let them have dominion over the fish of the sea, and over the fowl of the air, and over the earth, and over every creeping thing that crept upon the earth."[1]

The Christian community believes that the grant of man's 'dominion' over nature is a God-given decree. The Greek influence of Christian religion was reflected in the writings of the medieval scholastic philosopher, St. Thomas Aquinas, who blended the Christian theology with the philosophical ideas of Aristotle. Aristotle conceived the objects of nature in a hierarchical order, in which the objects with less reasoning capacity exist for the sake of those objects with more reasoning capacity, and placed humans at the highest position in the order. This type of attitude and thinking of St. Thomas Aquinas towards the natural world led to the following implications.[2]

- God gave humans dominion over the natural world, and God does not interfere how humans treat it.
- Natural world exists for the needs, and benefit of human beings.
- The destruction of plants, animals, and inanimate objects is not sinful, unless this destruction leads to harm humans.
- Nature by itself has no intrinsic value. Natural world derives its value only in so far as it is good for the sake of well being of humans.
- Humans are only morally significant beings of the natural world.
- Humans are unique, and fundamentally separate from the rest of nature as superior to, and in-charge of the rest of creation.

Paganism and Christianity

The victory of Christianity over paganism brought a tremendous change in the attitude of Western culture. In Antiquity, every tree, every spring, every stream, every hill had its own guardian spirit. Any man before he cuts a tree, or mines a hill, or dams a stream, it was important to placate the spirit in-charge of that particular situation. By destroying pagan animism, Christianity made it possible to exploit nature with an indifference to the feelings of natural objects. The concept of a 'sacred groove became alien to Christianity, and to the ethos of the West.'

In recent times, some religious leaders and theologians began to express the view that man is symbiotically interrelated with all living things. Frederick Elder, an American theologian, in his book on "Crisis in Eden", rejects the dichotomy between man and nature, and proposed the development of asceticism, that is, "a sense of reverence for all life". He felt that such asceticism would ease the strain on an exploited, and over-crowded biosphere, and would hopefully improve not only our quality of life but also the prospects of future generations.

The Impact of Age of Reason

In modern times, the idea of man-over-nature was emphasised in the philosophies of Bacon, Descartes, Leibnitz and Kant. They believed that man is not only different from nature, but also stands superior to nature on account of his rational capacity. They conceived man's control of nature, or man's mastery over nature was beneficent, and it was a mark of progress of human civilization. The philosophies of these thinkers have alienated man from the natural world through a sharp ontological division between rational minds, and the rest of nature. They maintained a dichotomy between the realm of man, and the realm of nature arguing that nature must be dominated by human rationality and purpose.

The Impact of Technology

In the history of humanity, technology played an important and active role in the development of man's domination over nature. The science and technology in the west have grown out of Christian attitude toward man's relation to nature. Modern technology is an important source of environmental problems. It equipped man with enormous power to control, and exploit nature ruthlessly to satisfy his greed. Environmental deterioration due to the effects of technology can be found mainly in the form of — pollution, depletion of natural resources, and overpopulation.

Industrial and mechanical wastage emissions are the most obvious sources of environmental contamination. Man assaults nature and pollutes environment through the use of pesticides and internal combustion engines. Technology contributed much to an increased consumption of resources like food materials, minerals and fossil fuels, which are rapidly being depleted. Finally, technology has contributed to the recent population explosion through increased food production, and longevity of human life, and a reduced infant mortality rate. Unlimited growth of population may lead to increased resource depletion and pollution.

The Impact of Darwinism

Darwin saw balances and harmonies in nature. His theory of evolution provided a basis for reconsideration of man's place in nature. His idea of webs of life, what we call them as ecosystems, has been a great challenge to the traditional dichotomies such as – man against nature, or man versus nature. Darwin's restatement of the concept of unity and harmony of nature provided the basis for building of modern ecological theory.

Anthropocentric and *Non-anthropocentric* Morality

Environmental issues can be addressed from two different standpoints – *anthropocentric* and *nonanthropocentric* morality.

Anthropocentric morality ordinarily presumes that moral obligation is essentially a function of human interest. It ascribes all values ultimately to human interest and concerns. The nonhuman world obtains its value only in so far as it is good for the sake of the well-being of human beings. It is merely a means to an end, and that end is man. Thus the nonhuman world has only instrumental value, that is, a means to some valued end, and that end is the human world. It has no intrinsic value because it is not held to be good, or valuable in itself. The predominant western attitude towards the nonhuman world, therefore, is decidedly *anthropocentric* bias.

The extension of moral consideration to the nonhuman beings and things of the natural world is said to be *non-anthropocentric* morality. It rejects the view of the *anthropocentric* morality that we are masters of nature, and nature is there to be exploited by us. It also rejects the view that all value, ultimately, resides in human interest and concerns. Its moral approach is not what benefits human community as a whole, but what benefits the biotic community as a whole. It is considered as a "holistic ethic", which maintains that our duties are not merely confined to human community, but to the whole of biotic community. It recognizes the intrinsic worth of every being and object of nature. It is based on nature–centred morality, rather than human-centred morality.

The Land Ethic

Aldo Leopold, an American ecologist, argues that there is a need for a 'new ethic', an ethic dealing with man's relation to land, to plants and animals which grow upon it. In his concept of 'Land Ethic', humans are considered a part and parcel of a wider community, which Leopold calls as 'biotic community', or an enlarged community, which includes not only all the living species but also all the members of the ecological system, including water, air and soil, or collectively – the Land. Leopold summed up the basis of his new Land ethic as:

> "A thing is right when it tends to preserve the integrity, stability, and beauty of the biotic community. It is wrong when it tends otherwise."[3]

The significant feature of this theory is *non-anthropocentric* morality. It considers land not as a commodity, which belongs to us, but as a community to which we belong. This is a radical shift in the conception of nature. The land is still considered as a property. The land-relation is still strictly economic, entailing privileges but not obligations. Hence, Leopold considers, the extension of ethics to land is an evolutionary possibility, and an ecological necessity. Leopold observes:

> "The land ethic simply enlarges the boundaries of the community to include soils, waters, plants, and animals, or collectively, the land."[4]

According to Leopold, the source of land ethic is — ecology, the science of the interrelationships and interdependence among organisms, and their environment. We should value nature not because of its value to us but because of its inherent value. From the standpoint of economic interest, the destruction of a forest is unsound because we could never buy back the link with the past represented by the forest. This argument is not meant to show that there can be no justification for cutting any virgin forests, but it means that any such justification must take full account of the value of the forests related to the particular scenic, or biologically significant.

Deep Ecology

Ecology refers to the science of the interrelationships among organisms, and their environment. The term 'Deep Ecology' is coined by Arne Naess, a Norwegian philosopher. Deep Ecology goes beyond a limited piecemeal shallow approach to environmental problems, and attempts to articulate a comprehensive religious, and philosophical worldview. Its moral approach is *non-anthropocentric,* and regards humans as a part and parcel of the organic whole. In reality, there is no bifurcation between human and nonhuman realms. Deep ecologists wanted to preserve the integrity of the biosphere for its own sake, irrespective of the possible benefits to humans. It rejects the view of the *anthropocentric* morality that human community is superior to, and in-charge of the rest of the nature.

Biocentric Equality

In an article on 'Deep Ecology', Bill Devall and George Sessions supported a form of 'biocentric egalitarianism'. Explaining the concept of 'biocentric equality', they wrote:

> "The intuition of biocentric equality is that all things in the biosphere have an equal right to live and blossom and to reach their own individual forms of unfolding and self-realization within the larger self-realization. This basic intuition is that all organisms

and entities in the ecosphere, as part of the interrelated whole, are equal in intrinsic worth."[5]

In the realm of biocentric equality there is no hierarchical order of species with humans at the top. Since it is intimately related to the all-inclusive self-realization, if we harm anything in nature, then we are harming ourselves. We have to respect all human, and nonhuman members in their own right as parts of the whole. The practical implications of this intuition suggest that we should live with minimum, rather than maximum impact on other species on the Earth.

The Value of Wilderness

Under the influence of Leopold, William Godfrey-Smith, an Australian Philosopher, rejected the Western tradition of anthropocentric morality, which is inadequate to provide a satisfactory basis for ecological obligation. He developed a sound biologically based morality, which could provide a satisfactory justification for ecological obligation and concern. In his essay on "*The Value of Wilderness*", Godfrey-Smith calls for the development of an ecologically based morality, which recognizes the intrinsic value of the natural systems. He explains wilderness as:

> "... Any reasonably large tract of the Earth, together with its plant and animal communities, which is substantially unmodified by humans and in particular by human technology."[6]

Godfrey-Smith says that the natural systems, or economically useless species, do possess an intrinsic value. We have to appreciate the symbiotic interrelation, and interdependence of the natural world. The holistic conception of natural world contains the possibility of extending the idea of community beyond human community, which includes all animate and inanimate beings and objects of nonhuman world. He asserts:

> "The holistic conception of the natural world contains, in my view, the possibility of extending the idea of community beyond human society."[7]

There is a conflict of interest between the lovers of wilderness for recreational use, and the economic interests of the miner, the farmer, and the timber merchant. The cost-benefit analyses of the economists tend to overlook some important inherent values of wilderness. Then, what is the use of the wilderness? It is valued as something of immense beauty, as a laboratory of scientific knowledge still to be gained, for recreational purpose as people like to know and enjoy something natural, which is relatively untouched by modern civilization. From a genuinely ecocentric view, Godfrey-Smith says, the question, 'what is the use of wilderness?', — would be as absurd as the question — 'what is the use of happiness?'

Duty to Future Generations

All thoughtful people agree that we *ought* not to make the world a much less pleasant place for our descendants than the world we have inherited from our ancestors by dumping our wastes into rivers, lakes, and oceans, cutting down our forests indiscriminately, and polluting the atmosphere with noxious gases. As temporary inhabitants of this planet, we do have certain duties to perform for future generations such as – not to pollute the atmosphere, to protect threatened plant and animal species, to preserve the beauty of the wilderness areas, and artistic treasures of earlier human civilizations. These are certain valuable objects, and things what we have inherited from our ancestors, and we must preserve them for our descendents.

In speaking of duties to future generation, we imply that future generations have rights, which are morally obligated to respect. Joel Feinberg, in his essay on *'The Rights of animals and Unborn Generations'*, emphasizes the interests of future generations to preserve endangered species. He says, "surely we owe it to future generations to pass on a world that is not a used up garbage heap."[8] We as temporary inhabitants of this planet, therefore, have certain duties to perform for future human beings to leave a livable planet.

The Need for Environmental Ethics

The environmental ethic holds the view that the humans have certain duties to the beings and things of natural world, or the environment has a right to be protected. In order to protect and preserve the environment, the humans should extend certain legal and moral rights to animals, trees, forests, rivers, and other natural objects. The beings and things of nonhuman world must have legal status at par with the infants, estates, corporations, and institutions, which cannot speak for themselves. To say that the environment should have rights does not mean to say that it should have the same rights the human have, but it means that the beings and things of the non-human world must have a right to continuance, or right to exist for them.

Christopher D. Stone, a Professor of Law at the University of South California, argues that natural objects such as trees, forests, streams, rivers should be given legal rights, and represented by legal friends, who protect their interests. He says that this is a radical idea, but no more radical than the idea of extending rights to women, and other sections of human society in the past. The basic idea underlying this suggestion is that at the practical level the environmentalists could more easily protect the beings and objects of natural world. Thus Christopher D. Stone asserts:

> "...the rightlessness of the natural environment can and should change; it already shows some signs of doing so...we should have a system in which, when a friend of a natural object perceives it to be endangered, he can apply to a court for the creation of a guardianship."[9]

In recent times, suits in the names of corporations are taken for granted. Inanimate objects are sometimes parties in litigation. The river, for example, is the living symbol of all the life it sustains, or nourishes — fish, aquatic insects and plants, a variety of animals including man, who are dependent on it, or who enjoy it for its sight, its sound, or its life. The river as a plaintiff speaks for the ecological unit of life, which constitutes a part of it. The people, who have a meaningful relation to that river, whether he may be a fisherman, a biologist, or an environmentalist, must be able to speak about the value of the river, which is threatened with pollution, or destruction.

Human-centred ethics is based on a false assumption that humans alone have intrinsic value and worth, whereas the non-human beings and objects have only instrumental value, or utility value. In contrast to human-centred ethics, the environmental ethics is based on the assumption that human existence and survival inevitably depends on the non-human world, or the good and welfare of humans invariably linked with the good and welfare of non-human world. The non-human world is to be protected not merely for the sake of human interest, but also for its own intrinsic worth. The non-human world, indeed, constitutes the very foundation for the existence of humans. This fact of necessary dependence of humans on the non-human world suggests that the humans have certain moral obligations towards the beings and things of non-human world.

Why do environmentalists call for a radical change in our ethical thinking? Our appeal towards environmental ethics has two reasons.

1. The belief that *anthropocentric* ethics and law are inadequate to deal with a variety of environmental problems that face us.
2. The belief that nature, wilderness, and non-human life have their own inherent value, and therefore deserve moral consideration.

Thus, in traditional western theory of morality there is no moral obligation to environment. Even if we have certain moral obligations *concerning* the environment, these obligations are directed *to* the interest of other humans. For example, we ought not to kill other person's pet dog because it is the property of another person, and our obligations to that person forbid us to destroy his property.

Critical Evaluation

The religious and philosophical traditions of the West have been obsessed with racial superiority, and the idea of dominance —— the dominance of one race over another race, masculine over feminine, wealthy and powerful over poor and powerless, humans over non-human forms of nature, western culture over non-western cultures. This type of attitude and thinking is erroneous and dangerous delusion. A human–centred environmental approach to environmental issues is a great challenge to environmental values.

In the domain of ethics no important changes have ever taken place without an internal change in our mindset, allegiance, inclination and convictions. At present, the most urgent task of moral philosophy is to develop a plausible biologically based ethic, which provides a satisfactory justification of ecological obligation and concern.

We are familiar with the moral revolutions occurred within the domain of human history. The acceptance and extension of 'rights' to racial, sexual and underprivileged classes of people, is a great revolution in the moral sphere. The struggle against racial discrimination led to eradication of racism; the fight against sexual discrimination contributed to women's liberation; and the war against special privileges to certain classes of people led to the freedom and equality to all its citizens in France.

To a limited extent, the extension of moral principles has already taken place with regard to the treatment of animals. Now, it is generally accepted that we have at least a *prima facie* obligation not to treat animals cruelly and sadistically. Cruelty to animals is accepted as intrinsically wrong. This shift in our moral thinking and attitudes in the treatment of animals is certainly an extension of our obligations from humans to animals. This extension of moral obligation is a recent innovation. From the standpoint of an evolutionary view of ethics, it may be possible to extend our obligations, in the years to come, to the whole of biotic community.

Environmental contamination possesses a great threat to human survival. Protection of natural environment is an essential condition for the very survival, and existence of humans. In fact, human life crucially depends on such necessities as breathable air, drinkable water, and eatable food. By reference to human needs and interests, we can make out a *prima facie* duty not to pollute the environment because it damages public welfare. The *prima facie* duty not to pollute may be understood as based on a basic human right, the right to a liveable environment. William T. Blackstone, an American moral theorist, asserts that every person has a right, a human right, to a livable environment. He argues:

> "Every person has this right *qua* being human and because a livable environment is essential for one to fulfill his human capacities."[10]

He says that this right has emerged as a result of changing environmental conditions, which are threatening the very survival of human life.

The Clash between Environmental and Economic Interests

Environmental interests very often clash with economic interests such as strong economy that will produce goods, jobs, and tax revenues; we like air-conditioning; we like the highways to drive our cars on them; we need projects, or dams for irrigation and electricity; we like the convenience of plastics and disposable goods. We weigh the collective human interest in a non-polluted environment against interests of humans. The following example illustrates some of the complexities involved in the problem.

An industrial plant with large financial investment, producing a product essential to society, and providing a large number of jobs, pollutes the environment to a larger extent. How far is the continued operation of the plant morally acceptable? In such a situation, certainly the general public interest in the quality of environment must be recognised. But what about the economic interests of the owner, the employees, and the consumers? Most of us with utilitarian conception and thinking are inclined to appeal for better cost-benefit analysis. Utilitarian thinkers look at environmental issues in terms of consequences, that is, in terms of cost-benefit analysis, which is a subject of debate.

The critics of utilitarian thinking and approach argue that a cost-benefit analysis is an inadequate system because it calculates only economic costs and benefits. In fact, certain objects or goods cannot be measured in terms of economic value. For example, how much does a human life worth? How much does a beautiful view worth? How much does an ornamental artefact like Taj Mahal worth? How much money it costs for hundred people from dying prematurely each year because of pollution? How much is it worth to swim, or fish in a river? It is not possible to identify all the relevant costs and benefits to assign economic value to such goods. Utilitarian calculation to fix a price for everything, including human life, is wrong. The issues of human world involve questions of *risk* rather than *cost.*

We have to appreciate the symbiotic interrelation and interdependence between the members of the biotic community. The holistic conception of natural world contains the possibility of extending the idea of community beyond human society. If we regard a community as a collection of individual members, who are engaged in cooperative behaviour, Leopold's extension of obligations to biotic community seems to be legitimate. The biotic community is like a human community. The first principle of any community is cooperation. Since an ethic is no more than a code of conduct designed to ensure cooperative behaviour among the members of community, the members of a biotic community will respect, and cooperate with each other.

Ecology teaches us that human life is crucially intertwined with ecosystem as a whole. The destruction of one part of the ecosystem may lead to a chain of events that ultimately culminates in disastrous consequences to human well–being. Hence we have to make every effort to preserve our environment for human welfare. Frederick Engels, a close and lifelong associate of Karl Marx, warned in this respect and said;

> "Let us not, however, flatter ourselves overmuch on account of our human victories over nature. For each such victory nature takes its revenge on us. Each victory, it is true, in the first place brings about the results we expected, but in the second and third places it has quite different, unforeseen effects which only too often cancel the first."[11]

The continued existence of endangered species, and wilderness areas bring enjoyment and satisfaction, or has utility for humans. A moral obligation to preserve them is firmly based on the interests of the human community. A virgin forest is the product of millions of years, and if it is cut-down, we may grow up another forest in its place, but the continuity of the forest has been broken down, the link with the past has gone forever. Hence the wilderness areas, at least some of them, with good scenic beauty, or biologically significant should be taken care of, and kept as 'world heritages'. We have inherited these forests from our ancestors, and it is our responsibility to preserve them for our decedents. If we loose these things, no amount of money can bring them back.

The tropical rain forests are the Earth's richest, oldest, and complex ecosystems. They are major source of biodiversity, and contain as many as five million species of plants, insects and animals. Already half of the world's original rain forest has been destroyed for commercial and other purposes. Human commercial activities affect the integrity of ecosystems. Therefore, to justify the destruction of an ancient forest on economic consideration of cost-benefit analysis of a utilitarian is unreasonable and unjustifiable. The future generations will value wilderness areas for the same reason that we value them. Just as we largely spend to preserve cities like 'Venice', or artistic treasures like 'Taj Mahal', so also we should preserve wilderness areas even though future generations care little for them.

The vital material needs of humans are probably simpler than what we generally conceive. The overwhelming propaganda and advertisements which we experience in technocratic–industrial societies are encouraging false needs, and promoting destructive desires among people to foster increased production, and consumption of goods. The fundamental assumption of environment ethic is based on the principle that it finds *virtue* in saving and recycling resources, and *vice* in extravagance and unnecessary consumption. Of course, the emphasis on simple living does not mean disapproval of one's pleasure, but it means that pleasure must not come from the multiplication of desires, and the needless use of the materials which are non-renewable.

The critics of environmental ethics, very often, raise the question — why environmental ethics is necessary and for what? If all the people living on this planet care about the survival of the planet, perhaps environmental ethics is unnecessary. But, if we care little about the survival of the planet, environmental ethics is necessary to preserve the majesty, integrity, stability, and beauty of the nature.

Concluding Remarks

The relation between man and nature constitutes the ultimate basis for all environmental issues. All natural beings, whether they are plants, animals, or humans, are dependant on nature for their sustenance and survival. Therefore, no natural being is independent of, and separate from nature, but it constitutes an integral part of nature. The beings and objects of natural world are interconnected and interdependent on one another, and there is perpetual action and reaction between them. Thus, all natural beings, including humans, are regarded as members belonging to one community, that is, a biotic community.

Every natural being, whether it is tiny, or giant, has its place, purpose, and worth in the vast web of life. Though mutual predation is a biological fact of life, if one natural being lives at the expense and sacrifice of other beings beyond certain limits, then the equilibrium or harmony in nature is disturbed, which may eventually lead to a variety of natural disasters.

In the hierarchy of evolution, or in the process of creation, humans occupied the highest place in the natural world. Humans are gifted with a number of unique qualities like reason, intelligence, self-consciousness, conceptual thinking etc; and these qualities distinguish them from all other beings of natural world. The possession of such unique qualities does not entitle humans to treat the entire non-human world as a means, or a resource exclusively obtainable for their own benefit and purpose. Indeed, the unique qualities of humans place certain obligations on them to protect the interests of less evolved, or lower beings and things of natural world.

By and large, human attitude to nature appears to be based on an erroneous presumption. The superiority of humans over the non-human world made them to believe that they are alone possess intrinsic value and worth, whereas the beings and things of natural world have only instrumental value, or utility value. This false view of humans made them to regard that the entire natural world is for the sake of satisfying their needs and greed.

Of course, it is true that nature feeds on nature itself, or the beings of the natural world feed on one another for their sustenance and survival. Respect for the beings and things of natural world does not mean complete discontinuation of the use of these beings and objects for human need and purpose. Since human survival necessarily depends on the non-human world, it is impossible for humans to exist without dependence on the natural world. However, it is morally unjustifiable to exploit, or damage the natural world for the sake of human greed, rather than human need.

The spectacular development brought about in science and technology, equipped humans with enormous power to control, and exploit nature not only to satisfy their needs, but also to quench their thirst for profit, or accumulation of wealth. No doubt, the natural world has sufficient physical material to satisfy human needs and comforts, but it does not contain adequate resources to satisfy the greed of humans. In order to maximize comforts, and luxuries of life, humans are engaged in employing their talents and skills to exploit the natural world to the maximum extent possible, without mindful of or concern for the damage they are doing to the environment.

In contrast to the Judo-Christian view of man's relation to nature, Hinduism lays more emphasis on the unity between man and nature. According to Hinduism, humans are neither separate, nor independent of nature, but constitute a part and parcel of the natural world. This viewpoint of Hinduism contradicts the Judo-Christian standpoint that man is the master of nature, or man is superior to nature.

Hinduism extends love and respect, care and concern, for the welfare of all beings and things of natural world. Traditionally most of the Hindus, if not all, worship many things and beings of nature as deities. For instance, it is a common practice among Hindus to worship the earth, rivers, fire, air, trees, and animals. The fundamental doctrine underlying the Hindu Scriptures is, "everything that exists in this universe is pervaded by one Supreme Reality." This doctrine of oneness is explicitly expressed in the Vedas, Upanishads, Gita and Puranas. In a dialogue between Yajnavalkya and Gargi in the Brhadaranyaka Upanishad, Yajnavalkya says: "O Gargi! That one universal imperishable consciousness (Brahman) has penetrated everything in this universe."[12] The same idea is expressed in the Bhagavadgita. Lord Krishna says: "I have interpenetrated this Universe like a thread connecting pearls."[13]

Of all the major religions of the world, perhaps no other religion lays more emphasis than Hinduism on the need for extending human obligation to the non-human world. Hinduism insists on man's responsibilities to nature, or protection of all animate and inanimate things of natural world. This idea is explicitly expressed in the *Bhoomikhanda of Padma Purana.* It says:

> "A person who is engaged in killing creatures, polluting wells, ponds and tanks, and destroying gardens, certainly goes to the hell."[14]

Hindus worship the Earth, and consider it as equal to one's own mother. There is a common belief among Hindus that one's own mother *(janani)* and one's own birth place *(janmabhoomi)* are more pleasant, and greater than the heaven. Hinduism advocates the idea of oneness, and it conceives all beings and things of the universe as members of one family (*Vasudaiva Kutumbakam).*

Environmental ethics warns us about the risk, or danger involved in contamination of natural environment, and the senseless exploitation and devastation of natural world. Although every living organism affects the environment to a limited extent, the humans possess the power to upset drastically the stability and integrity of natural world. The human commercial activities have destructive affects on the environment.

At present, a real threat to human survival is posed by the factors such as excessive pollution of soil, water and air; industrial wastes and toxins which are dangerous to life; ruthless exploitation of minerals; destruction of tropical rain forests; soil erosion as a result of cutting down the trees and forests; heat emissions from industrial installations into the atmosphere; growing application of various chemical fertilizers and pesticides in agriculture; the danger arises from nuclear wastes and nuclear-plant accidents; the upsetting of the equilibrium between various organisms and things of nature; ozone depletion or green house affect; excessive acid content in the atmosphere resulting in acid rains; global warming etc. These factors are contributing much for the deterioration of natural environment.

In the interest of present and future generations, it is necessary to take certain appropriate measures to protect natural environment. In this direction, we may suggest measures such as — preservation of the purity of land, water, and air; conservation of the natural resources; introduction of eco-friendly technology; recycling of resources; protection of endangered plant and animal species; preventing the abuse of animals for commercial purposes; protecting wilderness areas and tropical rain forests; discontinuation of the use of high quantity chemical fertilizers and pesticides in agriculture; and vigorous campaign to reduce the growth of population.

The ecological situation of a region, to a large extent, depends on the demographic position of that region. Population growth at a faster rate becomes a serious threat to the ecological condition. Since overpopulation leads to greater pressure on the natural world, the demographic factor is contributing greatly to the deterioration of ecological situation in many nations all over the world. The statistics available reveals the fact that the world's population is increasing at a faster rate during the last half-century than ever before in human history.

The planet Earth is just like a huge ship with a definite capacity to accommodate people. It cannot accommodate more and more people beyond its capacity. A journey in an overcrowded ship is always a risky proposition, and it may sink at any time in the course of its journey. Just as a ship with a definite capacity cannot accommodate people over and above its capacity, so also the planet Earth cannot sustain the burden of overpopulation beyond its capacity.

It would be immoral to make the world uninhabitable to the present as well as to the future generations. Man's ever expanding desire for a more comfortable and luxurious life, and his greed for maximization of profits, or accumulation of wealth is the root cause for deterioration of natural environment. The scientific and technological progress by itself is not an evil, but its improper use, or inaccurate application that is evil. Humans must learn how to use the scientific and technological knowledge judiciously to serve human needs and purposes, without causing harm to the natural world.

Just as a bee extracts honey from a flower without causing harm to the fragrance, or to the beauty of that flower, so also humans must learn to extract beings and things from nature, without inflicting damage, or causing harm to the natural world.

Humans, like all other living beings, are temporary inhabitants of the planet Earth. Humans must realize the fact that the beings and objects of the non-human world existed much before they came into existence on the planet Earth. The beings and objects of the nonhuman world can exist without humans, but humans cannot exist without them. The superior status of humans in the order of evolution, and the possession of rational faculty place certain responsibilities on the part of humans to protect the natural environment, and the beings and objects of natural world, not only for the sake of their own survival, but also for maintaining the majesty, integrity, stability and beauty of the nature.

References

1. Bible, Genesis, chap-1, verse 26.
2. Cf. Peter Singer, "*Practical Ethics*", (Cambridge, Cambridge University Press, 1993), pp.267-68.
3. Aldo Leopold, "*The Land Ethic*", in "A Sand County Almanac", (New York, Oxford University Press, 1949), p. 224-225.
4. *Ibid.*, p. 204.
5. Bill Devall and George Sessions, "*Deep Ecology*", in Daniel Bonevac (ed.) "Today's Moral Issues", (California, Mayfield Publishing Company, 1992), p. 195.
6. William Godfrey-Smith, "*The Value of Wilderness*" in Thomas A. Mappes and Jane S. Zembaty (eds.), "Social Ethics: Morality and Social Policy", (New York, McGraw-Hill, 1987), p. 498.
7. *Ibid.*, p. 501.
8. Joel Feinberg, "*The Rights of Animals and Unborn Generations*", in James E. White, (ed), "Contemporary Moral Problems", (New York, West Publishing Company, 1994) p. 434.
9. Christopher D Stone, "*Should Trees have standing? Toward Legal Rights for Natural Objects*", in James E. White, (ed) "Contemporary Moral Problems", (New York, West Publishing Company, 1994), p. 440.
10. William T. Blackstone, (ed) "*Philosophy and Environmental Crisis*" (Athens, University of Georgia Press, 1974), p. 35.

11. Frederick Engels, "*Dialectics of Nature*", (Moscow, Progress publishers, 1974), p. 180.

12. Brhadaranyaka Upanishad, 3.8.11

13. Bhagavadgita, VII.7.

14. O.P. Dwivedi, (ed) "*World Religions and the Environment*", (New Delhi, Gitanjali Publishing House, 1989), p. 96.

3

MAN AND NATURE: AN APPROACH FROM BUDDHIST ETHICS

Prof. Dilipkumar Mohanta

There is no greater threat today to the security of life on this earth than environmental degradation covering all aspects of Nature—plants, animals and human beings. We face today many challenges to our survival, such as, draught caused by deforestation, flood and soil erosion, increase in global warming, serious threat to ozone layer from chloroform carbon discharged by refrigerator along with many others. To address such environmental problems an integral relation between man and Nature has been advocated by the branch of philosophy called Environmental Ethics. It is also called 'Eco-sophy' because of its content is the moral relationship of human beings and Nature with its non-human contents. There is no doubt that armed with the knowledge of science and technology if we do not link ourselves with ethically skill–full ways of using our achieved powers we will destroy ourselves and destroy the happiness of the future generations to come. Material development divorced from moral and spiritual concern tends to develop selfish individualistic outlook and makes man greedy exploiter and polluter of Nature. As a result of over exploitation of natural resources, the replenishing capacity of Nature becomes impair. It is ultimately human beings who suffer as a result of greed, aggression and delusion. So, according to Eco-sophists, how to live a better life depends upon how to establish a balanced relation between our ways of living with nature. If we look at nature, we shall see that nature as a whole maintains a rein of harmony and interdependence. Our moral degradation badly affects our external environment .We have no right to disturb the harmony of Nature for the sake of our present happiness only and for meeting our greed. If we argue for our own happiness, by the same logic we cannot deny that the people belonging to future generations have the right to their happiness. We must change our short-sighted understanding of the word 'Development' to "Sustainable Development'. **Now it is imperative to take interest in future which lies beyond the boundary of our shortsighted outlook and self–interests. By extending love, compassion and non–violence in practice, according to Buddhism, we can take interest in protecting the right to happiness of the future generations.**

The Ethical approach of Buddhism towards Nature is similar to the **Deep Ecological Concern** of the Environmental Philosophy of today. The ethical teachings of Buddhism ask us to purify the mind to control our desire. It observes that being greedy, human beings want to take as much as they can from the earth and from others to satisfy their immediate wants, without consideration for the future. **Any kind of devaluation of other creatures and rating them in lower levels than human beings, empathetically disconnect us from the harmonious principle of nature and lead us to do harm to others as well as to ourselves.** It is this moral dimension of ecological problems which may be addressed from the ethical perspective of Buddhism. This paper is an humble attempt in this direction.

The Buddhist ethics is grounded on a broad naturalistic stance. All creatures – sentient and non–sentient, according to Buddhism, are subject to moral sensibility. Greed, hatred and delusion are considered as causal conditions for unwholesome actions and roots of *dukkha*, the fact of suffering. Buddhists texts contain references to different methodological devices to environmental crisis and emphasis on the inter-connectedness and interdependence of life upon earth. **Buddhism would view the spiritual crisis of self-centeredness and greed aided by the non-moral use of the knowledge of science and technology as the main source of**

environmental crisis. For Buddhism, any effort to eradicate environmental crisis must begin with purification of human conduct and mental attitudes. In its moral aspect Buddhism prescribes the precepts and virtues for ideal living. Let us concentrate on three such aspects of Buddhist Ethics, namely, the precept of non-violence, and virtues of loving kindness and compassion to address the environmental problems. Here **I propose two** different methodological **models** from Buddhist Ethics for an ideal relation between man and nature. The proposed models **may be called 'MOTHER-CHILD MODEL' and HONEY BEE MODEL'** .But before going to the precepts[1] and virtues[2] which lead to the models of our approach to Nature, let us refer shortly to some Buddhist textual evidences which support our contention.

In the *Sigalo–vāda suttanta* of *Dighanikāya* (Vol.-III, *Pātika vaggo* 31), thirty five sections have been devoted to elucidate the code of discipline for laymen. Killing, stealing, sexual misconduct, speaking untrue and intoxication have been prohibited. The canonical literature of Buddhism contains several references forbidding over exploitation of natural world. The *Dighnikāya* (I.5) prohibits doing any harm to 'seeds, plants and trees' and disobeying of prohibitory rules amounts to committing sin. *Vinayapiṅaka* (IV 34–5) also condemns doing harm or asking someone else to do harms to trees, plants etc. as offence. *Bahmajāla sutta* (*Dighanikaya*, I) condemns setting fire to fields, hills and woodlands' as sin *Anguttaranikāya* (II, 253) in order to dissociate people from violence urges that the result of killing animals or encouraging killing is the rebirth in hell. *Anguttaranikāya* (II, 208) also categorized the profession of a butcher, hunter or fishermen under wrong means of living. Deforestation has been condemned as an offence (*–bhutagāmapātabya tāya pacitti–yan ... bhūtagāmo nāma pañca bijajātani, mulabijāni, khandhabijąn, phalubijan, aggabijan, bijabijameva pañcamam — Pācittya, Nalanda* edition : 55). **The Buddhist's moral approach to environmental problem may be called a contribution to 'internal ecology'.** This consideration has been reflected in the life–pattern prescribed for monks and nuns during rainy season (*vassā–vāsa*), such as, to remain in monasteries as far as possible in order to reduce possible injury to and harming of small creatures like insects etc and green vegetations (*Mahāvaggo*, ed. Mahesh Tiwary, Delhi University edition : 144). The *Dhammapada* intensifies this teaching in 130 and 131

sabbe tasanti da ŏḋassa sabbesa ʂ jivita ʂ piyam/
attāna ʂ upama ʂ katvā na haneyya na ghātaye//
sukhakāmāni bhūtāni yo da ḋlena vihi ʂati/
attano sukhamesāno pecca so na labhate sukham//

All tremble at punishment because life is dear to all. Considering others feeling as good as the feeling of oneself, one should not kill or become cause of killing. (130). A person who seeks his own happiness harms other pleasure–loving beings with sticks, gets no happiness even in hereafter (131).

Suttanipāta refers to the incident of a *khira–offering* to the Buddha by a brahmin farmer named Bharadvāja. When the Buddha for some cogent reasons did not accept it, he advised the farmer not to throw it to any place where green grass would be harmed by it or in water where small insects would be affected (— *tain pāyāsai üappaharite vā chā ôḋhi, appā ḋke vā udake opilāpehi ti* — Bhikshu Dharmarakshita, 1977 : 20). This reflects on the concern of the Buddha for flora and fauna.

In Buddhism people are advised not to do any harm even to a leaf without exclusive necessity. *Petavatthu* (Nalanda edition: 163) contains many such instructions against what we call today deforestation and encouraging lessons for preservation of greens. *Vinayapa ṅka* records Jīvaka, the famous physician of the time of the Buddha as saying "I cannot find a single plant which does not possess any medicinal property" (1964 : 281). *Vinaya* also contains an instruction to Bhikkus to **'recycle old robes'** (II) and 'not to pollute water or green grass with urine or excrement' (IV). In Ashoke's Inscription, we find instruction for preservation of medicinal plants with special care because both human and animal species require these for getting rid of ailments. All these show that **the Buddhist way of living used to honour with gratefulness the inner rhythm of nature which is very close to a modern use of preserving *'bio–diversity'*.** The *Dharmapada*, 390 intensifies clearly the importance of non–violence in the following:

yatho yatho hi ṣamano nivattati,/
tato tato sammatimeva dukkham//

(the places where the mind is refrained from violence are places where there cannot by any more suffering). The precept of *ahimsā* — non–violence in Buddhist vocabulary is known as *pānātipāta–virati*. It is the precept of abstaining from killing, of not encouraging anybody for killing and of not sanctioning anybody's act of killing. It is a practicing precept both in thinking and action. **The extensional meaning of this precept will help us to address some of the ecological crisis we face today.** Now its meaning may be extended to include refraining from 'torture criminal intimidation, violent ideologies and activities' (Silva, 2001 : 48). It includes abstaining from all kinds of injury both–physical and non–physical to all creatures. It is in turn to be considered as an active attempt in recognizing the value of the lives of others and equal respect for all creatures. It is a positive virtue of doing good, because it is also a kind of resistance to evil through love. In this sense **it is essentially tied up with compassion and loving-kindness and such a tied up form of non–violence in spiritual sense can distill and unify the religio–cultural tradition of Buddhism into the bio–ethical ideals of living non–violently and with reverential attitude for all life. In ecological paraphrase, we may say that it is an indirect indication that we live in the world as interdependent** and **this is not only true in the context of other human beings but also of other beings, plants and of overall nature.** The extensional meaning of this precept would dissuade people from throwing any waste into river and lakes and would mean it obligatory to guard the lives of all creatures found in the process of natural environment This is strengthened by loving-kindness as a value and values are such that are to be realized by 'doing' as we become just by doing just acts. *Mettā–bhāvanā* is the practicing of unbounded consciousness of well–being from self (*sva*) to all (*sabba*)–(*hitesita parahita–kammata*). Cultivation of this is an antidote to any type of ill–will, hatred, fear, selfishness, greed, anger and all kindred states. **It is rather the extension of the first person experience of non–enmity (*avairi*), non–hatred (*avyāpada*), calmness (*anigha*) to all creatures, to all worlds** (*loka*) — **human, animal and plants.**[3] Its nearest enemy is lust (*kāma*).[4] If you practice loving kindness to somebody it would simultaneously become impossible for you to get angry with that body. Love means 'giving something' whereas lust means 'getting something' Buddhaghosa explains it with the metaphor of a mother's love to her only child when she wishes for the youth of that child. The mother protects her only child even at the cost of own life.[4] So goes the teaching of the *Dhammapada* 223,

> *akkodhena jine kodham asādhu § sādhunā jine/*
> *jine kadariya § dānena sacchenā alikavādinam//*

[—loving loving kindness kindness conquers anger, good conquers evils, donation conquers the stingy and truth conquers falsehood]. The *Dhammapada* 5, also stresses this when it goes as hatred never ceases through hatred, on the contrary hatred ceases through' love and this is the age–old–law.

> *[na hi verena verāni sammant' idha kudācanam/*
> *a verana ca sammanti; esa dhamma sanantano//]*

Again, compassion is called the basis for non–violence, because it eradicates *vihimsā*, the ability to become violent and there is nothing greater than doing goods to all creatures (*nāsti hi kammatar sabba lokahitatatpā*). It has been used as a verb and not as a noun. It is an antidote to cruelty and is rooted in wisdom.[5] The *Dhammapada* iv.49 says "*yathāpi bhamaro puppham va ōāgandham ahethayam/ Paleti rasam ā dī ya evam gāme munā care//*—" **Even as a bee gathers honey from a flower and departs without injuring the flower or its colour or scent, so let a sage dwell in his village**".(Eng.tr. Radhakrishnan,1950:75) become just by doing just acts.

In such a state of love, the dividing lines among oneself, beloved, foe and indifferent are blotted out and it is not subject to any conditions and which has no boundaries.

Now how to apply this ethics of virtues to meet the ecological challenges that we face today? The remedy Buddhism would suggest lies in changing our mindset and to bound us with loving-kindness and compassion connected with non–

violence to make "the paradigm shift so that our world–view is as world–sustaining as it is self–fulfilling." (Fox; 2001.164). *Aǵuttara nikāya* (II : 74–6) tells us that because of the unrighteous acts of the king and his people, (result of greed satisfaction in exploiting nature,) the environmental crisis arise in the form of little rainfall, poor crops and weak, short–lived people. We may extend it today to mean the "Whatever harm a foe may do to a foe or a hater to a hater, an ill–directed mind can do one for greater harm"

> (*diso disa yam ta kayirā veri vā pana verina/*
> *micchāpa āhita cittam pāpiyo na tato kare.//*

— *The Dhammapada*, 42). Out of greed people run after more and more possession; the same greed forces people to exploit others — to exploit nature beyond people's necessity; and the same greed makes people violent and aggressive. Instead of 'the attitude of possession.

Buddhism advocates a 'sense of belongingness' as the ideal relation on our part to nature. It tells us to change our mindset from 'having mode' to 'being mode' of life (Erich Fomm). The reality of human beings is to be realized as an integral part of his environment and in learning how to 'live–together' in this world of interdependence of humanity and nature in a harmonious balance. The story of *vyāghra jātaka* (no. 272) may be relevant here. It goes like this: Bodhisattva, one tree goddess, a tiger, and a lion were living in the same forest. Once without listening to the warning by Bodhisattva, the tree goddess drove the tiger and the lion away from that forest. Afterwards the greedy woodcutters came and destroyed the abode of the goddess. This story may be used in an extended sense to signify the model of protecting woodlands and forests with the help of wild animals.[7] We know that the deforestation along with loss of forest products cause many kind of natural disaster like soil erosion, flood, draught etc. *The Mahāyānasūtra* is eloquent in praising trees and plants. The Buddha was pictured as telling the seven daughters, "one hundred years old trees bore fruits and flowers...the birds could see...hundreds of birds and beasts were harmonious in their cries." (Paul,1979; 24). **We create environmental crisis when we are**

guided by any of the three *akusalamūla* — the roots of unrighteous states of greed, hatred and delusion. *Dasuttara–sutranta* of the *Dighanikāya* (III; 34 : 621–2) narrates that when a person is controlled by any of these, that person then does violence, steals (i.e. earns in non–righteous means), makes adulteration, speaks untrue and makes others to do similar non–righteous acts. This causes suffering for that person as well as for others. Since our mental determinations control our actions, it is our foremost duty to control over our mind:

> *(–manopubbamgamā dhamma manose ñṁā manomayā/*
> *manasā ce padu ñṁena bhāsati vā karotivā/*
> *tato nam dukkhamanveti cakka'va vahato pada Ṣ//*

— since mind precedes everything and if a person speaks or acts with an evil intention suffering as a necessary consequence follows that person just as the foots of full which draws the cart is followed by the wheels of the cart (eng. tr. mine) — *The Dhammapada*, 1; 1974; 1). In *Vinayapi ṁaka* (*sutta vigha ṁga* 1), we come across a sincere concern and encouragement for the protection of natural world. The dialogue between Maha Moggallana and the Buddha may be referred in this context. In this dialogue it is said that **for a Buddhist, humanity is never superior to 'the rest of the natural world'.**[7]

Let us now examine **the question of feasibility** of such an ethical approach founded on the precept of non–violence and on the virtues of loving-kindness and compassion to all — plants, animals and humans, without any discrimination. Buddhism advocates a middle path between excessive enjoyment/consumerism and extreme self mortification and in the light of this, we are to derive the barest minimum from nature to fulfill our needs. Precepts are meant to restrain ourselves from our greed–satisfaction. Here it may further be objected that what is called greed today will be considered as need tomorrow. In response to this, it is to be borne in mind that **when we speak of need, we speak of the minimum and what is due to us. Non–violence as a precept emphasizes on the avoidance of intentional violence and practice of non–violence as far as practicable.** Ashoke's declaration 56 non–

slaughter days is a step towards the reduction of active violence to animals. Vegetarianism is not mandatory but optional according to Buddhism. **We may develop an ideal model with the metaphor of 'mother–child' relation with regard to our relation to nature for satisfaction of our needs and not of greed. The mother out of affection feeds her child as per the requirement.** But an adult self–supported child does not require mothers' support any more. If now he demands still from the mother this is out of greed. If without adjusting with the harmonious course of nature we exploit nature, it takes revenge. Now extending the Buddhist teaching of interdependence, non-violence and compassion **we can change our attitude towards nature from one of 'domination' to 'co–operation'**. It covers forgiveness (*k ṣamā*), fearlessness (*abhaya*) and universal loving-kindness (*mettā*) for all forms of life. **The spirit of teaching of the Buddha would insist us to link commerce with morality, science and technology with humanity, knowledge with character, wealth with work and pleasure with conscience. This will enable us to live in a skill–full way and to preserve the planet from a realization of deep inter–connectedness of all things.**[9]

An ideal relation between our way of living and nature may be traced in *The Dighanikāya's* (II, 31; 26) *Simgālavādasutta* where the Buddha narrates it to *g ṛhapatiputta simgāloka*. Silva explains it in the following words :

> "A house holder should accumulate wealth as a bee collects nectar from a flower. The bee harms neither the fragrance nor the beauty of the flower, but gathers nectar to turn it into sweet honey. Similarly a human being is expected to make legitimate use of nature so that s/he can rise above nature and realize her/his innate spiritual potential." (see : Batchelor & Brown, ed., 1994; 22)

Following 'honey–bee–model' our right thinking and right doing should go hand in hand. Eco–catastrophe would be viewed by the Buddhist as a consequence of unrestricted exploitation of nature by human beings. External pollution originates from our attitude level corruptions. The key to happy living lies in

maintaining a balanced way of life among plants animals and human and in sincere wishing for happiness for all creatures — big or small, moving or immobile, visible or invisible, far and near.

"ye keci pānabhūtatthi, ta sā vā thāvarā anavasesā/
dīghā vā ye mahantā vā, majjhimā rassakā āukathūlā//
di ññhā vā yeva adi ññhā, ye ca dūre vasanti avidūre/
bhūta vā sambhavesī, sabbe satta bhavantu sukhitattā//"

(*Suttanipāta*, 1977; 36)

As Rabindranath puts this ideal of living with nature in harmony in his novel *'Yogāyog'*: "The woodcutter only knows how to cut the tree, so he does not get flower and gets only wood, the gardener knows how to nourish the tree, so he gets flower, fruits etc. (*ka ñhure gāchke kān ñe jāne, se gāch pay na, kā ñh pay. māli gāchke rākhte jāne, se pāy phul, pāy phal* — Rabindra Racanāvali, vol. 5: 1986 : 362). Let us wish to be gardener in Tagore's sense. Because of its illimitable scope, **the Buddhist ethics based on non–violence, loving-kindness and compassion "takes us beyond the polemics of dualities of animal versus human rights and human interests versus environmental protection and nature conservation.** It is surely from such an all–encompassing ethical sensibility that we can best consider, rationally and sensitively, the rights and interests of the entire life community of the planet... It is also enlightened self–interest because when we harm others, including the environment, we inevitably harm ourselves" (Fox, 2001; 179). In our times also the Buddhists are activity engaged in movement for *eco–centric* way of living against *ego centric* one. Moral way of living with universal responsibility and environmental compassion has been advocated by Dalailama. Thich Nhat Hant [8] has advocated another movement based on wisdom concentration as a necessary requirement for a balanced development of a sustainable natural habitat for all.

Let all creatures be happy. Let us not endanger ourselves by endangering the beauty of earth caused by pollution, deforestation and desertification. **To make our planet the abode/home for all**

in the real sense of the term, let us utilize the powers that we achieve in the field of science and technology skill–fully so that nature's harmony is not disturbed and this can be done to a large extent by linking ethical elements of restrains (*silasiksā*)and virtues (*bramha-bihāra-bhāvanā*) to our new powers. This would be the implication of middle way today. An ethical perspective from Buddhism would tell us that **environmental problems of today have deep roots in our misguided anthropocentric attitudes about the non-human domains of nature.** On the contrary, we should think ourselves as a part of nature. Work in harmony with it and use its resources for the normal sustenance and minimum requirements. In this way we may check our indisciplined voluntary actions to make our environment suitable for us as well as for future generations to come. It is interesting to see how in accordance with the traditional precepts a Zen teacher of California in USA has developed some **eco-precepts.**[9] The imaginative restructuring of Buddhist practice intertwines traditional virtue Ethics with environmental concern. **Prescribing simultaneously the eco-friendly way of life and recycling of materials, Buddhism contributes much to what we call today 'Deep Ecology'.** We need to see the presence of deep-level connection between religion and environment and this should not be restricted to academic thinking only. It must meet the field of interdisciplinary study where the field must meet the force, theory must meet practice, and academic must meet a sense of community. This relationship is not simply a field of study, but is also a matter of personal involvements and face to face relationships. Today we need to connect our new powers of science and technology with values imbedded in our cultural heritage through education of environmental protection. Environmental Study, where ethics constitutes an integral part, should no longer remain as an ornamental subject as we see especially in our university system today. Today we need a proper blending of ethics with our material achievements. Buddha's teaching integrates all aspects of eco-sphere, particular individuals and general species, in terms of mutual interdependence, which in a sense is an attempt to institutionalize care and welfare ethics beyond human domain reaching animal and plant worlds.

Notes and References

1. Precepts are prohibitions on conduct. It tells us what not to do as well as what we should do. Values refer to things we aim towards.

2. According to Pali Text Society Published *Pali–English–Dictionary* (New Delhi Oriental Books Reprint : 1975 : 503; London–edition 1921–1925) the word '*bhāvanā*' stands for "producing, dwelling on something putting one's thoughts to, application, developing by means of thought or meditation, cultivation by mind." In case of *brahma–vihāra*, it seems to be used in a non–technical sense of practicing or gradual development of virtues. *Suttapiṅaka* uses it in all these senses. *Anguttaranikāya* regards it as '*bodhipakkhika dhamma*, the constituents which are conducive to enlightenment. see, PTS, IV, 1900 : 125–6). *Brhmavihāra* is also known as *āryavihāra* in the sense of noble. In the sense of developing or actualizing the four fold noble virtues — love, compassion, empathetic joy and equanimity are very much in use. In Buddhist dominated countries like Srilanka, Maynamer (i.e. estwhile Burma), we see that many *bhāvanāsālā* exist. It may also be understood as the cultivation of any particular aspect of the Buddhas' teaching.

   In *Theragātā* Sthavira Revata emphasizes on this spirituo–moral state of love towards all creatures without any discrimination in the verse no 648. It goes as follows :

   sabba–mitto sabba–sakho, sabba bhutānukampako/
   metta§ citta§ ca bhāvemi avyāpajjha–rato sadā//
   (ed. H. Oldenberg, PTS 1966, (1883).

3. See, *Vissuddhimaggo* (tr. Maung Tin : 1971; 367); Anuruddha (1913; 82–83) also emphasized the universal and unconditional feature of loving kindness (*mettā bhāvanā*) in verses nos. 1335, 1336, 1343 and 1345. However he tries to hint to a special feature of practicing compassion, namely, the feature that constitutes a border–line case with *mettā*. For him *karunā–bhāvanā* can only be meaningfully practiced when it is preceded by *mettā–bhāvana*. The following two verses may be cited in support of our claim.

   'tathā' sevitasantāno, mettācetovimuttiya/
   karuõā–bhāvanā yoga ārabheyya tato param/ (1348)

sukhitesu ca medhāvi, dukkhākāram anussara/
pavatteya dayāpanno, karuõā bhāvanappaõam// (1360)

4. The word *bhāvanā* etymologically means 'making become'.[3] It is also used to mean meditational practice or gradual cultivation of four cardinal virtues which have deep implications for individual conduct and one's relationship with others including environment. These virtues are loving kindness (*mettā*), compassion (*karuõā*), empathetic joy (*muditā*) and equanimity (*upekkhā*). Buddhism recognizes the immeasurable 'power of our mind and developing these virtues through meditation is the highest spiritual roaming one can have in this world. It is interesting to note that *Karuõā* or compassion is recognized as the highest virtue in Buddhism. In both the senses of *means* and *goal*, *karuõa* as a virtue has been used in Buddhism. There are three kinds of practice of compassion and there are three ideals recognized through meditational practice. The first is called *srāvaka*. Here the goal is to eradicate the suffering of the individual following the eight–fold path of enlightenment. Experiencing the suffering of all that exist, a *srāvaka* becomes compassionate. He is aware of the non–substantiality (*anātta*) of everything that arises conditionally. The second stage of realization makes him aware of the universal impermanence that everything that exist is suffering is a fact and this makes the *srāvaka* compassionate. It is designated by the term *dharmāvalambanākaruõā*. It is the stage of lonely Buddha (*Patyek Buddha*). But the most comprehensive stage is called the stage of *Samyak Buddha*. His compassion transcends all conceptualization (*lokottara*). This compassionate Buddha is devoted to the service of all creatures. According to Nāgārjuna, the great compassion (*mahā karuõā*) that arises after enlightenment is boundless and can greatly save and help countless being.

5. In *Ariyapariyesana sutta* of *Majjhima Nikāya* the Buddha recognizes the importance of forest both for meditators and for laypeople. After realizing enlightenment (*buddhatva*) he set down for meditation in a delightful forest. Continuous rising of agrarian economy in and through deforestation and rising of commercial urbanization were matters of concern to the Buddha. So we see in different sermons the Buddha taught people to be compassionate to take due care for and love to all creatures. The

Jātaka stories testify Buddha's life in earlier births as birds and animals. In the Buddhist world view we see various types of inter relatedness and dependence of the total bio–community.

6. *Vinayapiňaka*, *sutta–vighanga*, para–1, contains the following dialogue which expresses respect for nature. "The venerable Maha Moggallana went to the Blessed One. He said : 'Lord, alms food is hard to get in Veranja now. There is a famine and food tickets have been issued. It is not easy to survive even by strenuous gleaning. Lord, this earth's under–surface is rich and as sweet as pure honey. It would be good if I turned the earth over. Then the bhikkhus (monks) will be able to eat humus that water plants live on. ... But, Moggallana, what will become of the creatures that depend on the earth's surface?

   ...Lord, I shall make one hand as broad as the Great Earth and get the creatures that depend on the earth's surface to go on to it. I shall turn the earth over with the other hand...Enough, Moggallana, do not suggest turning the earth over, Creatures will be confounded." — (Batchelor & Brown : 1992; 13)

8. The thoughts and experiences of a Vietamese monk Thich Nhat Hanh have been edited by Martine Batchelor may be seen for further details in this context. Water is a natural gift and there are passages for the proper use of it and skillful use of water contains the message of using all natural resources judiciously and act judiciously in using new methods and techniques discovered by the adventures of science for the good of all has been beautifully expressed in the following stanza :

   "Water flows over these hands.

   May I use them skill-fully

   to preserve the planet." (Batchelor & Brown, 1992; 106); it is also interesting to mention what Fox(2001:148) translated into English ,a stanza of a poem from Gagudju language of Australia as

   "If you feel sore——headache, sore body

   that means ,somebody killing tree or grass

   you feel, because your body is in that tree or earth.

   Nobody can tell you

   You get to feel it yourself."

9. Christopher Reed (1990:235) recently being a Zen teacher prescribe some moral codes and which are as follows,

   "I vow to recycle everything I can. This includes glass, cardboard, plastic, paper and motor oil. I vow to be energy efficient. This includes lowering the thermostat on the water heater, fixing all leaks immediately, using rechargeable batteries and cloth diapers.—I vow to be an active and informed voter. Learn how your representatives have voted on environmental issues. Let them know when you do not agree with them and when you agree —I vow to exercise my purchasing power for the benefit of all sentient beings" among many others.

Bibliography

1. *Anguttara Nikāya* (ed. E. Hardy, London, The Pali Text Society, 1900).
2. *An Introduction to Buddhist Ethics* (by Peter Harvey. Cambridge University Press, 2000).
3. *Buddhism and Ecology* (ed. M.E. Tucker and D. Williams, Harvard Center for the Study of World Religions, 1997).
4. *Buddhism and Ecology* (ed. Martine Batchelor and Kerry Brown, Motilal Banarasi Dass, 1994 (London 1992, Cassell)).
5. Buddhism and Environment (Simon P. James & David Cooper) in *Contemporary Buddhism*, Vol. 8, Issue 2, 2007 (Department of Philosophy, Durhan University, U.K.
6. *Buddhist Ethics (* Hammalawa Saddhatissa, Wisdom Publication, Boston, 2003 (1970).
7. *Bringing Life of Ethics : Global Bio ethics for a Humane Society* (Michael W. Fox, State University of New York, 2001).
8. Christopher Reed in his '*Dharma Gaia: A Harvest of Essays in Buddhism and Ecology,* 1990:235).
9. *Digha Nikāya* (Bengali tr. Bhiksu Silabhadra, Mahabodhi Book Agency, Kolkata, 1997 ed.).
10. *Dhammapada Aṅṅhakathā* (ed. H.C. Norman, London, The Pali Text Society, 1970 edition).
10. *Elegant Saying* (Nāgārjuna; ed. by Sakya Pandit, Dharma Publishing Emenyville, 1977).
11. *Encyclopedia of Environmental Sciences* (Vol.-6, ed. P. R. Trivedi & Gurdeep Roy, Akashdeep Publishing House.

12. *Environment* (R. N. Basu, University of Calcutta, 2000)

13. *Engaged Buddhism as Peacemaking* (ed. Christopher S. Queen, Wisdom Publications, 2000).

14. *Elegant Saying* (Nāgārjuna; ed. by Sakya Pandit, Dharma Publishing Emenyville, 1977)

15. *Fifty Key Thinkers on the Environment* (ed. J. A. Pahneer, Routledge, London 2001)

16. *Illustrated World Encyclopedia* (Vol.-5, New York, 1971)

17. *Jātaka* (ed. V. Fousboll, London, The Pali Text Society, 1963)

18. *Love in Action* (Nhat Hanh, Thich, Berkeley, C.A. Paralax Press, 1993)

19. *Man,Plant and Animal Interaction* (K.Chakraborti, Darbari Prakasan, Calcutta,1992)

20. *Mahāvagga* (ed. Mahesh Tiwary, Delhi University edition)

21. *Majjhima Nikāya* (ed. Lord Chalmers, London, The Pali Text Society, 1899)

22. *Namā–rūpa–pariccheda* of Anuruddha, (ed. A.P. Buddha datta, *Journal of Pali Text Society*, Vol.-VII, 1913)

23. *Non–violence to Animals, Earth and Self in Asian Tradition* (C.K. Chapple, Delhi, Satguru Publication, 1995)

24. *Pali–English Dictionary*, (London, The Pali Text Society, 1921–5)

25. *Rājā–parikathā–ratnamālā* of Nāgārjuna (tr. J. Hopkins & Lati Rinpoche; *The Precious Garland and the Song of the Four Mindfulness*, London, George Allen & Unwin, 1975)

26. *Rabindra–racanavali,* Visva Bharati, (Vol. 5),Kolkata,1986 *27. 27.Saddharmapuõóarikasutra* (ed. P.L. Vaidya, Buddhist Sanskrit Text, no. 6, Mithila, 1960)

28. *Samyutta–Nikāya* (ed. M. Leon Freer, 5 vols, London, The Pali Text Society, 1960; (1884–98))

29. *Spirit of the Environment* (ed. David E. Cooper & Joy A. Palmer, Rout ledge, London, 1998)

30. *Sutta Nipāta* (Bengali tr. Bhiksu Silabhadra, Maha Bodhi Book Agency, Kolkata, 2002)

31. *Sutta–Nipāta* (tr. Bhikkre Dharmarakshita, Motilal Banarasi Dass. Delhi, 1977).

32. *The Dhammapada* (Eng. tr. S. Radhakrishan. London, Oxford University Press, 1950).

33. *Theragātha* (ed. H. Oldenberg, London, The Pali Text Society, 1966 edition.

34. Toward a Buddhist Environmental Ethics (by Rita Gross, *Journal of the American Academy of Religion*, 65(2), 1997)).

35. *Uposatha* (Dipak Kumar Barua, Bharitiya Vidya Prakashan, 1991.

36. *Vinaya Piṅaka* (ed. H. Oldenberg, London, The Pali Text Society, 5 vols. 1964 edition).

37. *Vibhaḷga* (ed. C.A.F. Rhys Davids, London The Pali Text Society, 1934).

38. *Women in Buddhism : Images of the Feminine in Mahāyāna Tradition*, (D. Y. Paul : Berkeley, California, Asian Humanities Press, 1979.

4

NATURE AS THE 'OTHER'

Tarique Islam

The freedom man enjoys both determines and is determined by his attitude towards nature, which is primarily the result of his social being and corollary his political practices. Environmental studies, as a study of life forms, with its essentiality of interdisciplinarity, has been largely confined to the study of interaction between the sciences. However, this focus is changing to be more inclusive by making social sciences a part of it, especially politics, in order to comprehend the effect of socially organized humans on environment, which impacts the environment through its cultural attitudes, modes of social and economic organization and political practices. Politics, the sum total of political practices in a given society, is conventionally defined as the regulation of society, in other words, the concern with governance. This narrow definition has developed for the politicians a separate niche as professionals representing the citizens in parliament concerned with and determining governmental processes. These political practices obviously are in public sphere, where the politicians can be seen to negotiate and compromise in order to fulfill their role of representatives. Politics has therefore come to acquire the aura for the citizen of being distant; the citizen avoids any direct involvement. However, the definition has, as an overbearing necessity, transcended its conventionality to become more inclusive. Leftwich rightly depicts the inclusion as

"...[political] activities are not isolated from other features of social life. They everywhere influence and are influenced by, the distribution of power and decision making, the systems of social organization, cultural and ideology in society, as well as its relations with natural environment...Politics is therefore the defining characteristic of all human groups and always has been" (1983: 11). The attitudinal change effected by this broadening, by inclusion, of the definition of politics subverts its institutional character impacting attitude towards environment, which otherwise would only be a consideration of environmental policies and administration, whereas the need of the day is involvement of the masses in the issues and complexities faced with regard to environment. Therefore, the centrality of politics in environment and its study cannot be reasonably denied. But then this in turn requires delineating environmental studies as not a study of non-human universe or as an 'external', in short as the 'other'. Leftwich has rightly contended, "...the major organising activity at the heart of...history...[is] the...production and distribution of resources [which] has been and still is *politics* (italics in the original) (1983: 12). This view will enable, as Doyle and McEachern hope, an attitude so that nature will no "...longer be seen as resource but as more holistic construct that is far more open to interpretative possibilities...[such as] our relationship with the non-human world are socially as well as (on occasions) biophysically constructed...[which would be] more integrative...[and] non-anthropocentric..." (2008: 22).

The latter half of the eighteenth century witnessed the industrial revolution, which deeply ingrained 'modernity', the modern way of organising and legitimating social, political and economic life. This enlightenment project, where progress, was the basic aim, has resulted in the present ecological crisis and the ensuing debate is the result of this modernity, which has been lucidly and aptly portrayed by Carson as that "The 'control of nature' is a phrase conceived in arrogance, born of the Neanderthal age of biology and philosophy, when it was supposed that nature existed for the convenience of man" (1962: 100). The notion of nature revolves around the 'philosophy of man' in Western thought. The Cartesian dualism of the physical and the non-physical, with emphasis on the latter sealed the fate of nature, the physical environment or biophysical going ons. The question of identity in the Cartesian framework depended entirely on non-physical aspects of man. This brought the great divide between nature and man, by placing man outside nature, with freedom from nature's laws deeming him a moral agent. Man became absolutely different from nature and nature then became the 'other'. The view is related by O'Brian and Cahn, "Humans have long been interested in discovering our place in the hierarchy of nature" (1996:5). This reflected the broad Judeo-Christian view of the great 'Chain of Being' with its emphasis on a hierarchy within nature with man at the top having the privilege of exploiting nature, the 'other', to its advantage, which became the predominant 'philosophy of man' in Western thought. Nature then, as part of the 'Chain of Being', appeared in Western thought as the 'other' to be overcome, dominated and exploited to man's purposes. The domination became urgent and more emphatic with the fast growing capitalist society structured around the general dual principle of exploitation and domination.

The non-Western thought was not quite as impacting on environment as the Western with its advances in sciences and development of technology, which became primarily the tool to dominate physical nature. Most of the non-Western thought was more integrated with nature and its 'philosophy of man' did not galvanise around any hierarchical structures of being. However, the most commonly held view, now a days, whether one likes it or not, are those arising out of Western metaphysics and these form the corpus of contemporary thought on the present subject. By this I do not deny the importance of non-Western thought but simply suggest that environment has been brought into focus by two different principles operating simultaneously. The domination of nature and thereby deep exploratory concern with it, both are products of Western Judeo-Christian outlook.

The paper is a modest attempt to historically trace out the treatment of nature as the 'other', in social theorising, and attempt an understanding of the result of such a treatment. The paper will conclude by providing an alternative that may go some way towards achieving an understanding.

I would first of all point out that the advocacy of theories of 'inclusivity' is gaining currency and is in vogue today arguing for animal rights in environmental ethics. For our purpose the debate is somewhat uninteresting. However, it may be remarked in passing that talk of animal rights primarily reflects a deferred extension of the homocentric view point, animals being the nearest to man. Further, it springs up all sorts of arguments leading to absurdities such as non-animate rights. Still further, the more serious arguments come in where it is suggested that since the populace is now in a position to enjoy the fruits of nature the need has arisen to control it. In short to argue to stop progress in terms of technological advancement and availability of its fruits to all is absurd and can never be a practical regime.

However, there is no denying that humanity is faced with an environmental crisis of unprecedented nature. The awareness of this crisis brings with it the moral responsibility to control the immense capacity, through science and technology, of radically altering the physical nature. As Koestler, in the context of Hiroshima and Nagasaki, has rightly pointed out in his book 'Janus' that humanity has now the capacity to completely annihilate itself through atomic and other weapons. The interesting part is that we are the first generation aware of the transformation of the environment we are effecting and its implication for the posterity and future generations; the notion of 'sustainable development'. The environmental crisis has forced upon us to consider our relationship with nature and analyse its role in our lives. Therefore, there is a need for incorporating social sciences as part of environmental studies if it is going to be a meaningful discourse. The addition of social theorizing about nature is the only way for a more integrative approach otherwise nature will always remain the 'other' for us.

Environment has been used in social theory and one of the most common way, as Barry mentions, is "...in terms of 'reading-off' principles or how society should be from observations of how the natural world operates" (1999: 2). Barry goes on to claim that environment is essentially contested concept. An essentially contested concept is a concept whose definition in essence cannot be agreed upon, such as democracy, being evaluative and therefore evoking different irreconcilable views. Barry is wrong to classify environment as essentially contested for it is not an evaluative term the hall mark of such concepts. However, the concept of 'environment' may be polymorphous, in the Rylean sense, in that it can have a number of different connotations, refer to a heterogeneous variety of things, entities, processes, episodes, etc., but then this concept only comes into play if Wittgenstein's notion of family resemblance fails to yield results. However, not entering into the controversy over the status of definition of environment, it must be admitted that in theorising about nature the relation of human social existence has to be interrogated, which has always been a central concern of philosophy. It is crucial to first of all demarcate the concept 'environment' from its cognately related concepts like 'nature' and the 'natural' in social theory. For example, the term 'nature' cannot, as Raymond Williams has noted, be restricted to depict the nonhuman world, in fact it is, "...perhaps the most complex word in the language" (Williams, 1988:221). It is this complexity which led social theory trends in the nineteenth century to "First, an interest in the nature or social development and social origins. Second the merging of history and philosophy into a 'science of society' and third, the attempt to discover rational-empirical causes for social phenomena in place of metaphysical ones" (May, 1996:13). It must be noted that social theory is both descriptive and prescriptive, that is normative elements are present in it. It is this aspect which rightly prompts Barry to point out that "...thinking about the environment as something that can and does mean more than the 'natural world' can both help us in thinking about the natural world as well as revealing the complexity of social theorising about the environment" (Barry 1999:15). Soper has argued that in modern social theory, there is a marked tendency simply to equate the environment with the 'natural', the two terms being used virtually as synonyms (Soper, 1995). It is this treatment that keeps the social theory at a descriptive level lacking the normative aspects. The 'givenness' of nature has proved to be specially attractive, like in deep ecology, and natural processes are treated simply as if this is the way things ought to be, with any alteration as being not desirable. However, the problem with this approach again is treating nature as the 'other' as Smith points out, "The authority of 'nature' as a source of social norms derives from its assumed externality to human interference, the givenness and inalterability of natural events and processes and behaviours" (1996:41).

We will have to, however, learn to live with reading into nature for sometimes it is described as place of harmony, cooperation and balance, but then again as nasty, brutish, a rule of the might, competitive, survival of the fittest. This is because we project social claims, aims and positions on to the natural world. This is because social theory does not have any specific determinate readings of the environment without being value laden. As mentioned earlier the enlightenment project concerned with human progress and improvement, to bring about the plenty, depended on the effectivity in exploitation of the natural environment by use of scientific knowledge and technology. Till Enlightenment the social theorising about the environment primarily assumed religious or mythical overtones and with this perspective discussed the relationship between the natural world and humans. It was 'modernity' which effected a decisive change in Western thought about nature and with the advent of the industrial revolution, nature became 'disenchanted'.

Modernity is the first seat of engagement between social theory and environment, which primarily accepted nature as the 'other', describing it as being apart from humans and something to contend with. Anarchists therefore argued that humans in state of nature are naturally harmonious, co-operative and in no need for coercive state. This was contrasted by the contract theory of the state with Hobbes arguing that life in state of nature was 'solitary, poor, nasty, short and brutish' with no security. But Locke argued a different point and suggested that nonhuman environment, untouched by humans, is 'valueless' and human society required improvement and advancement, which had far reaching consequences on how the nonhuman environment was viewed by later social theorists. Locke's main argument was that humans could claim parts of the non-human environment as their private and exclusive property, which rationally justified an instrumental attitude towards and evaluation of natural environment as the 'other'. Barry is right in pointing out that, "So coupled with Hobbes's view of the 'state of nature' as something to be viewed with horror, Locke's view of nature as worthless in its untouched state, together produced the dominant attitude of social and political theory to the nonhuman environment up until the modern era." (1999:54)

However, not all social theorists agreed with the view and Rousseau, an early critic of Enlightenment, swam against the currents with his notion of 'noble savage' to argue that 'man' is naturally cooperative and preferred primitive societies as being the best for man. He asserted that the pre-civilised stage of human development and character was more virtuous, morally good, sincere and admirable than the 'advanced' civilised and cultured stage of social advancement. Rousseau argued that civilization and economic growth are the culprits for it is always accompanied by costs that by far outweigh the benefits, it corrupted our minds in proportion to the advances in our sciences. Rousseau came to be seen as a precursor of later Romantics and as Barry points out, "Rousseau was one of the first in this period to reverse the view that the 'Natural' was inferior to the 'Artificial', that a less complex society was necessarily inferior to an advanced civilized society such as those which existed in eighteenth century Europe. Going against the 'progressive'...his critique of modernity and its conception of progress is something that is at the heart of the later emergence of green social and political thought in the twentieth century. At the same time, his use of an evolutionary framework anticipated the work of Charles Darwin..." (1999: 55).

The successes in science went deeper to affect social theorizing and attempts to imitate the method of physical sciences into studies of human society assumed urgency. The scientific method was attractive since it presented a systematic study of phenomena, seeking universalisations, generalisable and law-like principles of explanation of cause and effect, using testable hypotheses which can be verified or falsified empirically. The success of science was its explanatory power and it was expected that adopting the scientific method would bring success in the study of society, which led to the birth of social sciences and to the first attempts to 'read off' how society is, and ought to be, from observations of the natural world.

The application of the scientific method to social studies led to the emergence of the 'self-regulating' lesse faire market as the liberal principle of organising the economy. It was this principle coupled with the freedom to acquire unlimited wealth or private property that led to production for profit and gave industrial society its 'capitalist' character. The uprising market strategies coupled with Nietzsche's proclamation of 'death of God' made progress of humanity an urgent project, to the extent of justifying as Arnold has written "...the indefinite continuance of imperial rule [in India]" (1996:174). As Marx and Engels pointed out, "The bourgeoisie, during its rule of scarce one hundred years, has created more massive and more colossal productive forces than have all preceding generations together. Subjection of Nature's forces to man, machinery, application of chemistry to industry and agriculture, steam-navigation, railways, electric telegraphs, clearing of whole continents for cultivation, canalization of rivers, whole populations conjured out of the ground-what earlier century had even a presentiment that such productive forces slumbered in the lap of social labour?" (1967: 85).

The scientific approach was also claimed by Malthus attack on whose notion of population affecting environment formed the basis Marxist concerns about nature. Marxist argue that non-social ecology is against the enlightenment project of ridding the scarcity through industrialisation, use of science and technology, which is not in the interest of the working class, which Marx pointed out was amply apparent in Malthus's work with its ideological tenor. Marxist presented a materialist social theory, the basic tenet of which is that the material conditions and relations determine the character of a society. Marx argued that it is not ideas that change societies but the material relations which organises the economic life that determine ideas in society.

Marx distinguishes other animals from the human by its characteristic of being capable of producing its needs and means of subsistence. Therefore, he held that human beings transform through their labour the natural resources into its needs for survival. According to Marx there is no nature of man as an abstract entity he is the product of his material conditions, which include environmental resources needed in order to survive. Man's consciousness is social consciousness, which includes awareness of nature, which is why humans do not simply take from nature whatever their natural environment provides but they transform the 'raw materials' of their environment through their labour power to fulfill their needs.

Habermas has succinctly pointed out that, "...the new conflicts are not sparked by problems of distribution, but concern the grammar of forms of life..."(1981: 33). Habermas is describing the political concerns of the day and not prescribing a route environmental politics should take. It has been a standing criticism of the Marxists that the grand narratives have been decidedly done away with in late capitalism to divert the attention to small, but very manageable social movements, such as gay rights, feminism, etc. Beck too suggests and agrees with Habermas that "What was at stake in the older industrial conflict of labor against capital were positives: profits, prosperity, consumer goods. In the new ecological conflict, on the other hand, what is at stake are negatives: losses, devastation, threats" (1995: 3). However, a theme that is emerging rapidly in social theorising, through the works of Habermas and Giddens, in critical theory, is to connect social theorising about external nature with internal or human nature and this is in order to bridge the gap between human and the 'other'. The Marxist construct of including within it the nonhuman world is beginning to gain as Vogel says, "What is wrong with the way nature appears to us (and our natural science) today is that it seems utterly independent of us and even opposed to us. Its sociality is hidden: we see it as separate from us, as dangerous (and impossibly complex, as always taking its revenge), and fail to see that rather it is always something in which we are deeply and actively enmeshed" (1997:188) It is precisely because nature appears as 'other', apart from us, that we fear it and there is a desire to control and dominate it. Marx had argued that social relations include the nonhuman world and not just relations between man and man and that external nature is in fact always already social, since it is partly the product of human transformative practices. Vogel argues, "Only a nature viewed as so separate from us would be something we would feel the (frightened) need to 'dominate' or the (equally frightened) need to 'preserve'. In either case it appears as alien, something to be either overcome or propriated – not simply as part of the (social) world that we both inhabit and continuously transform" (1997: 188). The Marxist depiction of the environment as socially constructed makes nature known and then not be understood as the 'other'. The modern conditions create a distance from the production of our needs and global capitalism has increased this distance, as Barry (1999: ch. 6) puts it, between production and consumption.

The requirement of the day then is more social theorising about nature and opening up the doors of the laboratory through more democratic accountability and popular participation. According to Beck, "Industrial society has produced a 'truncated democracy', in which questions of the technological change of society remain beyond the reach of political-parliamentary decision-making. As things stand one can say 'no' to techno-economic progress, but it will not change its course in any way" (1992b: 118). Our country has recently passed the Right to Act, 2005 which can be utilized fruitfully to bring in more accountability in the functioning of the corporate and government and inculcate greater participatory democracy with regard to environment.

Bibliography

Arnold, D: The Problem of Nature: Environment, Culture and European Expansion, Blackwell Oxford, 1996.

Barry, J: Environment and Social Theory, Routledge, 1999(a).

Beck, U: Risk Society: Towards a New Modernity, London, Sage, 1992.

: From Industrial Society to Risk Society: Questions of Survival, Social Structure and Ecological Enlightenment, Theory, Culture and Society, 9:1, 1992b.

: Ecological Enlightenment: Essays on the Politics of the Risk Society, Princeton, Humanities Press International, NJ, 1995.

Carson, R: Silent Spring, Greenwich, CT: Fawcett Premier, 1962.

Doyle, T and McEachern, D: Environment and Politics, Routledge, 2008.

Doyle, T and Walker, K: Looking for a world They Can Call Their Own, Campus Review, Australia, February 1-7, 1996.

May, T: Situating Social Theory, Open University Press, Buckingham, 1996.

Marx, K and Engels, F: The Communist Manifesto, Penguin, Harmondsworth, 1967.

Marx, K: Economic and Philosophical Manuscripts, in L. Colletti (ed.), Karl Marx: Early Writings, Penguin, Harmondsworth, 1975.

Goldblatt, D: Social Theory and the Environment, Polity, Cambridge, 1996.

Habermas, J: New Social Movements, Telos, 1981.

Leftwich, A: Redefining Politics: People, Resources and Power, Methuen, London, 1983.

Polanyi, K: The Great Transformation: The Political and Economic Origins of Our Time, Beacon Press, Boston, 1947.

Smith, N: The Production of Nature, in G. Robertson *et al* (eds), 1996.

Soper, K: What Is Nature? Blackwell, Oxford, 1995.

Vogel, S: Habermas and the Ethics of Nature, in R. Gottlieb (ed.), 1997.

Williams, R: Keywords: A Vocabulary of Culture and Society, Fontana, London, 1988.

5

PROTAGORAS, FREEDOM AND ENVIRONMENTAL CRISIS

Prof. S.E. Bhelke

Great truths appear simple, but in an attempt to understand them fully, one realizes how complex and difficult they are, being profound. Such truths have multiple interpretations which lead to a difference of opinion without allowing unanimity on their content and meaning. Nevertheless, they seldom get falsified, though their understandings and interpretations assume various forms as per spatio, temporal, historical or cultural contexts. One such truth was advocated as a basic principle by Protagoras before some millennia. He had said, "Man is the measure of all things, of the things that are, that they are, of the things that they are not, they are not". (Theaetetus, 152, Plato) This doctrine has been interpreted in various ways with opposing extremes, mainly because of the meaning of the term 'man'. Is it a particular man? Or, is it a man in general referring to the entire humanity as such? Which is this man? Who is this man? Is he that selfish and narrow minded person who does not recognize anybody without himself in the universe as a point and direction of activities in the universe? Or, is he that person who is a spring-head of all ideas and activities that enhance and enrich the existence and functioning of the universe? In fact, if a historical review is taken, man has been appearing in both these roles from time to time and in these varying roles of man vis-à-vis the human problems have been increasing and getting more and more complicated. In order to investigate into nature and causes of these problems we enter into another area for investigation, viz., human nature.

When we discuss the topic of human nature, it is discussed in a specific context and with a particular view or end in mind. The context for the present investigations is the context of the current environmental crisis in which we are required to re-define man's relation with nature and for these investigations, a certain concept of human nature is presupposed.

To begin with, we have to understand human nature on the physical or body level. Man being a living organism needs support and supply for his living from the nature. His living basically is a process of taking air, water and food in the body, absorbing that part of the intake which helps to maintain and enhance his life and then give away the remaining part of the intake. Thus the products from nature pass through his organism and this cycle continues till he is alive. In fact, this cycle is necessary for his living. He lives on energy and he absorbs the energy from nature through these intakes. His organism is designed in such a way that the need is made known through signals. They are instincts like thirst and hunger. The signals are so powerful that they motivate the organism to fulfill the needs. This is the functioning on the physical level. But body and sense-organs get habituate to demands and develop a continuous demand for fulfilling the needs of the organism, even in the absence of the genuine needs. The organism, thus, develops a tendency to keep on making demands. This takes us to the higher order of mind. Mind takes up the tendencies, develops attitudes and transforms needs into cravings. It is difficult to draw a line of demarcation between needs and cravings. Man is Free with needs, he can abstain himself from fulfilling needs; but he comes under the pressure of cravings and looses his freedom, since cravings are so powerful and dominating that they do not allow the man to control them, rather they control man by overpowering man's discriminatory powers. This is with objects concerned with body.

Beyond physical needs he has psychological needs which is a higher level of his organism and its living. He receives not only physical things like air, water and food but also receives favorable responses from other men in the society around him. As a living organism he has emotions which are concerned with his psychological needs and social needs, though fulfillment of his semi-physical needs are rooted in his physical existence. As he needs food for the existence and maintenance of his organism, he also needs to be cared by others where in return he cares for others. This mutual need is originated in him as his need and gets completed in its reciprocation. Thus he gets attracted by others and attracts others. This physical attraction is necessary for the life of an organism as it makes possible the reproduction, duplication or multiplication of his organism which is another dimension of the continuity of his existence. Not only the existence is to be maintained in a sound and healthy form but also is to be continued. He has sense to maintain his existence and he also continues it in such a way that it becomes more and more pleasant. On the physical level the sense of fulfillment gives satisfaction and it is articulated as pleasure.

The sensation of pleasure has one prong in physical body and another in the psychological. Man wants to increase and repeat the moments of pleasure. He is capable of increasing, repeating and abstaining from it. Although the natural course is to get pleasure, he has a capacity to alter, modify and vary the modes and directions of the natural course. This capacity is his freedom in which he does not follow the natural course blindly but evolves his own course, of his imagination or thinking. His freedom, thus, consists in being creative. He conceives and creates orders which do not exist in nature. He creates his own world and lives in it. The substance out of which he creates his world is the natural world. His capacity to conceive and construct a different and new world is his freedom. In doing this, he uses the natural world. The real ethical issue arises when he chooses the mode in which he uses the natural world for creating his own world.

Everything has its own dignity and sovereignty and violation of anybody's dignity and sovereignty is an immoral act which leads to exploitation. It is undesirable because ultimately it harms the life-interests of the agent who violates the dignity of others. It is not only the human beings who have dignity and sovereignty but animals, plants and the entire nature has it. Although man has freedom to use nature and change the natural course, he is not expected to violate the dignity and sovereignty of the nature. The complex situation in which the nature is around man to interact with, is the environment. Man has been experimenting and handling the environment for his own purpose for making his life more convenient and pleasurable. However, it becomes a delicate task to draw a line between the use and misuse or use and over use of the environment for his own purpose. Nevertheless, man has to make a judgement and decide whether and how he is exploiting his environment by going beyond using and handling it. In an excess of exercising his freedom man ultimately loses his freedom by bringing his existence in difficulties. He is supposed to enhance and enrich his existence by exercising his freedom; but in an over use of freedom his quality of life deteriorates. Man is free by nature and also has discriminatory power. He has to take a judgement to the extent till what he can be free if he has to be moral. An immoral behaviour annihilates the conditions of cxistence of the agent and hence the morality which is made possible due to his freedom, needs an exercise of discrimination and judgement.

Man is bestowed with several capacities and some of them are astonishing. Although many human capacities cannot be scientifically analysed and explained or justified, they are widely experienced. Man does not have only instincts but also has an intuition, a logic of which cannot be recursively and objectively explained or developed. Many of the discriminatory decisions and judgements are based on intuition rather than instincts or reason. He often gets a feel of the situation and also the anticipation of the future events and those feelings turn out to be true. The situations are so complex that many times his reason falls short of taking a right decision, because his reason cannot cover the vast area of the complex situation. Nevertheless, at times he gets an intuitive feel which turns out to be true when the happening takes place. Usually the intuition does not make man either to take morally wrong decisions or curtail his freedom. However, we can not depend upon intuition as a reliable and regular source for getting the grasp of the situation and making a judgement of decision about it to follow a certain course of action. It is not reliable in the sense that it may not be necessarily available for use whenever required. Its occurrence is unpredictable.

The other capacity man has is his reason. Its function is recursive. It is objective and the results obtained through its functions have certainty and necessity. Its results are also universal, i.e., they are a-spatial and a-temporal. This capacity or faculty makes discrimination, analysis and critique possible. It is rigorous in its function and it demands to be operated rigorously and also recursively. It has its own discipline which does not allow it to function irregularly. Its consistent use makes the agent disciplined-discipline in thought and action. However, a disciplined way poses a problem of freedom. It is usually believed that discipline and freedom are not compatible with each other. A disciplined person is not considered as a free person. In operations of reason there are restrictions and deviations are not allowed once reason begins its operations. Reason always has a direction and it keeps the direction as it functions rigorously.

As against reason another faculty of imagination is considered and accepted to be free in its operations. However, the purpose of both these faculties is different and hence one should not see or impose antagonism between them. The operations of the faculty of imagination consist in visualizing many possibilities and the operations of the faculty of reason consist in being recursive in drawing conclusions. Reason is penetrating and hence undertakes analysis while imagination is encompassing wider and wider ranges of possibilities and hence constructs unprecedented structures and super-structures. It is to be noted that these faculties of human nature, viz. instincts, intuition, reason and imagination, though discussed independently, their functions and operations are not undertaken so exclusively and singularly. It is the same human nature or potential which functions with all these faculties simultaneously, but at a time one of them predominantly and other supporting it remaining on the background and much less active. Hence, none of them affect the freedom of man as far as his intellectual capacities and functionings are concerned.

All natural happenings show a certain pattern. It is cyclic in nature. At every moment it takes a different direction and it turns.

Finally, it meets with the point where it had begun. This is its completion. In fact this is a two dimensional depiction of the happening. In a three dimensional depiction, it is spiral where circles keep ascending. This gives a model of growth and it is unending growth. The unending growth in a spiral model gives the understanding of infinity. Thus, truely speaking all processes or happenings or becomings or even being are infinite by nature. The being qua being is not limited to any (finite) number of dimensions. However, ordinarily it is understood as three or multidimensional. The happenings are known or understood as happenings in slices and cross-sections of the being. Living organisms are parts of the being and so exhibit the patterns of the being as a whole. In parts of being the happenings are in a spiral model and the entire being as a whole also has a spiral model. This means that between any two modes of happenings there is a rhythm. The dynamic aspect of the happening is rhythmic. As movements of each happening are rhythmic, the movements of many or all happenings too, are rhythmic in nature. The rhythmic spiral model of a happening is the proper nature of it. Any deviation or missings of a rhythm is something unnatural and problematic.

In the becoming aspect or form of the being a missing or loss of a rhythm is an indication of a problem. Loss of a rhythm leads to imbalance. The environmental crisis is to be understood as such an imbalance occurred due to a loss of rhythm. When man disturbs the rhythm between the human activities and the natural happenings, the course natural happenings take affects adversely the becoming, and upto some extent even being, of the human world. Except the human agency there is no factor which can cause the misfiring of the natural rhythm either in organisms or in the nature. It happens so because man makes or treats himself as the centre of happenings. To treat man as a centre of epistemology helps him better to understand the happenings and becoming on a practical and interactive level. This convenience impels man to treat himself as a centre for actions, norms and creativity. Even this situation does not lead to any crisis so far as the man at a centre is consistent with the nature and follows the course of natural mode as a part of the cosmic being. But when man treats himself outside the orbit of the course of natural happenings, his being a centre of the activities, norms and creations does not preserve the rhythm between himself as a part of the cosmic being and the cosmic being.

For an epistemic purpose man as a knower has to position himself outside the orbit of the cosmic being. But this distancing is imaginary and not real. This distancing is to create a space for interaction between a knower and a known where knowledge is or is an outcome of an interaction between knower and known. This distancing makes man separate from and independent of the cosmic being where man looses an awareness of a fact that the rhythm of man's happenings has to be in concordance with the rhythm of happenings of the cosmic being. The problem triggers at this point. When man treats himself at a centre by making nature and parts of the cosmic being as means to fulfill his own needs, the problem emerges. When the imaginary distancing of an epistemic purpose is employed for practical interactive purpose, man's being the centre and measure of all things create problems. Man's being the measure of all things is a perspective to understand the course of natural happening and this perspective enables man to understand because he thinks himself to be a finite being as against the infinite cosmic being. Hence the Indian approach invokes an understanding that man is potentially infinite being and he has to realize his infinite nature so that the interaction between man and the cosmic being assumes a different form. This also explains how and why the epistemology, praxiology, axiolagy and the discourse of creativity are radically different in the Indian tradition.

When man, with these faculties, confronts with nature, his interactions with nature and responses to nature become the matter of concern for philosophical investigations, especially when this interface becomes a ground for problems and challenges to man and nature both. Human nature has to have integrity as there is integrity in nature. In the interaction between man and nature, if both of them preserve their integrity, there is harmony and balance. The present problem of environmental hazards is due to man's undue manipulation of nature and aggressive role to deal with nature resulting into disharmony and imbalance. There is disharmony not only in the relation between man and nature but also in the nature itself. Man has generated and accumulated large energy which he uses to control and conquer nature so that he can enslave and use nature for his own purpose. This has become possible because of his various faculties and the freedom he has to use his faculties and direct the accumulated energies. Hence what we have to think more and seriously is the phenomenon of human freedom.

Freedom is a scope or space for infinite possibilities without determining to adopt any one of it out of any limitation. Man is free means he can choose any of the possibilities without any limitation and constraint which could be either internal or external. Usually interests by whom man is guided and directed in his course of life suggest him to choose a possibility in the given wide spectrum. When he delimits his interests with the narrow interests out of his selfish attitude the choices he makes, harm the harmony of the nature. The most basic fact is ignored that although for the sake of explanation man and nature are treated different from and antagonistic to each other, they are, in fact, united in one whole. Man is a part of nature; but due to his capacities he can distance himself from nature to interact with it. Man also forgets that the freedom he has, is within the scope of nature to which he belongs to as its part. When man segregates himself from the context to which he belongs to as a part, he can use and handle it by keeping a distance from it and exploit it for his limited and personal purpose. He does this because he thinks that he is free to do it. But the question is whether he is right in his understanding. If in an exercise of choosing one possibility, if he looses every chance to choose further any possibility, is his first choice a result of a genuine freedom? When man has to exercise his freedom in choosing possibility, he has to foresee consequences and be sure that in the further course his freedom will not get curtailed by his first or initial choice. If it so happens, then it will be a pseudo freedom and not a genuine one.

Man has to act physically, mentally, intellectually, socially and spiritually. His life is not completely determined. Hence his acting has to have a space and a multiple possibilities of modes in which he has to act. He chooses a mode out of the multiple possibilities. This is his freedom. An exercise of his freedom makes him creative which is the essence of his being. Nevertheless, being a part of the nature, scope of his being and acting is within the still larger scope of nature. The laws of nature govern and determine his actions but certainly not the modes of actions. So far he belongs to the larger frame of nature he is free. As soon as he breaks or demolishes the frame of nature, he looses his freedom because his very existence comes into difficulties and the multiple possibilities of modes go on reducing. The excess and indiscriminate exercise of freedom proves to be self-annihilating for his freedom as well as existence. His narrow selfish interests make him indiscriminate in his exercise of freedom. This is seen in the present scenario where man is too much playing with nature with a result to disturb and destroy the environmental balance.

This raises still basic problems to be discussed philosophically. Is man's freedom absolute? If it is not absolute but context relative, then how far is it to be accepted as freedom? In fact, the purpose and function of freedom decides the nature, genuineness and futility of freedom. Since man is not totally governed by nature and natural laws, he contributes to the world by creating novel structures. However, whatever existence we think of and speak about is always within a frame. If we think of the absolute existence of man and nature, there are no problems whatsoever to be faced. So far as man is considered as an agent of actions and knowing, he belongs to a context which has a certain frame of it. Man's actions and freedom are meaningful and intelligible only within the frame to which he belongs to. In exercising his freedom he is creative and his being creative makes him happy. His freedom, thus, is to be viewed in the parameters of creativity and happiness. Whatever act, situation, factor, cause or direction obstructs or annihilates his creativity and happiness destroys his freedom. The freedom has such a great potential that it can keep man continuously creative or make him self-destructive. Hence, the mode which gives a direction to freedom to lead it to its destruction is not really the freedom.

Although man is bestowed with great potentials and freedom, he is also bestowed with the power of discrimination. What can save him from his destruction is this power of discrimination. He is free to use or unuse and direct the way he wants to his power of discrimination. This freedom of using the power of discrimination to use freedom itself is to be recognized as the real freedom which alone can preserve his freedom to be creative and happy. Thus man is free as an agent and he himself has a standard to set the exercise of his freedom with discretion. Rather, the latter part is more important, viz., man being the source of standard to create and establish a measure to know and deal with the objects in the world. In this way the doctrine of Protagoras needs to be understood that man is the measure of all things, of the things that are, they are, of the things that they are not, they are not.

As per the Indian tradition nature is not inanimate. There is life everywhere. Even stones, mountains, rivers and similar inanimate beings have life. Of course the levels of life may differ, but there is life everywhere and in every object. Hence man's relation and interaction with all objects or things in the nature or with the nature as a whole are on an equal footings. When man establishes a relation with others, where the other may be either human being or living creature or nonliving thing, he has in his mind, consciously or unconsciously, an idea of his own status and the status of the other with whom he enters into a relation. He may think himself either superior or inferior or equal to the other for whatever reason. However, there has to be a moral dimension to the relation which is possible when the sense of dignity is introduced to the status of both relata. The sense of dignity in relations is seen quite often when the other is superior on moral and spiritual grounds. But, if the entire nature is seen as living i.e., in a form of consciousness, any relation gets the ground of dignity. The sense of dignity restricts the atrocious exploitation of the other and orients human freedom in such a direction where the wellbeing and happiness of all relata is the prime consideration. The proof of the foundation of dignity to relations is seemed when the other is personified, especially when the other is not a human being. Even when the other is a human being, when the other is treated just not a human but as a person while entering into a relation, the relation gets the foundation of dignity. Our interactions have to be with the sense of dignity of the other. Such a mode preempts exploitation and misuse of freedom.

The tendency of personification of every thing in the world is not a naïve attitude in the Indian tradition, but it is a way to acknowledge the dignity of everything in the world. This attitude has given rise to the notion of divinity and deity. It must be noted here that the consideration of deity and divinity is not theological in the Indian culture. When we treat the other with an element of divinity in it, naturally we respect and treat it with dignity. In this mode of interaction the attitude is that of adoring the other and hence exploiting, enslaving, and controlling the other does not take place. In this context freedom of the agent is exercised not to make drastic alterations in nature, but to direct the nature with such a moderate attempt that the agent gets support from the nature to enhance and enrich his life. In this situation one is free to be just a dispassionate spectator with devotion in mind and so he does not interfere with nature, just accepts the course of nature and makes his life harmonious with nature by making required modifications, alterations and innovation in his own life. In another mode of exercising freedom one does make alterations, modifications and innovations in the nature and natural course without disturbing the basic structure of the nature and the framework in which the nature functions. This is done to enhance one's aspirations, but keeping them in harmony with the nature and nature's functioning. As if there are two streams, one is of the life of man and the other is of the functioning of the nature. Both these streams are kept parallel to each other and in harmony with each other.

When man feels certain limitations in his life, he tries to overcome them by introducing innovations in himself as well as in the nature. He is free to accelerate operations and functions of the nature within himself and also in the world. But these attempts have to be moderate. It is difficult for man to slow down his accelerating the attempts to gain more and more pleasure and it becomes a challenge to him to moderate the acceleration so that his needs, passions, emotions etc. do not turn into greed or lust or cravings. He can moderate his needs etc. only if he is free. His freedom, thus, also consists in moderating his extreme and excess tendencies which override man and enslave man. Are we aware of and serious about this aspect of freedom? Freedom and its exercise has to be such that it should not turn out to be self-annihilating. Man is free to improve the quality of his life, but he can do so regularly and not for a short, i.e., if he is improving the quality of his life then for it he should not improve it in such a way that in future the way would get permanently blocked.

Man is not supposed to enslave the nature because firstly he is a part of the nature and secondly, in such an attitude, he develops rivalry with the nature. In principle man is free to develop rivalry with the nature; however is it desirable? To be moral is to enhance life and conditions of life. By developing rivalry no one can enhance either life or conditions of life and hence it will not be moral. When we think of responsibility, in fact, it is a moral commitment. To understand the responsibility associated with freedom is to understand the moral commitment involved in it. The moral commitment is to protect and preserve both freedom and life. It is said that man has made a great progress in civilization mainly because he is free to allow and motivate operations of his traits. However these developments have transgressed their limits so much that his modifications in the nature and natural course have posed threats to his life and existence. Innovative changes and artistic creations are different from artificialities in life and nature. We have to radically re-think, therefore, about freedom, progress, prosperity, pleasure and happiness.

One of the reasons for regression in man's status in the wake of the high scientific and technological developments is his continuous focus on and involvement in the material aspect of life. Spirituality indicates here higher and purer levels of life. Spirituality indicates here higher and purer levels of awareness which make creativity possible, which makes man happy by transgressing pleasures and sensuous levels of material life which gives moral pleasure and aesthetic joy and which elevates man from carnal life to higher life. When man's ego melts into wider consciousness, when his attachments to personal interests loosen and when he aspires for higher goals which are beyond mundane plane, he attains spiritual level. His spirituality is neither a mystic nor an occult phenomenon but it is a trans-empirical level of his being and experiencing. His interactions with others and the world on this level make his life spiritual and make him happy in his life. Since there are no carnal and sensuous bondages or limitations on this level, his freedom can be exercised in an unrestricted way without making his life immoral. Man having been elevated, thus, on a spiritual level exercises his freedom in a right way without getting self-annihilated and without getting trapped into immoral situation.

Man has been playing with nature. His playful attitude has taken various forms through which man has various kinds of creations to his credit. Religion is one such creation which is a result of his playing with the cosmos with respect and reverence. Hence man adorns nature by seeing in it divinity. Another creation of man is science which begins with a curiosity to know and penetrate into the depth. This play has enabled man to discover several laws of nature and man has tried to predict and control nature by using its laws. Art is still another creation of man when he plays with nature to enjoy it on spiritual level. His creations make his life and world aesthetic and beautiful. Man has also played in another way and created values, the moral values, though a super-structure over the nature but a base structure for social life. All these creations are results of human freedom where man has played with nature by altering, modifying or innovating novel structures in and over it. When he transgresses his limits of freedom, he is in peril. His freedom is absolute, it is not limited or determined by any external condition but it is restricted and moderated by itself to abstain it from turning self-annihilating. The philosophical attitude moderates the freedom to get exercised in its natural and proper form. This attitude makes freedom disciplined and creative, it is this aspect of freedom which is spiritual and in its spiritual aspect freedom makes man moral to deal with himself, others and nature.

Man has been indiscriminate in the exercise of his freedom not only when he deals with the society and nature but also when he deals with himself. When we think of an environment, usually we think of the external conditions and situations in the world or nature. But there is also a social environment as well as a psychological environment. The social temper and emotional set-up or moods are the forms of environment man lives in. He has to be very careful in exercising his freedom in these forms of environment. Whatever man does and gets in return, he is responsible to it. He is at the centre of the world, the natural world and also the world(s) of his creation. He creates and sets standards in the world. He knows the world and he justifies the world by keeping himself at the centre of the world as a spring-head of creations, creations of processes, procedures, explanations, justifications, standards, parametres and also the ends. The life for man begins with himself and ends with himself. He himself is the goal or end of all his activities. This world and life is free because it is determined not by any external factor but by aspirations emerging from within himself. When man truly becomes aware that he is the measure of all things, he becomes the balanced and responsible agent to initiate interactions with him and the other. As he creates problems, he alone solves them. He is in bondage because he is not aware of his nature and freedom. He liberates himself when he exercises his freedom which is innate to him. The realization that freedom and creativity are the essences of his nature makes him to exercise his freedom and actualize creativity. These processes are never ending. If these processes get arrested, it means that he has slipped from the right path and direction in exercising his freedom. Through freedom he creates his environment and lives in it. His environment is a form of the world, social and natural, to which he belongs to. This is a world of his creations and hence his enjoyment, not the sensuous but spiritual enjoyment which is also called by a word like happiness. In his life man is the measure of his creations, happiness and also freedom - a man not captivated by selfish ego but the man who encompasses the entire world within himself by merging himself into the cosmos.

6

"VEDANT AND CONSERVATION OF BIO-DIVERSITY"

Prof. Mridula Ravi Prakash

Philosophy in the ultimate analysis denotes love for knowledge, which is what characterizes the importance of Philosophy in today's world. In fact, ever since human being has started thinking and questioning. Philosophy had impact on individual and society, generally one of the forms of social consciousness. It includes the conceptions of the general laws of being and cognition and of the relation of thought to being. Therefore, the principal functions of philosophy are the cognitive i.e. worldview, the methodological and lastly the ideological. A worldview is interpreted as a historically shaped system generalized views of the outside world, social like and the attitude of man to this world and to himself. Application of the worldview principles to the process of cognition and transformation of reality is referred to us methodology.

The most important function of philosophy is closely linked with ideology which means a system of ideas and views expressing the position and needs of a definite class, social group or the whole of society and acting as a guideline for social action. Philosophy performs a similar function. The overwhelming majority of Philosophy give an affirmative answer to the most challenging question of class, society and world that it is the only science which is capable in its ideas and notions of the real world to produce a correct reflection of reality. Although it needs some enthusiastic revisitations and reconstructions of metaphysical and epistemological theories of Indian Philosophy and also a similar strong creative attempt for reflective awareness of the need for reshaping Indian ethics with a fresh scientific conceptual insight which seems to be absent in the Philosophy of contemporary India. In the present age it has been named an age of scientific achievements, which have made mankind to think that sky is their limit, this is regrettable, at least- for two reason. One is that the recent concern with value based education would look some what sankhya without a solid theoretical foundation that can be provided only by a philosophical ethics. The other and more important reason is that Indian ethics cries out for its redefinition and reformulation in terms of more systematic theory-centric expositions of rich ethical resources scattered in the multifarious aspects of the Indian traditions.

Mankind today is in an epoch of transition. Although we may be too close to the event to grasp in full significance, but it is now quite clear that we are in the process of a major change. Advancement in science and many other conceptual revolutions have compelled the revitalization of ethical philosophy in modern India. The predominant consciousness of the human race reflects its evolutionary situation, and it would be true to say that at this crucial cross-roads, when modern philosophers are spreading the idea of none party and supra class spirit of philosophical thought, mankind is looking for a philosophical help, a paradigm to solve the daunting challenges of society and nation as well.

In this reference we should not forget the contributions of our traditional Indian philosophical systems. The Vedic environmental ethical code springs from sarvajivadaya. The Vedic seers recited the sacred lores like what is bad for you, should not be done to others (Atmanam pratikulani paresham na samacharet). Emmanuel Kant's 'categorical imperative' is a positive assertion of this ethics. It touches every form of existence. It therefore, provides solid basis for ecological concerns. Instinctive love and respect for and protection of nature and environmental awareness are deeply rooted in Vedic traditions as a part of Indian tradition. All life is scared, meaningful and valuable. It proves that that environmental ethics not only regulates human conduct in relations to one's own self and in relation to other fellow human beings but also goes a step further to bring in human conduct in relation to all living beings and natural environment. Every existence has intrinsic worth and it must be respected. Therefore, Vedic seers reveal organism and the existence of 33 crore deities. It includes all organism elements (Panchmahabhuta) like air, fire, earth, sky, water, birds, animals or (in water worlds all macro and micro elements which surround all sentient) beings. The Vedic environmental ethics also has to be spiritualistic aiming at Universal well-being based on the enlightened principle of selflessness of all existence. It does not mean that during the Vedic period there were no selfish and materialistic people. However, in those days there was a general notion, which functioned as an important part in their environment that self-centeredness and other negative attitude were not something to be cherished. That value system gave a distinct shape to the Vedic environmental ethics and its inculcation of, it was the prime objective of Vedic lifestyle.

Therefore there is a need of launching the purification of livelihood, the best way of livelihood is that of a honey bee. As s honey bee moves to the different flowers and without causing any harm either to the shape or colour of the flowers, collects sustenance and maintains its living, similarly one should eke out his livelihood without inflictive any injury to any one.

Where something exists there is biodiversity and where there is nothing there is no biodiversity. Therefore biodiversity is defined as the variability among living organism from all sources. Including terrestrial marine and other aquatic eco-system and the ecological complexes of which they are a part, this includes diversity within species, between species of which they are a part; this includes diversity with in species between species of ecosystem. So biodiversity is part of daily life and livelihood and constitutes resources upon which families, communities, nations and future generation is surviving and will depend.

Loss of biodiversity has serious economic and social costs for any country. Conservation and sustainable use of biodiversity is fundamental to ecological sustainable development. Every country has the responsibility to conserve, restore and sustainable use the biodiversity, within its jurisdiction.

India is one of the 12 mega diversity countries of the world. The experience of the past few decades has shown that with the rise of science and technology, nature has been commoditized and exploited. Our comforts have been achieved at the expenses of all life forms: large scale masses have been displaced by civilization advances countless species are perpetually facing the extinction; the earth is burning and groaning, we face the global warming. Indiscriminate conduct of the so called modern and civilized human being is compared to a donkey who carries burden of sandalwood without knowing its value or utility. As the donkey bears the burden of sandalwood but has no share in the wealth of his load, similarly a person knows to fly in the sky, but he does not know how to live on the earth along its biodiversity.

India 'a Mega biodiversity country' has been sensitive to need of conservation and hence is still rich in biological resources. Ethos of conservation and harmonious living with nature is very much ingrained in the life style of Indian people; because the vedic environmental ethics provides a value based life style rather than a consumerist one. In the wake of globalization, environment along with biodiversity is facing a threat of survival. Environmental ethics and policies enunciated by the Vedas provide a solution to this challenge.

The modern society whether national or international has enough resources and technology to ensure for every human being on earth, the physical, intellectual, material, and spiritual, inputs necessary for full and healthy life but on the other hand surely the poison is also upon us. It is in this context that the necessity for an alternative philosophy of life becomes so intense and because of the universal values that it enshrines, the Vedanta represents precisely such an integrated and universal philosophy. Vedanta is basically based upon the great source of knowledge, the Upnishads and the Bhagvatgita, a testimony to the magnificent spiritual endeavour to solve the problems of present society. It provides insights which can be of crucial value for the survival of humanity in this nuclear age. The basic principles of Vedanta provide the framework for a Philosophy to sustain the emerging global consciousness on our planet.

The first important concept of the Vedantic knowledge is that of all-pervasive Brahnisa Vasyam Sarvam Yat Kinca jagatyam Jagat i.e. what ever exists and wherever it exist is permeated by the same divine power and force. This is in a way parallels the realization of modern science which rejects the incurable dichotomy between matter and energy and accepts that whatever exists is really the same energy although it may appear in different forms of matter, particle or wave. So the united field theory towards which the scientists are desperately probing already has its spiritual counterpart in the concept of the all pervasive Brahman of the Upnishads.

The another important keynote of Vedantic teaching is the relationship between the Atman and the Brahman. Vedant believes that Bhraman recites with in each individual consciousness is the Atman and Atman is the reflection of Brahman in individual consciousness. Both are not separate from each other. All the four Yogas- the Gyana Yoga, the Bhakti Yoga, the Karma Yoga and Raj Yoga are directed towards bringing about a union between the Atman and the Brahman. The concept of Ishwarah Sarvabhutanam hrddeserjunatisthati is a great insight of current challenges in the context of globalization.

The above concept also reflects the essence of Adaita philosophy which is the philosophy of monism or non duality.

"Brahman Satya Jagat Mithyat" i.e. Bhraman is the only thing which is true. Everything else is Maya. Ultimately every soul merges with the Brahman. All human beings are members of a single extended family as they shared the same spirituality. All are Amrtasya Putrah (Childern of immortality). A famous verse 'Vasudhaiva Kutumbkam' points out that the division between 'mine' and your's is a small and narrow way of looking at reality indulged in by people with immature minds. Tatvamasi is another expression which stresses the ultimate oneness of things. If we are able to remove the barriers which come in the way of this unity of we remove differences and give the idea of looking at things as not being connected but look at them as part of a single whole then we must be able to go beyond the apparent differences and arrive at the latent unity. The concept of oneness or unity is a philosophy which cuts across barriers of hatred and the fanaticism that have been built in the name of religion. Our traditional philosophy confirms the essential unity of all religions and spiritual paths as it is said in the Vedantic concept "Akam sad Viprah bahudhaVadanti" means Truth is one, the wise call it by many names as the Rig Veda has it. The Mundaka Upnishad explains the unity of all religions by a beautiful verse which says: as streams and rivulets arise in different parts of the world but ultimately flow into the same ocean, so do all these creeds and religious formulation arise in different times and areas but if they have a true aspiration, ultimately reach the same goal. Vedant, as a Universal religion, accepts the infinite possibilities of movements towards the divine. This philosophy believes that once we really start moving upwards in the fields of spiritual Endeavour, we will find our denominational and intellectual differences gradually losing their importance and as we rise to the summit, we will realize the spiritual oneness of humanity.

Next the cosmic vision of Indian philosophy is also very important to rescue humankind from the octopus grip of excessive greed, inordinate ambition and selfish pursuit of the shams and shows of life. Welfare of all beings "Bahujana Sukhay Bahujana Hitay" is the salient feature of Indian philosophy. This slogan seeks the welfare of all creation, not- only of human beings but also of what we call the lower creatures. Our arrogance and ignorance, have destroyed the environment of this planet. We have not only unbreathable air, polluted ocean but also we have desecrated nature and decimated wild life. But it is our great Indian philosophical tradition which believes man is not something apart from nature and therefore it believes in compassion for all living beings and preaches us that while we are working for our own salvation; we must seek to develop both elements of our psyche, the inner and the outer, the quietist and activist. Indeed, both are two sides of same coin.

In short, it is these valuable concepts and teaching of Indian philosophy which provides us a comprehensive world view which will greatly help to solve the problems and the challenges of globalization. Gradually a world civilization is being born, and it has to be born if mankind is to survive in this nuclear age. Although science and technology have given us tremendous power but at the same time we must never forget that the worship of power of science is not enough, we also need to recapture wisdom, compassion and understanding. We can now survive only if we have an alternative ideology to the one which has led mankind to this position and we boldly stand at in harmony with that ideology, the rich traditions of Indian philosophy provides such an alternative world view and if even at this late hour we can imbibe some of its universal truths, we can perhaps reverse the mad rush towards destruction and begin the long, slow climb back to sanity. Let us close than with that immortal Indian values which provide the basic frame work of their approach to tackle the problems of current challenges in Indian context and in the context of globalization as well.

7

ENVIRONMENTAL ETHICS

Prof. Asha Maudgil

Bioethics is the interface of biology, technology, healthcare and ethics. This area requires revision and updating often as biotechnological developments, changes in healthcare occur at a rapid pace and the emergence of new voices in a rapidly expanding field require attention.

The field of environmental ethics concerns human beings' ethical relationship with the natural environment. While numerous philosophers have written on this topic throughout history, environmental ethics only developed into a specific philosophical discipline in the 1970s. This emergence was no doubt due to the increasing awareness in the 1960s of the effects that technology, industry, economic expansion and population growth were having on the environment.

Of course, pollution and the depletion of natural resources have not been the only environmental concerns rather: dwindling plant and animal biodiversity, the loss of wilderness, the degradation of ecosystems, and climate change are all part of a raft of "green" issues that have implanted themselves into both public consciousness and public policy cver subsequent years. The job of environmental ethics is to outline our moral obligations in the face of such concerns. In a nutshell, the two fundamental questions that environmental ethics must address are: what duties do the humans have with respect to the environment, and why? The latter question usually needs to be considered prior to the former. In order to tackle just what our obligations are, it is usually thought necessary to consider first *why* we have them. For example, do we have environmental obligations for the sake of human beings living in the world today, for humans living in the future, or for the sake of entities within the environment itself, irrespective of any human benefits? Different philosophers have given quite different answers to this fundamental question which, as we shall see, has led to the emergence of quite different environmental ethics.

A. Extending Moral Standing

As noted above, perhaps the most fundamental question that must be asked when regarding a particular environmental ethic is simply, *what* obligations do we have concerning the natural environment? If the answer is simply that we, as human beings, will perish if we do not constrain our actions towards nature, then that ethic is considered to be "anthropocentric." Anthropocentrism literally means "human-centeredness," and in one sense all ethics must be considered anthropocentric. After all, as far as we know, only human beings can reason about and reflect upon ethical matters, thus giving all moral debate a definite "human-centeredness." However, within environmental ethics anthropocentrism usually means something more than this. It usually refers to an ethical framework that grants "moral standing" solely to human beings. Thus, an anthropocentric ethic claims that only human beings are morally considerable in their own right, meaning that all the direct moral obligations we possess, including those we have with regard to the environment, are owed to our fellow human beings.

While the history of western philosophy is dominated by this kind of anthropocentrism, it has come under considerable attack from many environmental ethicists. Such thinkers have claimed that ethics must be extended beyond humanity, and that moral standing should be accorded to the non-human natural world. Some have claimed that this extension should run to sentient animals, others to individual living organisms, and still others to holistic entities such as rivers, species and ecosystems. Under these ethics, we have obligations in respect of the environment because we actually owe things to the creatures or entities within the environment themselves. Determining whether our environmental obligations are founded on anthropocentric or non-anthropocentric reasoning will lead to different accounts of what those obligations are. This section examines the prominent accounts of moral standing within environmental ethics, together with the implications of each.

B. Human Beings

Although many environmental philosophers want to distance themselves from the label of anthropocentrism, it nevertheless remains the case that a number of coherent anthropocentric environmental ethics have been elaborated (Blackstone, 1972; Passmore, 1974; O'Neill, 1997; and Gewirth, 2001). This should be of little surprise, since many of the concerns we have regarding the environment appear to be concerns precisely because of the way they affect human beings. For example, pollution diminishes our health, resource depletion threatens our standards of living, climate change puts our homes at risk, the reduction of biodiversity results in the loss of potential medicines, and the eradication of wilderness means we lose a source of awe and beauty. Quite simply then, an anthropocentric ethic claims that we possess obligations to respect the environment for the sake of human well-being and prosperity.

Despite their human-centeredness, anthropocentric environmental ethics have nevertheless played a part in the extension of moral standing. This extension has not been to the non-human natural world though, but instead to human beings who do not yet exist. The granting of moral standing to future generations has been considered necessary because of the fact that many environmental problems, such as climate change and resource depletion, will affect future humans much more than they affect present ones. Moreover, it is evident that the actions and policies that *we* as contemporary humans undertake will have a great impact on the well-being of future individuals. In light of these facts, some philosophers have founded their environmental ethics on obligations to these future generations. Of course it is one thing to say that human beings in the future have moral standing, it is quite another to justify the position. Indeed, some philosophers have denied such standing to future people, claiming that they lie outside of our moral community because they cannot act reciprocally (Golding, 1972). So, while we can act so as to benefit them, they can give us nothing in return. This lack of reciprocity, so the argument goes, denies future people moral status. However, other philosophers have pointed to the fact that it is usually considered uncontroversial that we have obligations to the dead such as executing their wills and so on, even though they cannot reciprocate (Kavka, 1978). While still others have conceded that although any future generation cannot do anything for us, it can nevertheless act for the benefit of its own subsequent generations, thus pointing to the existence of a broader trans-generational reciprocity.

However, perhaps we do not have obligations to future people because there is no definitive group of individuals to whom such obligations are owed. This argument is not based on the simple fact that future people do not exist yet, but on the fact that we do not know who they will be. Derek Parfit has called this the "non-identity problem" (Parfit, 1984, ch. 16). The heart of this problem lies in the fact that the policies adopted by states directly affect the movement, education, employment and so on of their citizens. Thus, such policies affect who meets whom, and who has children with whom. So, one set of policies will lead to one group of future people, while another set will lead to a different group. Our actions impact those who will exist in the future, making our knowledge of who they will be incomprehensible. Since there is no definitive set of future people to receive the benefits or costs of our actions, to whom do we grant moral standing? Secondly, and of particular importance for environmental ethics, how could any future people legitimately complain that they have been wronged by our environmentally destructive policies? For if we had not conducted such policies, they would not even exist.

In response to the non-identity problem, it has been argued that while we do not know exactly who will exist in the future, we do know that some groups of people will exist and that they will have interests. In the light of this, perhaps our obligations lie with these interests, rather than the future individuals themselves. As for the second aspect of the problem, we might claim that although future generations will benefit from our environmentally destructive policies by their very existence, they will nevertheless have been harmed. After all, cannot one be harmed by a particular action even if one benefits overall? To illustrate this point, James Woodward gives the example of a racist airline refusing to allow a black man on a flight that subsequently crashes (Woodward, 1986). Isn't this man harmed by the airline, even though he benefits overall?

Even if we do decide to grant moral standing to future human beings, however, that still leaves the problem of deciding just *what* obligations we have to them. One set of difficulties relates to our ignorance of who they are. For not only do we lack information about the identity of future people, but we have neither knowledge of their conceptions of a good life, nor what technological advances they may have made. For example, why bother preserving rare species of animal or oil reserves if humans in the future receive no satisfaction from the diversity of life and have developed some alternative fuel source? Our ignorance of such matters makes it very difficult to flesh out the content of our obligations.

By way of reply to such problems, some philosophers have argued that while we do not know everything about future people, we can make some reasonable assumptions. For example, Brian Barry has argued that in order to pursue their idea of the good life - whatever that happens to be - future people will have need of some basic resources, such as food, water, minimum health and so on (Barry, 1999). Barry thus argues that our obligations lie with ensuring that we do not prevent future generations from meeting their basic needs. This, in turn, forces us to consider and appropriately revise our levels of pollution, resource depletion, climate change and population growth. While this might seem a rather conservative ethic to some, it is worth pointing out that at no time in human history's history have the needs of contemporaries been met, let alone those of future people. This unfortunate fact points to a further problem that all future-oriented anthropocentric environmental ethics must face. Just how are the needs and interests of the current generation to be weighed against the needs and interests of those human beings in the future? Can we justifiably let present people go without any concern for the future humans?

Clearly then, the problems posed by just a minimal extension of moral standing are real and difficult. Despite this, however, most environmental philosophers feel that such anthropocentric ethics do not go far enough, and want to extend moral standing beyond humanity. Only by doing this, such thinkers argue, can we go beyond the narrow and selfish interests of humans, and treat the environment and its inhabitants with the respect they deserve.

C. Animals

If only human beings have moral standing, then it follows that if I come across a bear while out camping and shoot it dead on a whim, I do no wrong to that bear. Of course, an anthropocentric ethic might claim that I do some wrong by shooting the bear dead – perhaps shooting bears is not the action of a virtuous individual, or perhaps I am depleting a source of beauty for most other humans – but because anthropocentrism states that only humans have moral standing, then I can do no wrong to the bear itself. However, many of us have the intuition that this claim is wrong. Many of us feel that it is possible to do wrong to animals, whether that be by shooting innocent bears or by torturing cats. Of course, a feeling or intuition does not get us very far in proving that animals have moral standing. For one thing, some people (hunters and cat-torturers, for example) no doubt have quite different intuitions, leading to quite different conclusions. However, several philosophers have offered sophisticated arguments to support the view that moral standing should be extended to include animals.

Peter Singer and Tom Regan are the most famous proponents of the view that we should extend moral standing to other species of animal. While both develop quite different animal ethics, their reasons for according moral status to animals are fairly similar. According to Singer, the criterion for moral standing is sentience: the capacity to feel pleasure and pain. For Regan, on the other hand, moral standing should be acknowledged in all "subjects-of-a-life":

that is, those beings with beliefs, desires, perception, memory, emotions, a sense of future and the ability to initiate action. So, while Regan and Singer give slightly different criteria for moral standing, both place a premium on a form of consciousness.

For Singer, if an entity possesses the relevant type of consciousness, then that entity should be given equal consideration when we formulate our moral obligations. Note that the point is not that every sentient being should be treated equally, but that it should be considered equally. In other words, the differences between individuals, and thus their different interests, should be taken into account. Thus, for Singer it would not be wrong to deny pigs the vote, for obviously pigs have no interest in participating in a democratic society; but it would be wrong to subordinate pigs' interest in not suffering, for clearly pigs have a strong interest in avoiding pain, just like us. Singer then feeds his principle of equal consideration into a utilitarian ethical framework, whereby the ultimate moral goal is to bring about the greatest possible satisfaction of interests. So there are two strands to Singer's theory: first of all, we must consider the interests of sentient beings equally; and secondly, our obligations are founded on the aim of bringing about the greatest amount of interest-satisfaction that we can.

Tom Regan takes issue with Singer's utilitarian ethical framework, and uses the criterion of consciousness to build a "rights-based" theory. For Regan, all entities who are "subjects-of-a-life" possess "inherent value". This means that such entities have a value of their own, irrespective of their good for other beings or their contribution to some ultimate ethical norm. In effect then, Regan proposes that there are moral limits to what one can do to a subject-of-a-life. This position stands in contrast to Singer who feeds all interests into the utilitarian calculus and bases our moral obligations on what satisfies the greatest number. Thus, in Singer's view it might be legitimate to sacrifice the interests of certain individuals for the sake of the interest-satisfaction of others. For example, imagine that it is proven that a particular set of painful experiments on half a dozen pigs will lead to the discovery of some new medicine that will itself alleviate the pain of a few dozen human beings (or other sentient animals). If one's ultimate norm is to satisfy the maximum number of interests, then such experiments should take place. However, for Regan there are moral limits to what one can do to an entity with inherent value, irrespective of these overall consequences. These moral limits are "rights", and are possessed by all creatures who are subjects-of-a-life.

But what does all this have to do with environmental ethics? Well, in one obvious sense animal welfare is relevant to environmental ethics because animals exist within the natural environment and thus form part of environmentalists' concerns. However, extending moral standing to animals also leads to the formulation of particular types of environmental obligations. Essentially, these ethics claim that when we consider how our actions impact on the environment, we should not just evaluate how these affect humans (present and/or future), but also how they affect the interests and rights of animals (Singer, 1993, ch. 10, and Regan, 1983/2004, ch. 9). For example, even if clearing an area of forest were proven to be of benefit to humans both in the short and long-term, that would not be the end of the matter as far as animal ethics are concerned. The welfare of the animals residing within and around the forest must also be considered.

However, many environmental philosophers have been dissatisfied with these kinds of animal-centered environmental ethics. Indeed, some have claimed that animal liberation cannot even be considered a legitimate environmental ethic (Callicott, 1980, Sagoff, 1984). For these thinkers, all animal-centered ethics suffer from two fundamental and devastating problems: first of all, they are too narrowly individualistic; and secondly, the logic of animal ethics implies unjustifiable interference with natural processes. As for the first point, it is pointed out that our concerns for the environment extend beyond merely worrying about individual creatures. Rather, for environmentalists, "holistic" entities matter, such as species and ecosystems. Moreover, sometimes the needs of a "whole" clash with the interests of the individuals that comprise it. Indeed, the over-abundance of individuals of a particular species of animal can pose a serious threat to the normal functioning of an ecosystem. For example, many of us will be familiar with the problems rabbits have caused to ecosystems in Australia . Thus, for many environmentalists, we have an obligation to kill these damaging animals. Clearly, this stands opposed to the conclusions of an ethic that gives such weight to the interests and rights of individual animals. The individualistic nature of an animal-centered ethic also means that it faces difficulty in explaining our concern for the plight of endangered species. After all if individual conscious entities are all that matter morally, then the last surviving panda must be owed just the same as my pet cat. For many environmental philosophers this is simply wrong, and priority must be given to the endangered species (Rolston III, 1985).

Animal-centered ethics also face attack for some of the implications of their arguments. For example, if we have obligations to alleviate the suffering of animals, as these authors suggest, does that mean we must stop predator animals from killing their prey, or partition off prey animals so that they are protected from such attacks (Sagoff, 1984)? Such conclusions not only seem absurd, but also inimical to the environmentalist goal of preserving natural habitats and processes.

Having said all of this, I should not over-emphasize the opposition between animal ethics and environmental ethics. Just because animal ethicists grant moral standing only to conscious individuals, that does not mean that they hold everything else in contempt (Jamieson, 1998). Holistic entities may not have independent moral standing, according to these thinkers, but that does not equate to ignoring them. After all, the welfare and interests of individual entities are often bound up with the healthy functioning of the "wholes" that they make up. Moreover, the idea that animal ethics imply large-scale interferences in the environment can be questioned when one considers how much harm this would inflict upon predator and scavenger animals. Nevertheless, clashes of interest between individual animals and other natural entities are inevitable, and when the push comes to shove, animal ethicists will invariably grant priority to individual conscious animals. Many environmental ethicists disagree, and are convinced that the boundaries of our ethical concern need to be pushed back further.

D. INDIVIDUAL LIVING ORGANISM

As noted above, numerous philosophers have questioned the notion that only conscious beings have moral standing. Some have done this by proposing a thought experiment based on a "last-human scenario" (Attfield, 1983, p. 155). The thought experiment asks us to consider a situation, such as the aftermath of a nuclear holocaust, where the only surviving human being is faced with the only surviving tree of its species. If the individual chops down the tree, no human would be harmed by its destruction. For our purposes we should alter the example, and say that all animals have also perished in the holocaust. If this amendment is made, we can go further and say that no conscious being would be harmed by the tree's destruction. Would this individual be wrong to destroy the tree? According to a human or animal-centered ethic, it is hard to see why such destruction would be wrong. And yet, many of us have the strong intuition that the individual would act wrongly by chopping down the tree. For some environmental philosophers, this intuition suggests that moral standing should be extended beyond conscious life to include individual living organisms, such as trees.

Of course, and as I have mentioned before, we cannot rely only on intuitions to decide who or what has moral standing. For this reason, a number of philosophers have come up with arguments to justify assigning moral standing to individual living organisms. One of the earliest philosophers to put forward such an argument was Albert Schweitzer.

His influential "Reverence for Life" ethic claims that all living things have a will to live", and that humans should not interfere with or extinguish this will.

But if we recognize moral standing in every living thing, how are we then to formulate any meaningful moral obligations? After all, don't we as humans require the destruction of many living organisms simply in order to live? For example we need to walk, eat, shelter and clothe ourselves, all of which will usually involve harming living things. Schweitzer's answer is that we can only harm or end the life of a living entity when absolutely necessary. Of course, this simply begs the question: when is absolutely necessary? Taylor attempts to answer this question by advocating a position of general equality between the interests of living things, together with a series of principles in the event of clashes of interest. First, the principles state that humans are allowed to act in self-defense to prevent harm being inflicted by other living organisms. Second, the basic interests of nonhuman living entities should take priority over the nonbasic or trivial interests of humans. Third, when basic interests clash, humans are not required to sacrifice themselves for the sake of others (Taylor, 1986, pp. 264-304).

While Albert Schweitzer can be regarded as the most prominent philosophical influence for thinkers who grant moral standing to all individual living things, Aldo Leopold is undoubtedly the main influence on those who propose "holistic" ethics. Aldo Leopold's "land ethic" demands that we stop treating the land as a mere object or resource. For Leopold, land is not merely soil. Instead, land is a fountain of energy, flowing through a circuit of soils, plants and animals. While food chains conduct the energy upwards from the soil, death and decay returns the energy back to the soil. Thus, the flow of energy relies on a complex structure of relations between living things. While evolution gradually changes these relations, Leopold argues that man's interventions have been much more violent and destructive. In order to preserve the relations within the land, Leopold claims that we must move towards a "land ethic", thereby granting moral standing to the land community itself, not just its individual members. This culminates in Leopold's famous ethical injunction: "A thing is right when it tends to preserve the integrity, stability, and beauty of the biotic community. It is wrong when it tends otherwise" (Leopold, 1949/1989, pp. 218-225)

Now while many holistic philosophers do explicitly condone sacrificing individuals in some situations, for example by shooting rabbits to preserve plant species, they are reluctant to sacrifice human interests in similar situations. But isn't the most abundant species destroying biotic communities Homo sapiens? And, if human individuals are just another element within the larger and more important biotic community, is it not necessary under holistic ethics to kill some of these "human pests" for the sake of the larger whole? Such considerations have led Tom Regan to label the implications of holistic ethics as "environmental fascism" (Regan, 1983/2004, p. 362). In response, proponents of such ethics have claimed that acknowledging moral standing in holistic entities does not mean that one must deny the interests and rights of human beings. They claim that granting moral standing to "wholes" is not the same thing as taking it away from individuals. While this is obviously true, that still leaves the question of what to do when the interests of wholes clash with the interests of individuals. If humans cannot be sacrificed for the good of the whole, why can rabbits?

E. Social Ecology

Social ecology is of the view that the foundations of the environmental crisis lie in the dominant ideology of modern western societies. Thus, social ecology claims that in order to resolve the crisis, a radical overhaul of this ideology is necessary. However, the new ideology that social ecology proposes is not concerned with the "self-realization" of deep ecology, but instead the absence of domination. Indeed, domination is the key theme in the writings of Murray Bookchin, the most prominent social ecologist. For Bookchin, environmental problems are directly related to social problems. In particular, Bookchin claims that the hierarchies of power, prevalent within modern societies have fostered a hierarchical relationship between humans and the natural world (Bookchin, 1982). Indeed, it is the ideology of the free market that has facilitated such hierarchies, reducing both human beings and the natural world to mere commodities. Bookchin argues that the liberation of both humans and nature are actually dependent on one another.

The Future of Environmental Ethics

Given the increasing concern for the environment and the impact that our actions have upon it, it is clear that the field of environmental ethics is here to stay.

However, it is less clear in what way the discipline will move forward. Having said that, there is evidence for at least three future developments. First of all, environmental ethics needs to be and will be informed by changes in the political efforts to ameliorate environmental problems. Environmental ethics concerns formulating our moral obligations regarding the environment. While this enterprise can be, and often is, quite abstract, it is also meant to engage with the real world. After all, ethicists are making claims about how they think the world ought to be. Given this, the effectiveness of states and governments in "getting there" will affect the types of ethics that emerge. For example, the Kyoto Protocol might be regarded as the first real global attempt to deal with the problem of climate change. However, without the participation of so many large polluters, with the agreed reductions in greenhouse gas emissions being so small, and with many countries looking like they may well miss their targets, many commentators already regard it as a failure. Ethicists need to respond not just by castigating those they blame for the failure. Rather they must propose alternative and better means of resolving the problems we face. For example, is it more important to outline a scheme of obligations for individuals rather than states, and go for a bottom-up solution to these problems? Alternatively, perhaps businesses should take the lead in tackling these problems. Indeed, it may even be in the interests of big business to be active in this way, given the power of consumers. It is quite possible then, that we will see business ethics address many of the same issues that environmental ethics has been tackling.

However, the effects of environmental ethics will not be limited to influencing and informing business ethics alone, but will undoubtedly feed into and merge with more mainstream ethical thinking.

After all, the environment is not something one can remove oneself from. In light of this, once it is recognized that we have environmental obligations, all areas of ethics are affected, including just war theory, domestic distributive justice, global distributive justice, human rights theory and many others. Take global distributive justice as an example: if one considers how climate change will affect people throughout the world so differently – affecting individuals' homes, sanitation, resistance from disease, ability to earn a living and so on - it is clear that consideration of the environment is essential to such questions of justice. Part of the job of the environmental ethicist will thus be to give such disciplines the benefit of his or her expertise.

Finally, environmental ethics will of course be informed by our scientific understanding of the environment. Whether it be changes in our understanding of how ecosystems work, or changes in the evidence concerning the environmental crisis, it is clear that such change will inform and influence those thinkers writing on our environmental obligations.

The problem of environmental ethics is an imported problem, it is a problem of the western world which has a materialist bent of mind. It respects no one, if it stands to gain. Exploitation is the accepted system of working which has now resulted in the changes in the eco-system resulting in change of weather patterns, rise in pollution etc. In the Indian perspective there is no such problem because our philosophy and life are not separate. Our philosophy and religion has taught us to respect all plants and animals. The Indian system stresses the balance of nature. If one animal is killed by man he has to ask for atonement of his sin and he has to perform several other tasks to nullify the sin. These tasks are there for the maintainance of the balance of the eco-system. In India we co-exist with the bio-diversity. Holy status is given to many trees, plants and animals. We have the habit of feeding the birds, animals like dogs and cows. We find all these animals on the streets of our towns. In the case of the western world we hardly get to see any birds because they are killed, to avoid interference with air travel which is so popular there. Thus, Instead of discussing issues about which there is much hue and cry in the west, we must spend our energy on discussing those issues which are directly relevant here. In the land of Sunderlal Bahuguna a single individual can bring about a revolution of ideas when required and we do not have to wait for business houses to endorse our concerns. The idea of ecosystems which is integral to the Indian view is only now, slowly dawning on the thinkers of the west.

Bibliography

- Bookchin, Murray and Foreman, Dave, *Defending the Earth,* (New York: Black Rose Books, 1991).
- Passmore, John, *Man's Responsibility for Nature,* New York: Scribner's, 1974). Blackstone, William T., "Ethics and Ecology" in Blackstone, William T. (ed.).
- Callicott, James Baird, "Animal Liberation: A Triangular Affair", *Environmental Ethics* 2 (1980): 311-328.*Philosophy and Environmental Crisis,* (Athens, University of Georgia Press, 1972): 16-42.
- Gewirth, Alan, "Human Rights and Future Generations" in Boylan, Michael (ed.), *Environmental Ethics,* (New Jersey: Prentice Hall, 2001): 207-211.
- Golding, Mark, "Obligations to Future Generations", *Monist,* 56 (1972): 85-99.
- Kavka, Gregory, "The Futurity Problem" in Sikora, R. I., and Barry, Brian (eds.), *Obligations to Future Generations,* (Philadelphia: Temple University Press, 1978): 186-203.
- Parfit, Derek, *Reasons and Persons,* (Oxford: Clarendon Press, 1984).
- DesJardins, Joseph R., *Environmental Ethics: An Introduction to Environmental Philosophy,* (Belmont CA: Wadsworth, 3rd ed., 2001).
- Regan, Tom, *The Case for Animal Rights,* (Berkeley: University of California Press, 2nd ed., 1983/2004).

- Singer, Peter, "All Animals Are Equal", *Philosophical Exchange,* Vol. 1. No. 5 (Summer, 1974): 243-257.
- Sagoff, Mark, "Animal Liberation and Environmental Ethics: Bad Marriage, Quick Divorce", *Osgoode Hall Law Journal* 22, 2 (1984): 297-307.
- Schweitzer, Albert, (translated by Naish, John), *Civilization and Ethics: the Philosophy of Civilization Part II,* (London: A & C Black Ltd, 1923).
- Rolston III, Holmes, "Duties to Endangered Species", *Bioscience,* 35 (1985): 718-726
- Leopold, Aldo, *A Sand County Almanac: And Sketches Here and There,* (Oxford: Oxford University Press, Special Commemorative Edition,1949/1989).
- Taylor, Paul W., *Respect for Nature: A Theory of Environmental Ethics,* (Princeton NJ: Princeton University Press, 1986)

8

ANTHROPOCENTRIC CUM ECO-CENTRIC NATURE OF ENVIRONMENTAL VALUES

Prof. D.N. Yadav

There can be no ethics without value, the study of which is called 'axiology'. Therefore, in this paper I am going to deal with the nature of value, especially as it concerns the ecological or environmental or the natural world. Value can be held to inhere in either single, discrete items, in which case it is individualist, or in sets of such items, in which case it is holist. The usual example of the former is an individual person, animal or living being; the latter may include species or biotic places, comprising at a minimum two or more individuals who are connected in some non-random or arbitrary way with species, genetically, or with places, eco-systemically.

Again, a more important distinction is made between instrumental value and intrinsic value. The first kind is the value someone or something has as a means to something else, where that something else constitutes, in effect, a good in itself or at least, is more valued than the means. In contrast, when someone or something has value as an end in itself, for its own sake, it has intrinsic value. **Callicott J.** introduces another form of intrinsic value as inherent value meaning that in order to exist, intrinsic value requires some one to value it.

But there has been a great deal of confusion around this issue. Let us briefly try to clear it up. In the first place, the distinction between instrumental and intrinsic value is necessary. Because each such term depends for its meaning on the contrasting one it is defined against. Furthermore, if there were only instrumental value, then every thing would only have value as a means to something else; but for something to have value as a means, that something else must, at least in practice be relative to the means, and have value in itself. In other words, it must have intrinsic value. But if there was only intrinsic value , it is not at all clear how it would actually be possible to live, i.e., without using anything or anyone.

Secondly this confusion relates closely to the subject of the realism and relativism,–there is the vexed question among environmental philosophers of whether intrinsic value is 'objective' or 'subjective'. Many debates have taken place between realists or objectivists, who assert that value is 'really there', 'actually there' or even 'out there', and relativists or subjectivists, who argue that we 'project', 'create' or 'construct', it. The former use their assertion to argue for the pre-eminence of science among all the ways of knowing. The subjectivists, believe that there is such a thing as True Knowledge but that we cannot have it. Thus any agreement is therefore arbitrary.

The problem is that both sides, or rather dogmatic proponents of both these views, tend to talk past each other. The resulting stalemate is unnecessary, however, for the same reasons. On the one hand, there can be no value that is objective in the sense of being 'out there' whether we know it or not. Any such value has no reality, it has meaning only for us, in other words, reality just is reality-for-us whoever 'us' might be it certainly need not be just human.

On the other hand, neither is value created, or conjured by us out of nothing, and out of whatever we wish. Neither is it subjective in the sense of being purely our personal creation; we only exist in, nor apart from, a world of others which exercises constant constraints. We should therefore abandon the untenably extreme views according to which value must either be completely independent of human apprehension, in order to qualify as objective, or 'merely' subjective meaning arbitrary or trivial, and therefore, in another form, in need of some kind of other support, usually scientific. But this is a false choice. Value requires both a world and participation by one who values it to be real. It is both objective and subjective for us.

In short, whatever has intrinsic value is that which is valued for its own sake, without any reference to its usefullness in realizing some other goal. Now it may be too strong to maintain as John Fowles holds that, "We shall never understand nature or ourselves, and certainly never respect it, until we dissociate the wild from the notion of usability-however innocent or harmless the use."[2] But there are certainly good grounds for holding that nature must not be seen as only of instrumental value.

With this in mind, we can turn to the next major distinction between anthropocentrism, which limits most if not all intrinsic value to humans, and eco-centrism, which finds intrinsic value in nature.

Thus, there is a spectrum of perceived proceedings from that we have two main types of concepts in Environmental Ethics: (1) Anthropocentric-which is entirely restricted to humanity-meaning thereby human centered value, thoroughly (2) Eco-centric meaning thereby- Earth centered value. It follows then, that we must concentrate increasingly on the latter as we proceed through that spectrum, looking at the strengths of each major position on it, but also with limitations that point to the need, for a more eco-centric alternative. However, let it be made clear that ecological ethics is not intended to replace traditional human centered ethics- which has a perfectly legitimate and important role in intra-human relationships or its extension to animals and other non-human living beings.

Therefore, we cannot prefer either value over the other; rather we should have to deal with both natures of value i.e. eco-centric through the anthropocentric and vice-versa or anthropocentric cum eco-centric nature of value.

Anthropocentrism, which literally means human centeredness, is one of the most contentious ideas. Therefore, it has an important place in ecological ethics. There have been several attempts to replace it, but none has been particularly convincing, and since some such concept is definitely needed, it would probably be better to deal with this one while being careful about exactly what we mean by it.

Sometimes one objection to the term is leveled against which can be cleared up right way. It goes something like this : 'For us, everything is necessarily human-centered. Therefore, there is no alternative, and the term is meaningless'. This point is then used to argue that all value is human, and that ethics should therefore, have human beings as it principal or even sole focus as Jordanova has stated as follows; "Man never left centre stage, nature never has been, and never will be, recognized as autonomous".[3]

Thus, the premise is true here that all value, for us, are anthropogenic-generated by human experience, although always co-created by both man and nature. But because value is generated by human beings, it does not follow that humans themselves must be the main repository or central concern of value. Similarly, recognition of the intrinsic value of the natural world may require a human valuer. Again, it does not follow that such value is therefore, itself purely human. As David Wiggins put it as follows, "In thinking about ecological things we ought not to pretend and we do not need to pretend that we have any alternative, as human beings, but to bring to bear upon ecological questions, the human scales of values.... The human scale of values is by no means exclusively a scale of human values."[4]

However, there are those who maintain that as a matter of existential or metaphysical fact, humanity is the principal or sole thing of value, and that the only appropriate or possible scale of value for humans is a scale of human values.

Now, the use of 'anthropocentrism' has been criticized, not without reason, as too far-reaching. After all, there is nothing wrong with a concern for human beings as such, nor is it necessarily inconsistent with a concern for non-human nature. For this reason, alternative terms have been suggested such as human chauvinism, speciesism and human racism.[5]

All these terms have some merit, although the first term is awkward, the second an insufficient neologism and the third involves too narrow an analogy However, still more important is that the term 'anthropocentrism' is pretty well established. Also, there is already a reasonably good word for a healthy and non-exclusive appreciation of human value, namely 'humanism'. For these reasons, I think, we, should retain, anthropocentrism' to refer to the unjustified privileging of human beings, as such, at the expense of 'other forms of life'.

Thus, it is vital to recognize how dominant this mindset is, whether in politics, economics, science or culture. Neil Evernden, in 'The Natural Alien', calls it 'resourcism', so to quote him as follows; 'Resourcism is a kind of modern religion which casts all of creation into categories of utility to humans, whereby there is literally nothing in the natural and human world which cannot be transformed into a resource. It is the ideology par excellence of modernity, and thus of ecocrisis."[6]

Now, we come to the opposite position, and it is a very important one, both in itself and as a counter pole to anthropocentrism. There are intermediate positions of course. One is Zoocentrism as mentioned by Patrick Curry[7] according to which the principal locus of value is animals-in practice, non-human animals. Another, less limited and arbitrary concept is biocentrism which has been dealt with, in detail by Arne Naess, Sessions, George and Paul Taylor, which are worth special treatment, but this is not my concern in this paper. Briefly speaking, biocentrism means life itself as value, in all its forms. There is co-existent and identity relationship between man and nature.

Again, the question arises regarding the intermediate position why this position. The simple answer is that, life is itself dependent on components aptly summarized in the ancient elements, earth air, water, fire (Sunlight) and ether. Ecosystems thus, comprise a complex ongoing activity of interrelationships not only with other organisms but with the non-organic. For this reason, eco-centrism is the more inclusive concept and value.

Like anthropocentrism, eco-centrism is also at least equally contentious and delicate matter. At first sight, it seems that its meaning should be simple i.e. placing or finding, value in the natural world as Robyn Eckersley[8] has also stated. But again a crucial question is, does or should that include human beings? Critics of eco-centrism have charged it with a simple inversion of anthropocentrism which is not only misanthropic and strategically counterproductive but preserves the radical split between the human and natural worlds that we inherited from Platonism and Cartesianism. That split is one which ecologists in general see as an integral part of the problem. And the accusation of misanthropy is not always without justification where some Deep Ecologists are concerned. But there is no reason why compassion for human beings and compassion for non-human animals and nature should have to be mutually exclusive. Logically speaking, if humans are a part of nature, then they share, at least in part and/or potentially in nature's intrinsic value. And in practice the two kinds of compassion are likely to reinforce each other.

Eco-centrism does not necessarily exclude humanity, and there are powerful reasons-strategic as well as ethical- why it should not. In this connection Warwick Fox has rightly said that, "Being opposed to human centeredness is logically distinct from being opposed to humans per se."[9]

And misanthropy is as unjustifiable as it is unattractive. As Robyn Eckersley writes, respecting the Earth's boundary, "The principle of common entitlement makes it clear that humans are not expected to subvert their own basic needs in order to enable other life-forms to flourish".[10]

Humanity poses a riddle or problem in this respect, being plainly part of the natural world and, at the same time distinct from other animals in the degree to which individual reflective consciousness, and its socialization as culture, affects to a relatively unique extent how otherwise 'purely' natural factors play themselves out. Let us note here that no superiority or special privileges necessarily follow from this uniqueness as G. Snyder[11] also points out.

Ken Jones also puts up an excellent discussion as follows; "But it does mean that ethically, humankind does have a unique responsibility for the well being of other creatures and the whole ecosystem, yet is at the same time a dependent and integral part of that system."[12] Thus, in the light of above points, let us say that neither exclusive anthropocentrism nor exclusive eco-centrism is a defensible, or desirable option.

However, it is vital to recognize that even with an inclusive eco-centrism, there can be serious conflicts between humans and non-human nature, and an arrangement, in which the former cannot lose, if and when there are such conflicts, cannot be called eco-centric. Some social ecologists, like Murray Bookchin,[13] maintain that the 'liberation of nature' necessarily follows from the liberation of oppressed humans. But this wishful thinking obscures the real conflicts and hard choices that can occur between what are at least perceived as humans' interest interest and nature's interests, which makes it harder to evaluate and decide between them.

Indeed, even within the broad movement to protect the non-human world, there are clashes between proponents of animal liberation/rights i.e. trying to protect individual animals and ecologists/environmentalists like Hargrove[14] trying to protect species and/or ecosystems. Patrick Curry has also established the dependence of both systems i.e. anthropocentrism and eco-centrism as he states; "Alliances between different progressive and emancipator movements do not come readymade; the hard work of forging them is unavoidable. And it should be added that in many perhaps even most of the situations, an appeal to anthropocentric value (human self-interest) maybe an unavoidable part of the argument for an eco-centric outcome."[15]

It follows that an eco-centric ethic alone will probably not suffice to save an earth fit for life as we know it, but that also would not happen without it. In our unprecedented circumstances, the dominant philosophy of the last two millennia either in religious or secular form, is now in drastic need of change. Eco-centrism recognizes as anthropocentrism does not, that human beings live in a more than-human world, of which they are only one part.

Thus, anthropocentrism's denial of such a fundamental point cannot be corrected by 'enlightened self-interest', through limited measure. The problem with 'enlightened anthropocentrism' is exactly the same as with 'enlightened egoism' as Mary Midgley says; "egoism by its nature is rather unenlightened and hard to enlighten".[16] The important thing now, as Sylvan and Bennett state is, to "Set anthropocentric concerns within ecocentric concerns".[17]

At last to conclude in the words of Patrick Curry as follows; "An eco-centric horizon' to our concerns, in contrast, would help avert ecological disaster, and do so in a way that also furthers anthropocentric interests; if humans learn to care about what happens to other species and ecosystems, that is, to treat nature as if it mattered-then the repercussions of ecological destruction to humans will be lessened".[18]

We have now arrived at a conclusion via value, at ecological ethics: that is, principles concerning how human beings ought to behave in relation to non human nature. Here, too, there is a spectrum. At one end, corresponding to instrumental value, consideration for the non human is only indirect, insofar as the well-being of humans is affected. In middle, there is consideration for non human individuals. At the other end, corresponding to intrinsic value, we find consideration for the well-being of non-human places and eco-systems.

References

1. J. Baird Callicott, "Intrinsic value, Quantum Theory, and Environmental Ethics;" Published in Environmental Ethics 7, 1985, pp. 357-75.

2 John Fowles; "The Tree"; St. Albans : The Sumach Press; 1979; pp. 43-44.

3. Ludmilla Jordanova; "The Interpretation of Nature (1987)" quoted by Patrick Curry in 'Ecological Ethics: An Introduction'; Polity Press, U.K., 2006; pp. 42-43.

4. David Wiggins ; "Nature, Respect for Nature, and the Human Scale of Values"; proceedings of the Aristotelian Society, 2000, pp. 7-8.

5. Richard Routley and Routley; "Against the Inevitability of Human Chauvinism (1979), quoted by Patrick Curry in 'Ecological Ethics' *op.cit.*, p. 43.

6. Neil Evernden; "The Natural Alien: Human Kind and Environment" University of Toronto Press, 1985, p. 23.

7. Patrick Curry; *op.cit.;* pp. 44.

8. Robyn Eckersley; 'Environmentalism and Political Theory : Toward an Ecocentric Approach, Albany : State University of New Yark Press, 1992.

9. Fox Warwick; "Toward a Transpersonal Ecology: Developing New Foundations for Environmentalism", Fox hole: Resurgence; 1995, p. 19.

10. Robyn Eckersley; "Beyond Human Racism"; Environmental Values", State University of New York Press; 1998; p. 177.

11. Gary Snyder; "The Practice of the Wild"; San Francisco: North Point 1990, quoted by Patrick Curry; *op.cit.,* p. 45.

12. Ken Jones; "Beyond optimism: A Buddhist Political Ecology"; Oxford: Jon Carpenter Publishing; 1993; p. 97.

13. Murray Bookchin; "The Philosophy of Social Ecology"; Rawat Publications, New Delhi, 1996, pp. 37-69.

14. Eugene C. Hargrove; "Foundations of Environmental Ethics"; Denton, Tx , Environmental Ethics Books; 1989.

15. Patrick Curry; *op.cit.;* p. 46.

16. Mary Midgley; "Sustainability and Moral Pluralism"; Routledge-London; 1997, p. 94.

17. Richard Sylvan and David Bennett; "The Greening of Ethics: From Human Chauvinism to Deep-Gree Theory" Cambridge: White Horse Press; 1994, p. 90.

18. Patrick Curry; *op.cit.,* p. 46.

9

USE AND MISUSE OF FREEDOM OF MAN: CASE STUDY OF HYDROPOWER

Bharat Jhunjhunwala

The Framework

The purpose of this universe appears to be 'evolution of consciousness' as seen in the meaning of the word 'Brahman'—to grow. It is obvious that man, being part of the Brahman, should act in a way that furthers the purpose of Brahman—to grow. Since Brahman is consciousness, it follows that growth must be defined as growth of consciousness. Brahman may here be defined synonymously with 'Nature' or 'Universal Consciousness'.

Man has higher degree of freedom than other living beings. It is man's solemn responsibility to exercise his freedom in a way that leads to evolution of his consciousness. Man is part of Brahman hence evolution of his consciousness spontaneously becomes evolution of Brahman.

There is a caveat, however. Man's consciousness can evolve in two ways:

- Evolution: While helping others in raising of their consciousness.
- Devolution: While hitting at others and reducing their level of consciousness.

An example will clarify the matter. Planting of trees on barren land leads to all-round increase in consciousness. The barren land has low level of consciousness. This is increased by growing of trees, animals, insects, etc. On the other hand, planting of the same trees in a beautiful garden would lead to lowering of level of consciousness. The scented flowers and flowing waterfalls will be replaced with a jungle of trees.

Man must exercise his freedom to modify nature in a way that leads to an overall evolution of consciousness and not to its devolution.

This seems to be the difference between Asuras and Devtas. Both are *bhogi.* But Asuras undertake bhoga while hitting at others while Devtas undertake bhoga by helping others evolve along with. Cutting of a forest for making charcoal may be done both by Asuras and Devtas. The Asuras will cut the forest and leave the land barren. Devtas will cultivate the land and grow wheat and paddy. Thus, Rig Veda mentions cutting of forests in a positive sense:

> "Goddess of the wild and forest... seemest to vanish from sight. And, yonder what seems a dwelling-place appears... another there hath felled a tree" (10.146).

The Asuric use of freedom leads to reaction from other elements of Universe. Let us say the civilization of Indus Valley collapsed because of over-exploitation of the forests. As a result the silt got deposited in the river beds and led to floods which destroyed the civilization. We may conclude from this that the loss of consciousness in the forests that were cut was more than the gain of consciousness by use of the forest resources. In the result nature—silting and floods—took revenge. The loss of consciousness due to the cutting of the trees was not compensated by an increase in consciousness brought forth by the use of that timber etc.

The main problem is that it is difficult to understand and comprehend whether consciousness is increasing or decreasing by a particular action. It requires one to connect with various players and appreciate the increase or decrease in their consciousness. People of the Indus Valley failed to connect with the consciousness of the

Table 1: Sources of power reckoned on the touchstone of consciousness

Sl No	*Parameter*	*Impact*	*Thermal*	*Hydro power*	*Nuclear*
1	Use of electricity	Students will be able to study etc.	+3	+3	+3
2	Methane	Global warming kills life forms. Bad smell lowers consciousness. Methane emissions by thermal are assessed at 800 grams/KwH against 2154 for storage hydro plants in Brazil.	-2	-3	-
3	Mining	Coal and uranium lying locked at lower level of consciousness is burnt and liberated into air. Large amount of coal is burnt.	+3	-	+2
4	Storage of Nuclear waste	Accidental release of nuclear waste can kill life and lower consciousness	-	-	-3
5	Quality of River Waters	Thermal and nuclear stations discharge hot water into rivers. Hydro deprives various living organisms of the kinetic energy of rivers; and lowers the quality of waters for bathing by pilgrims. Consciousness of flowing water is reduced by flowing it through canals and tunnels.	-1	-3	-1
6	Sediments	Sediments are trapped in hydro reservoirs and deprives fish, flood-recession agriculture,	-	-2	-
7	Forests	Forests are cut in mining; and are submerged in hydro reservoirs.	-2	-2	-2
8	Earthquakes	Mining of coal leads to subsidence of cities like Jharia. Hydro reservoirs led to reservoir induced seismicity.	-2	-2	-1
9	Displacement	Human beings are displaced in mining and hydro projects.	-2	-2	-1
10	Health	SOx emissions from thermal, mosquitoes from hydro reservoirs and radiation from nuclear plants.	-1	-1	-1
11	Biodiversity	Reduction of forest cover in thermal and hydro impacts negatively.	-2	-2	-1
12	Aesthetic value	Cutting of forests and damming of rivers reduces their aesthetic value.	-1	-3	-1
	Total		-7	-17	-6

forest and rivers and were, therefore, punished. They probably thought they were doing a great service to the Universe by cutting the forests for providing fuel wood to the artisans of Mohanjodaro and Harappa for making of beads. They did not appreciate that the increase in consciousness from wearing of beads is less than the decline of consciousness from the cutting of forests.

Application of the Framework to Power Sector

We can use this framework to assess which source of energy would be good. This author has ranked the impact of three main sources of power—thermal, hydro and nuclear—on various parameters. The change in consciousness has been ranked on a scale of (-)3 to (+)3. The figures are best estimates by author (table 1). The learned reader is welcome to make alternative estimates. The importance lies in the framework rather than the figures.

The difference in this method is brought in focus when we compare it with the comparative assessment of the three sources of energy made by the Planning Commission in its Integrated Energy

Table 2: Comparative assessment of sources of energy by Planning Commission

Sl No	*Option*	*SO2 NOx TSPs*	*Solid Waste*	*Liquid effluent*	*Thermal impact on receiving waters*	*Flora, Fauna impacts*	*Forest loss*	*Involuntary Resettlement*	*Total Impact, Nos Y = Yes is Negative Impact*
1	Thermal power (including Mining)	Y	Y	Y	Y	Y	Y	Y	7
2	Hydro-power	N	N	N	N	Y	Y	Y	3
3	Nuclear Power (including Mining)	N	Y	Y	Y	Y	Y	Y	6

Policy Report, 2006. It has concluded that hydropower is the least negative source of energy (table 2).

Such difference in assessment arises because the various impact on consciousness enumerated above are not accounted for. The differences are explained in table 3 below.

It will be seen that while thermal and nuclear energy raise the consciousness of dormant lying coal and uranium; hydro power reduces the consciousness of free-flowing waters. It is suggested that all developmental activities be reckoned on the touchstone of consciousness.

Table 3 : Unaccounted Impacts on Consciousness

Sl No	*Parameter*	*Planning Commission ignores impact of hydropower*	*Planning Commission ignores impact on consciousness*
1	Use of electricity	-	-
2	Methane	Methane emissions from hydro reservoirs ignored	-
3	Mining	-	**Increase in consciousness of coal and uranium is ignored.**
4	Storage of Nuclear waste	-	-
5	Quality of River Waters	-	**Decline in consciousness of flowing water is ignored.**
6	Sediments	Deprivation of sediments to downstream areas is ignored.	-
7	Forests	-	-
8	Earthquakes	Impact of hydro on Reservoir Induced Seismicity is ignored	-
9	Displacement	-	-
10	Health	Ignored	-
11	Biodiversity	-	Reduction in consciousness due to extinction of species is ignored.
12	Aesthetic value	-	**Reduction in aesthetic value of free flowing rivers is ignored.**

10

ECOTOURISM AND EMPOWERED COMMUNTIY DEVELOPMENT—DODITAL LAKE AREA IN GARHWAL HIMALAYA: BEYOND THE COBWEBS OF MASS TOURISM

Sanjay Singh Mahar and S.C. Bagri

Abstract

Mass tourism has been widely exploited as a development tool, resulting in numerous negative impacts. Present study area is an example of many ecotourism destinations in Uttarakhand where community development is strongly empowered and action-oriented. Local people have started banking upon the rich reservoir of Dodital Lake, where hundreds of thousands of tourists throng every year. Village Development Committees have been formed and a best route is charted out to sell Dodital on a sustainable basis. Various settlements of villagers' en route Dodital have been entrusted with a separated task to educate tourists' on environmental issues besides letting them feel the serenity of Dodital and surrounding area. Main components of ecotourism like nature-based, education, and sustainability, includes ethical and conservation principles where guest-host relationship needs to be trustworthy lest it reaches the zenith of extinction. Thus, it also investigates the importance of local population to preserve the natural resources having positive views.

Key words: ecotourism, environmental awareness, sustainability, education, community development

Introduction

As the earth is shaking with the tremors of explosions and calamities, there is a fear among mankind to let them free out of the shackles of their home periphery. Recently numerous negative impacts associated with mass tourism have been recognized. As a consequence, the concept of responsible tourism 'a better place to live in and to visit' is fast catching up and have sparked off debate and discussion among many tourism fraternity. Keeping this in view ecotourism, as an alternative form of tourism is transcended and has taken a quantum turn towards rural and natural areas. Though in its infant stages, ecotourism is increasingly one of the most popular forms of tourism (Wight, 2001). According to the World Tourism Organization, (UNWTO) ecotourists make up 20% of world travel (McKercher, 2001). The crucial life-supporting environmental services provided by mountain forests and highland pastures in vulnerable fragile terrain such as the Himalayas are qualities too often taken for granted by mid-altitude village communities (Sati, 2008).The importance of the world's mountain regions has been internationally recognized since the Earth Summit in Rio de Janeiro in 1992; Agenda 21 contains a chapter specifically devoted to mountains. Mountains constitute 25% of the earth surface (WSSD, PrepCom, 2002). Sustainability of the local culture, social structure, economic well-being and way of life are common goals that are inherently interconnected with the health of the natural resource base (Horochowski et al., 1999). Thus, ecotourism has become a major engine of economic growth and employment generation for the community members in the villages. Ecotourism is significantly helpful in conservation, preservation and maintenance of the floral and faunal wealth. Synergy with various tourism stakeholders is well perceived in nature based tourism where concerted efforts are done to accelerate the tourism growth in sync with local aesthetic values and serene sylvan surroundings. Sustainable tourism development has become an important tool to showcase the hidden jewel of rich forest wealth without any damage done. Eco-friendly resorts and accommodations are created to maintain the soothing environments of surrounding areas. Kabini Jungle Lodge and Resort (KJLR) in Karnataka have bagged several prestigious awards for promoting awareness among tourists and local people to protect, conserve and nurture as well as the natural wealth on sustainable basis. Looking back to the performance of the North Indian states in India since 2000, it is observed that Uttarakhand is all set to make a mark on the tourism map with a remarkable increase in ecotourist. Uttarakhand state has been attracting investments in the sectors like ecotourism. The state's vast resource remained unexplored till date. Rich natural resources, water, forests and mountains are enough to captivate the onlookers. Pro-active measures are the concomitant need of the hour to incorporate ecotourism in its scheme of diversifying its bouquet of tourism offering for the unsurpassed holiday sojourn of any travelers, beyond the memoirs of cyber tourism (Singh, 2007).

In concrete terms, sustainable management of mountain resources means enabling mountain populations to earn a livelihood, providing protection against natural hazards, enhancing conservation of natural resources, safeguarding social and cultural traditions, and supporting development that takes account of the special features of mountains regions and ensures the interest of mountain people (WSSD, PrepCom, 2002). Tourism has got concentrated in areas where there is severe pressure on local facilities. A great deal of pollution has been caused to the Himalayan water. Even treks are known to have left behind a lot of waste material on paths and trails. Around areas where there has been tourist concentration, forests have suffered a great deal because of high levels of demand for fuel wood. Many of these things have resulted in a turmoil situation (Dhar, 1976) which have been observed by the so many a large calamities. This creates a situation of jeopardy.

As regards to the present study area Dodital, one of the loveliest lakes in Uttarakhand is a very famous trek route, nestling at an elevation of 3,024 m. An emerald lake surrounded amid dense pine, deodar, rhododendron and oak forest. The lake is entirely filled with rare species of Himalayan Golden Trout, but angling is strictly prohibited to facilitate re-stocking. It provides an idyllic set up for rest and recreation activities like bird watching, wildlife photography, trail hiking, eco trekking, alpine traversing etc. It consist an immense vista of gently sloping hillsides, richly forested in patches, with a number of streams gushing and meandering, churns into the white milky water formed in the rocky hollows. The route to Dodital begins with a short drive of 15 km. from Uttarkashi district headquarters to Sangam Chatti (*Chatti* represent a transit point where one can have refreshment and relaxation). Dodital is at a distance of 22 km. from *Sangam Chatti*. The first day's trek involves a steep ascent of 6 km. to *Agora*, where a well established Forest Rest House (FRH) provides a homestay for a comfortable night's rest. From Agora, Bewra is at a distance of 1.5 km, *Kacheru* is at a distance of 9.5 km, *Manjhi* is at a distance of 11 km, a popular camping site and *Dodital* at a distance of 16 km. Bewra, a summer shelter for the people of Agora is situated at the bank of river Assi Ganga emerging from Dodital. One can use this site for tented accommodation and even wooden rooms (wooden rooms are made by local villagers for their stay with domestic animals during summer season) are available for the trekkers' stay overnight. There are 4 shops available which provides food and lodging facilities run by the villagers of Agora. The next day involves a long 14 km. trek along the hills, hillocks and dale, with some tempting but extremely steep short-cuts. The entire route is lined with a wide profusion of wild flowers. From Dodital one can ventures to Darwa Top (4131 m.), at a distance of 6 km which is extremely tough because of its inaccessibility. On the way are numerous camps of *Gujjars* (a nomadic tribe community moving around Himalaya with their herd of animals). Darwa Top, summer grazing pastures affords a glorious, wonderful and panoramic view of the Himalayan ranges (Bunder Punch range the emerging source of Yamuna) and to Dayara Bugyal and Bakriya Top, a trek further 3 km from Dayara. From Agora another route leads to Dayara which is 15 km away, a region which could be profitably developed for skiing on pattern of Auli.

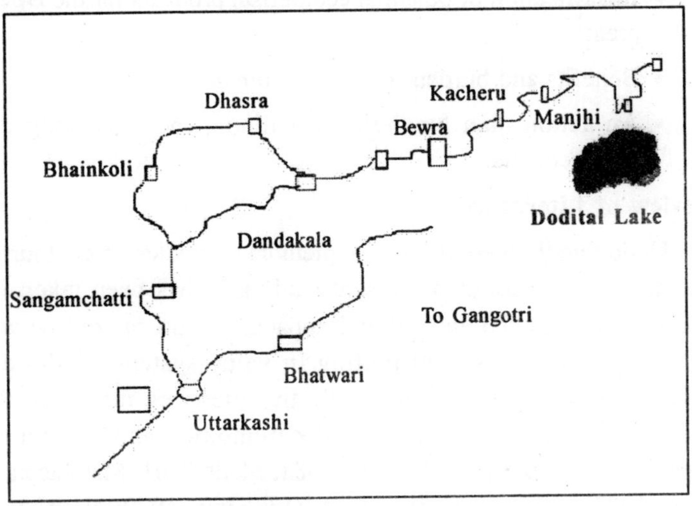

Map 1: Location Map of the Study area

Rationale and Objectives of the present study

As part of the long-term conservation strategy for surrounding villages of Dodital, Village Development Committees and village panchayat is considering ways to assist in developing income-generating mechanisms for vulnerable communities. Many communities without an alternative livelihood or food sources have started participating in ecotourism as both an economic and conservation strategy. It is hoped that opportunities provided by ecotourism development will contribute to assisting communities as well as protection of the natural resources. Present study was conducted to determine the viability of ecotourism in the Dodital area. Simultaneously education level of the villagers has been taken into account to assess the environmental sustainability and level of awareness. The purpose of the study was to gather information to identify potential ecotourism development opportunities, and the viability of those opportunities to offer direct benefits to conservation and community livelihoods.

Objectives of the study include:

- Level of awareness among local villagers about environmental management;

- Identification of potential ecotourism products for the Dodital area;
- Benefits and burdens of local communities; and
- An action plan for the area outlining short and long term requirements.

Review of Literature

Undoubtedly there have been plethora of studies on ecotourism, but not much account of present study area has been taken into consideration. Social and cultural impacts of tourism are 'the ways in which tourism is contributing in value systems, individual behavior, family relationships, collective lifestyles, moral conduct, creative expressions, traditional ceremonies and community organizations (Pizam and Milman, 1984; Modi, 2001; Matheison and Wall, 1982), socio-cultural impacts (Williams, 1979; Nash, 1981; Pizam, 1996; Singh, 1996; Diamantis, 1999). Conservation, sustainable development, protection of floral and faunal wealth, and environmental awareness is of prime importance if it is to sustain for a long time (Singh, 1989; Bose, 1968; Horochowski et al., 1999; Wallace and Pierce, 1996; Sati, 2008). Natural resource planning as well as incompatible social value have often felt local level (Getz, 1983; Joppe, 1996). Ceballos-Lascurain, 1996; The Ecotourism Society, 1991a, b; National Ecotourism Strategy of Australia, 1994; Tickell, 1994; Ecotourism Association of Australia, 1992 defines ecotourism as a responsible traveling to relatively undisturbed or uncontaminated natural areas to foster environmental and cultural understanding, appreciation and conservation managed to be ecologically sustainable without causing damage to either.

Research Methods: Field work for this study took place in Dodital (Uttarkashi) in the month of March and April 2008. This location was chosen owing to its key ecotourism status and popularity among the tourists. It comprised a combination of qualitative and quantitative research. As part of a broader study, convenience sampling designed questionnaire and first-hand interviews were conducted to collect the primary data, and secondary sources were compiled from research papers, compendiums, government reports, ecotourism policy of Uttarakhand, govt. archives, seminar proceedings, NGOs study etc.

Based on primary data, total of 40 respondents of 4 villages i.e., Bhainkoli, Dhasra, Dandakala, and Agora were selected based on convenient-cum-judgement sampling. Thus, 10 villagers from each village were the sample target. Forest officials and travel agents based at Uttarkashi were also interviewed to sketch a detailed description of the ecotourism potentials and possibilities. Few tourists were also asked to comment on the strengths and weaknesses of this destination. The survey instrument was self-administered. The question asked about respondents' socio-demographics i.e., gender, qualification, profession etc. The statistical techniques used for the analysis of the data include percentage method. Keeping in mind the importance of Dodital, this study was planned.

Research Results

As observed in the foregoing sample size of 40 respondents were selected with 10 villagers from each of the four villages. The age and gender characteristics of the respondents is exhibited by Table 1.

Table 1: Age and Gender Characteristics of the sample

Age	*Gender*		*Total sample*
	Male	*Female*	
Under 18	2	-	2
19-30	19	3	22
31-35	8	2	10
36-45	5	1	6
Total	34	6	40

Sources: Primary data collection

Among 40 respondents, 34 (85%) were male and 6 (15%) were female. Majority of the respondents falls in the bracket of 19-30 age groups with 19 male and 3 female. Education background in the villages is quiet low with 5 only having higher education (graduation and above), 20 having education upto intermediate, 10 having passed high school certificate and 5 were having no formal education. Incidentally all 5 illiterate respondents were catering to the needs of tourists by having engaged in eatery and tea stalls at Dandakala, Bewra, Manjhi and Dodital. Education level is quiet unsatisfactory in all four villages. Dandakala village has a least literacy rate of 40% where Agora and Bhainkoli primary and secondary education is quiet high. Dhasra village has a literacy rate of 50%.

Status of Villages enroute Dodital Trek

Bhainkoli, Dhasra, Dandakala and Agora are in the vicinity of Dodital lake and for the present study, sample of villagers were collected here in these four villages. Dandakala and Agora are the villages which are situated on way to Dodital. However Dhasra and Bhainkoli are the two other villages which are on the other side of the Dodital trek route. From Sangam Chatti one way leads to Dhasra, Bhainkoli and other goes to Agroa and Dandakala. Demographic profile, basic facilities and amenities, infrastructural development, employment generation through ecotourism, local people participation in environment preservation have been studied from ecotourism standpoint in present research paper.

Bhainkoli village is sparsely populated by 400 people of 120 families. 4 km away from Sangam Chatti Bhainkoli is one of the biggest Gram Panchayat in the area. The major crops are paddy, wheat, maize and potatoes. Dhasra village is 8 km away from Sangam Chatti and is deprived of basic amenities. Only one primary school is available here. For secondary and higher secondary education student moves either to Agora and Bhainkoli. This village is populated by nearly 30 families with a total population of 100. Dandakala one of the villages in gram panchayat is 6 km away from Sangam Chatti and is in the immediate vicinity of Agora enroute to Dodital. It occupies hardly 15 families and sparsely populated by a population of not more than 70 people. Bhuveneshwari Mahila Ashram centre, one of the reputed NGOs in Uttarakhand is working ceaselessly and tirelessly to educate men and women, assisting people to earn their bread and butter, thus alleviating poverty. Simultaneously it conducts workshops to educate people about health and sanitary conditions. Environmental campaigns and awareness programmes are run parallel to aware local people about environment and sustainability. Major agricultural crops and vegetables consists of potato, bajra, *rajma* (commond kidney beans), *mandua* (finger millets), wheat, *ramdana/chauli* (amaranthus), *moong* (green gram), *gahath* (horse gram), paddy, maize, *bhat* (soyabean), Jhangora *(oplismenus frumentaceurs)*, spinach, cucumber, garlic, ginger and tomato etc.

Village Agora, 6 km away from Sangam Chatti is the main halting point of Dodital Trek and is full of basic amenities. Total population of the village is 350 with having 100 families. Over the years, local communities have been viewed as being detrimental to development and have been pushed to the fringes and their homelands and the wildlife surrounding the same subjugated and exploited. Forest Department has laid due emphasize on workshops and trainings of the local people to cater ecotourists' venturing Dodital for employment generation. People of this village are well aware of the tourism development and its negative impacts. 80% villagers know about ecotourism and environmental impact. Local people gathers various information about the prose and cons of ecotourism promotion and development and disseminate it among all to prevent any loss to floral and faunal wealth. Current literacy rate of the village is 60%.

Following factors in ecotourism promotion, development and management vis-à-vis environmental awareness were assessed in the area. Summary of which is discussed in Table 2.

As observed in Table 2 the importance of natural sites in the area were treated very important by local people where 75% respondents agreed on its importance. 25% considered it to be important. As regards to cultural heritage and village ethnicity 45% respondents said that it is very important to showcase the cultural wealth and village tradition and ethnicity to outsiders so that tourist could get a glimpse of rich culture. 30% considered it important, 10% responded that it is not very important. It was observed that due to the cultural breakdown and loss of moral values these people are not very much interested to showcase their culture and tradition to tourists and even outsiders. Of those engaged in ecotourism activities, 45% (very important) and 30% (important) said that it is good to have numerous opportunities to gain economic benefits.

Table 2. Responses about ecotourism activities and environmental management

Factors	*Very important*	*Important*	*Not very important*	*Not important at all*
Natural sites in the local area	30 (75)	10 (25)	-	-
Cultural heritage & village ethnicity	18 (45)	12 (30)	10 (25)	-
Opportunities to gain economic benefits	18 (45)	12 (30)	4 (10)	6 (15)
Discover something new or interesting about the area	8 (20)	10 (25)	18 (45)	4 (10)
Participation in Environmental awareness programmes	34 (85)	6 (15)	-	-
Natural resources to mankind	32 (80)	8 (20)	-	-
Conservation and Protection of natural resources in the area	30 (75)	10 (25)	-	-
Govt. role in ecotourism promotion and development	28 (70)	12 (30)	-	-
Infrastructural development in ecotourism destinations	4 (10)	10 (25)	20 (50)	6 (15)
Role of village panchayats and Village Development Committees in ecotourism	34 (85)	6 (15)	-	-
Forest official participation in ecotourism promotion and development	30 (75)	6 (15)	-	4 (10)
Need for environmental ethics	36(90)	4 (10)	-	-

Sources: Primary data collection

Note: Figures in Parenthesis are percentage

Those not having any relationship with ecotourism provided negative responses.

While discussing one of the important variables with villagers in Table 2, participation in environmental awareness programmes were accorded top priority where 85% considered it very important and 25% of the respondents treated it important responsibility to protect and conserve the environment for their well-being. As a corollary, role of village panchayats and village development committees were considered of prime importance where 85% people surveyed said that it is very important to shoulder the responsibility of ecotourism promotion and development by local authorities for sustainable development. 15% considered it important. 70% respondents said that government role is very important in ecotourism promotion and environment conservation but hardly any measures are taken by government to execute the forest policies for the betterment of local people and forest wealth. For the need for environmental ethics and values 90% of the respondents were of the view that it is conscious oriented and all human beings should be conscious about other creatures and environment so that we could live in harmony.

Forest officials and travel agents based at Uttarkashi were interviewed and the mix response was sought. Forest policy for conservation and environmental management has been accorded top priority by forest department for all important eco destinations. They agreed that local people play a vital role in making a big success of these policies otherwise tend to be a complete failure to manage the forest wealth where local villagers inhibited the periphery of forest land.

Travel agents considered Dodital as one of the emerging ecotourism destinations and responded favorably to seek the support of local villagers of all four villages for their self-reliance. Simultaneously, environmental awareness campaigns are organized by them for all stakeholders to get knowledge about floral and faunal wealth of Dodital and other environmental issues.

Discussions

Department of Forest and Wildlife, Govt. of Uttarakhand selected eight villages in the State for the purpose of Ecotourism and Agora was one of the villages selected for various activities. In the wake of this Rs. 50 Lakh were sanctioned for this purpose in Agroa. Out of this Rs. 30 Lakh have been distributed and the balance amount has to be distributed after having an inspection of the flow of work. *Milan Kendra* (Meeting Point) was established in Bewra to display the local artifacts for the adventure enthusiasts and giving popularity to almost driven out crops such as maize, potatoes, chaulai, bajra and pulses etc. Rs. 15,000/- were given to the individual guest house owners to renovate the property and making it at par of the tourists expectations and providing them the village ambience and environment. In this Ecotourism project unemployed educated students were chosen from the village by the District Forest Department under the aegis of Department of Forest and Wildlife, Govt. of Uttarakhand to provide them guide and cooking training and making them highly skilled personnel at Ramnagar (Nainital). Now the future plan is to distribute water heater, solar energy system to the villagers randomly selected for different project. It is also working to develop the production and sale of local handicrafts, to promote area domestically and internationally as a tourism destination and to help ensure that the benefits of tourism are shared as widely as possible within the community.

Approaches to Ecotourism Planning

The International Ecotourism Society (TIES) defines ecotourism as: "responsible travel to natural areas that conserves the environment and improves the well-being of local people." Ecotourism can promote a positive attitude toward conservation among the local people as well as the tourists (WWF, 2001). Ecotourism (ET) is a form of sustainable tourism and Community-based Ecotourism (CBET) is ecotourism where local communities are the main actors. Some see ecotourism itself as a contradiction in terms. Others simply misunderstand and misapply the concept, leading to many critical problems. Ecotourism promotion in rural communities is still a focus of many agencies, both governmental and NGO, and some private sector operators (Leksakundilok, 2004). Following guidelines have been set up for the new national ecotourism policy of Ministry of Environment and Forest (MoEF), Govt. of India.

- Forest based ecotourism
- Ethnic ecotourism
- Harmonizing the infrastructure in National Parks
- Tapping of unexplored and restricted

As observed in the foregoing discussions an attempt has been made to highlight the problems and possibilities in sound ecotourism destination? Questions hover around policy makers to seize the interest of local people by allowing them to cash and carry the destination benefits and burdens. Let them open up more avenues of employment generation through Village Development Committees on their own. Are they not the real custodians of any destinations? Or else to put it who are the real stakeholders of any ecotourism product? Sound ecotourism policy can find the answer. Undoubtedly, government has to initiate actions, but people's confidence on the course of actions has to be earned. The policy planners often have to face the great many dilemmas in evolving balanced growth in strategies for mountain regions where the most difficult task lies "in achieving a certain balance between the considerations of the people who live there".

Conclusion and Recommendations

Climate change is a serious and long term challenge that has the potential to affect each and everyone of us. It is one of the biggest issues facing the world today- a global threat no nation can resolve alone. The Earth care awards are a pioneering step taken by JSW Energy Ltd. In response to the increasing need to provide credible and technically-sound leadership to identify and foster actions across several sectors with special reference to mitigation and adaptation imperatives related to climate change and global warning. Some of the harmful effects of mass tourism include "price rises…changes in local attitudes and behavior; pressure on people (crowding, disturbance, alienation); loss of resources, access, rights, privacy; denigration or prostitution of local culture; reduction of aesthetics; pollution in various forms; lack of control over the destination's future; and specific problems such as vandalism, litter, traffic, and low-paid seasonal employment (Blamey, 2001). To mitigate one of the detrimental impact of forest and environment misuse, The JSW-The Times of India Earth Care Awards is one such effort constituted to recognize local and relevant action in tackling challenges posed by climate change. The awards are technically supported by The Energy and Resources Institute (TERI) and Centre for Environment Education (CEE).

To prepare the local population for the upcoming challenges of environmental degradation, much education is needed to be offered. One of the issues to be addressed is the value of traditional practices and the importance of maintaining them when confronted with other practices. With the advent of widespread media use, tourism may not be the main instigator of the spread of western system, but it can be an aggravator. To mitigate these aggravating effects, attempts should be made to bring a heightened awareness of the worthy qualities of the traditional physical culture and culture ecology. There is an educational element to ecotourism, and it is a form of tourism that "minimizes negative impacts upon the natural and socio-cultural environment". Ecotourism generates alternative occupations for local people, while generating awareness of conservation issues among the host community and the tourists (UNESCO, 2003).

Earlier paragraph dealt with the possible chaos emerged with the massive exploitation of natural wealth by the stakeholders. There are a number of arguments used against ecotourism like getting to the destinations with a wrong perception, leading to climate change and global warming. Although ecotourism provides employment, the jobs offered to local people are often low quality/low paid jobs and are seasonal – only available at certain times of the year. Any form of tourism can impact on the culture and traditions of local people, either because they lose their meaning and simply become 'entertainment' for tourists (e.g. traditional dances) or because the customs tourists bring to an area threaten local culture and traditions. Thus, there is a pressing need for a paradigm shift in the planning process. The top-down process has to be replaced by a bottom-up one in planning and managing ecotourism in the mountain regions of Uttarakhand in general and of the present study area in particular.

Committees must be formed for the dual purpose of dispersing new information to the people, and getting the peoples' input. According to the World Wildlife Foundation (WWF) one of the best ways to strengthen the community's understanding of their rights and responsibilities in decision-making is to work within the structures that already exist in the community. Effective structures are required to enable the community to influence, manage and benefit from ecotourism development and practice. Schools, companies, artists, NGOs, community movements and associations, private practitioners, bureaucrats, researchers, academicians and other stakeholders must raise ecological awareness among local people to protect the natural wealth on their own. Insertion of the environmental issues in school curricula, particularly in the public education system, using the sustainable consumption manual to provide society with knowledge of present environment scenario so as to establish ties between nature and young people, is expecting them to extend this experience to the home environment, where consumption decisions are made.

Recommendations

Community-based ecotourism requires an understanding, and where possible a strengthening, of the legal rights and responsibilities of the community over land, forest resources and ecotourism development is a prerequisite. This should apply in particular to the tenure of community-held lands and to rights over tourism, conservation and other uses on these lands, enabling the community to influence activity and earn income from ecotourism activities.

To attain the common goal of resource sustainability and viability in a long run, the role of local people have diversified and carved a more meaningful niche. This is true and eventually will have a far reaching implications in the near future where climate change, environmental damage, rise in pollution, damage to forest wealth will take its toll to rip the whole world. Leading by example is more likely to bear better and fruitful results not only in the interest of villagers of Dodital area but also step ahead as a source of inspiration for other villagers to adopt the strategies formulated by them to nurture the nature. Likewise, the exchange of ideas and suggestions through systematic and regular meetings, and/or communications with group members could generate useful alternatives, if tourist arrival reaches the threatening limits. In a nutshell various issues can be addressed as mentioned follows:

- Ensure that local populations receive an equitable share of benefits from ecotourism resources;
- Further integrated and applied research on critical mountain issues, with particular attentions to spatial dimensions;
- Develop and implement policies to ensuring protection and sustainable management of mountain ecosystems and biological diversity;
- Improve the diffusion of knowledge;
- Increase exchange and learning among and between major stakeholders of ecotourism;
- Address the fragility of mountain ecosystems, particularly with respect to deforestation, land degradation, loss of biodiversity, as well as vulnerability to climate change of natural disasters;
- Mobilize sufficient resources, from national and international sources, for creating a real impact in poor mountain areas through investment and capacity buildings.

Suggestions

The creation of community-based, participation-oriented tourism management committees allow locals to participate in the decision-making process and influence the decisions that have a direct effect on their lives. At the same time, participation increases the support and cooperation of the locals for protection projects. Additionally, the amount of knowledge that the locals have of their environment and the ways to save it should not be underestimated as they are termed as the real custodians on any destination. To ensure the successful development and continued support for ecotourism in the Dodital lake area, it is important to involve the community from the beginning to ensure a sense of ownership and a level of responsibility. Gaining an understanding of residents' attitudes towards tourism development will assist in the development of tourism options as well as highlighting possible issues and impacts.

Awareness raising, educational programmes and conservation activities have begun to have a positive effect on the natural resources of the area. Local communities have reported positive differences in the amount of ecotourism activities during the peak season.

Acknowledgements

The author would like to thank the forest officials, villagers and travel agents who helped during survey to identify the various ecotourism assets in the area and providing important input into this paper.

References

Australian Department of Tourism (1994), "National Ecotourism Strategy", AGPS: Canberra.

Blamey, R.K (2001), "Principles of Ecotourism," In *The Encyclopedia of Ecotourism*, ed. David B. Weaver. New York: CABI Publishing, 2001.

Bose, S.C., (1968), "Land and People of the Himalaya, Indian Publication, Calcutta.

Ceballos-Lascurian, H., (1996), "Tourism, Ecotourism and Protected Areas", IUCN. The World Conservation Union. Gland, Switzerland.

Central Statistical Organization, Ministry of Statistics and Programme Implementation, Government of India, Women and Men in India, 2002, available from *http://mospi.nic.in/Women_and_Men_in_India 2002_Final%20Report.pdf;* Internet; accessed 10 October 2008, 41.

Dhar, T. N., (1976), "Environment-Friendly Tourism- Some Key Issues, SHERPA, Lucknow.

Diamantis, D., (1999), "The Characteristics of UK's Ecotourists", Tourism Recreation Research, Vol. 24 (2), 99-102.

Getz, D., (1983), "Capacity to absorb Tourism: Concepts and Implications for Strategic Planning", Annals of Tourism Research., 10: 239-263.

Horochowski, K., and Moisey, R. N., (1999), "The role of Environmental NGOs in Sustainable Tourism Development: A Case Study in Northern Honduras", Tourism Recreation Reserch, Vol. 24 (2), 19-29.

Hospitality Biz, Travel Magazine., Vol. 1 (4), February 1-15, 2008, Mumbai.

Joppe, M. (1996), "Sustainable Community Tourism Development Revisited", Tourism Management: 17 (7): 475-479.

Leksakundilok, A., (2004), "Ecotourism and Community-based Ecotourism in the Mekong Region" WORKING PAPER SERIES Working Paper No. 10, Australian Mekong Resource Centre, University of Sydney.

McKercher, B., "The Business of Ecotourism," in *The Encyclopedia of Ecotourism*, ed. David B. Weaver (New York: CABI Publishing): 569.

Sati, V. P., (2008), "Traditional Intramontane Mobility in Garhwal Himalaya: A survey of subsistence practices in the Pindar Basin, Uttaranchal", Singapore Journal of Tropical Geography, Vol. 29, pp. 173-185.

Singh, T.V., (1989), "The Kullu Valley, Impact of Tourism development in the Mountain Areas, Himalayan Books, Connaught Place, New Delhi.

Singh, T.V., (2002), "The Valley of Flowers: Beyond the World of Cyber-tourism", Asia Pacific Mountain Network (APMN) Bulletin., Vol. 7 (2), ICIMOD, Nepal, p.4.

"Unparalleled Uttarkashi", a handbook of Tourism Department, Uttarkashi.

United Nations Educational, Scientific and Cultural Organization (2003), "Education for Sustainable Development", Available from http:// *portal.unesco.org/education/en/ev.php-* accessed on 18 October 2008.

United Nations Educational, Scientific and Cultural Organization (2003), "Education for Sustainable Development." *Available from http:// portal.unesco.org/education/en/ev.php* accessed on 17 October 2008.

Wight, P.A., (2001), "Ecotourists: Not a Homogeneous Market Segment," in *The Encyclopedia of Ecotourism*, ed. David B. Weaver (New York: CABI Publishing): 38.

World Wildlife Fund, Guidelines for Community-Based Ecotourism Development, July 2001, available from *http://www.wwf.org.uk/ filelibrary/pdf/community_based_ecotourism.pdf;* Internet; accessed 7 October 2008; 6.

WSSD PrepCom (2002), "International Partnership for Sustainable Development in Mountain Regions", Draft for discussion during the 4th session of the World Summit on Sustainable Development (WSSD) Prep Com, May-June, 2002, Bali, Indonesia.

11

THE BIOSPHERE RESERVES: AN INSTITUTION FOR CONSERVATION, ENVIRONMENTAL RESEARCH, EDUCATION AND DEVELOPMENT

R.K. Maikhuri, S.L. Rawat, V.S. Negi, C.S. Negi, K.P. Chamoli, P.C. Phondari, Abhay Bahuguna

Abstract

When the Man and Biosphere (MAB) programme was launched in 1971 by UNESCO, a natural consequence of it was to have Biosphere reserves which can preserve and generate natural and cultural values, through management that is scientifically correct, culturally creative and operationally sustainable. The biosphere reserves were established and developed to fulfill the objectives such as (a) conservation of biodiversity, (b) research, monitoring, training and education, and (c) socio-economic development of local communities living in and around reserve. These objectives are associated together through a some degree of zonation system consisting of a core zone, buffer zone and transition zone. Though, ideally, the core zone is left free of human influence, in reality in India and many Asian regions, even the core zone may not be free from human interaction, though at a reduced level. The buffer zone and a transition zone surrounded by the human population usually involved in conservation linked with sustainable development. The world network of biosphere reserves, as implemented through the

Seville Strategy, is thus an integrating tool which can help to create greater solidarity among peoples and nations of the world (UNESCO, 1995) for linking conservation with sustainable development.

Keywords: Biosphere Reserve, Conservation and Management, Community Participation, Awareness Education, Sustainable Development.

Biosphere Reserve Concept

The biosphere concept has been refined over the years and more and more countries have discovered the usefulness of putting this multifunctional approach to nature conservation into practice in the field of biosphere reserves as protected areas of terrestrial and coastal/marine ecosystems displaying one or more characteristics viz., (a) representative examples of natural biomass, (b) unique communities or areas with unusual features of exceptional interest, (c) examples of harmonious landscape resulting from traditional patterns of land use, (d) examples of modified or degraded ecosystems that are capable of being restore to more or less natural conditions and are internationally recognized within the framework of UNESCO's programme on Man and Biosphere (MAB). This flexibility and creativity in biosphere reserve concept has simultaneously brought in even National Parks, World Heritage Site and other natural reserves, as an integral part of biosphere reserve. The humans being living in forested areas have always been an integral part of ecosystem function, living close to nature and the natural resources. Living within natural resources rich areas, traditional communities have derived many of their livelihood requirements from the rich biodiversity around them. Ecosystems such as forests not only meet a variety of livelihood needs of the forest dwelling traditional communities, through products such as timber and non-timber forest products (NTFPs), but also sustain traditional agricultural practices through resource flow between the two, and thus contributing to the food and nutritional security of the people within biosphere reserves. Reserves are nominated by national set of conditions before being included to the network. Each biosphere reserve is intended to fulfill three basic objectives:

- *In-situ* conservation of biodiversity (genetic resources, species, ecosystems) of natural and semi-natural ecosystems and landscapes,
- Contribution to foster sustainable economic development of the human population living within and around the biosphere reserve, and
- Provide facilities for long term ecological studies, environmental education and training, and research and monitoring related to local, national and global issues of conservation and sustainable development.

These functions/objectives are associated together through a zonation system consisting of a core zone, buffer zone and transition zone (Box 1).

Box 1. Elements of Biosphere Reserve (UNESCO, 1995).

- One or more core zones: securely protected sites for conserving biological diversity, monitoring, minimally disturbed ecosystems, and undertaking non-destructive research and other low-impact uses (such as eco-tourism and education).
- A well-defined buffer zone(s): which usually surrounds or adjoins the core zones, and is used for cooperative activities compatible with sound ecological practices, including environmental education, recreation and applied and basic research.
- A flexible transition area or area of cooperation: which may contain a variety of agricultural activities, settlements and other uses and in which local communities, management agencies, scientists, NGOs, cultural groups, economic interests and other stakeholders work together to manage and sustainably develop the area's resources.

Biosphere Reserve Functioning/Operation

Biosphere reserve designation, planning and management are strictly national prerogatives, though international leadership to establish reserves throughout the world and to promote and coordinate international cooperation in research, monitoring and information exchange has its role. Methods for designing and managing biosphere reserves are kept in general, so that the great variation in how the biosphere concept has been applied around the world would be easier. New technologies for involving stakeholders in decision making processes and resolving conflicts have been developed and emphasis has been given to the need to use the regional approaches for effective conservation and management. New kinds of biosphere reserves have evolved considerably, from a primary focus on conservation to a greater integration of conservation and development, through increasing cooperation among stakeholders (UNESCO, 1995).

A biosphere reserve should be large enough to be an effective conservation unit and to accommodate different uses without conflict.

- It should provide opportunities for ecological research, education and training, and it should have special value as a base line for measuring long-term changes in the biosphere reserve as a whole.
- It should have adequate long-term legal protection. In some cases, it may incorporate existing or proposed protected areas, such as national parks, sanctuaries, or nature reserves.
- It should seek the cooperation and participation of the local people in the management for without their agreement and support conservation cannot be achieved in the long run.

In brief the different objectives or functional attributes of the biosphere reserve is explained here one by one.

Conservation

Biosphere reserves contain a set of unique ecosystems identified on the basis of its natural resources – biodiversity, naturalness and effectiveness as a conservation unit. The natural or unique areas mostly form the core area of the biosphere reserve where as a rule no disturbance is allowed or are minimally disturbed. Recently the core area of many biosphere reserves of the world has been designated as a World Heritage Site due to unique natural and cultural values. Biosphere reserves may be the store house of highly valuable genetic resources such as medicinal plants, traditional landraces of crops and their wild relatives and ancient races of domestic animals. Therefore biosphere reserves may be very useful to conserve *in-situ* the precious/valuable genetic resources (Box 2).

Box 2. Ensuring local support for conservation-action plan for biosphere reserves (UNESCO. 1994).

- Recognise that local support is fundamental to the long-term conservation and sustainable use of biodiversity.
- Ensure that local populations participate as true partners in designing and managing conservation programmes.
- Allow local populations to identify their own socio-economic needs.
- Ensure that people who bear the costs of conservation projects (e.g., restrictions on fishing) also receive a high proportion of the benefits (e.g., tourist revenues).
- Initiate research activities that identify options for sustainable use of biodiversity.
- Use indigenous knowledge to manage protected areas to the extent possible.
- Ensure that local populations have maximum stewardship over local resources (rather than government agencies at the regional and national levels).
- Offer income-earning activities and/or services (e.g., improved access to markets, low interest credit, controlled access to resources) to local populations and others with a stake in conservation-development projects.
- Provide local population with the skills and resources needed to make lifestyle changes necessitated by conservation measures.
- Educate local populations about the rationale for conservation and the relationship between conservation actions and benefits.

Research, Education and Monitoring

Man and the Biosphere (MAB) programme of the UNESCO is devoted to international scientific cooperation and training and it is its one of the major concern. International biosphere reserve network is being increasingly recognized as a basic framework for activities involving a number of countries to undertake cooperative research/ studies to enhance knowledge on ecosystems, biodiversity, testing and assessing different land use systems and their management techniques, undertake in-depth scientific studies on species suitable for degraded land rehabilitation to attain sustainable development and monitoring changes in a particular or samples of ecosystems exist in the biosphere reserve.

Sustainable Development

Basically from the very beginning the idea of biosphere reserves is to link it with the development of land, water, forest, and many other resources in their research, training, demonstration and educational activities to promote social and economic development and provide direct benefits particularly to the community living in and around so that they support and encourage the very existence of the biosphere reserve in the longer term (Box 2). These benefits are either related to the food supplies, education, and health or can be related to the tourism and employment generation.

The link between conservation of biodiversity and the development needs of local communities – a central component of the biosphere reserve approach – is now recognized as a key feature of the successful management of most national parks, nature reserves and other protected areas.

Meanwhile, the concept of sustainable development was first articulated by the World Commission on Environment and Development, 1987, through the now well known 'Brundland Report entitled Our Common Future' which has been about a sharp shift in our thinking on the concept of economic development. Until recent times, industrial human societies had assumed that natural resources are inexhaustible and is available to be exploited for human welfare. Sustainable development is now seen as that processes of development aimed to meet the needs of the present generation without compromising the ability of future generations to meet their own needs.

Arising out of these developments, what has now come to be known as the Seville Strategy (UNESCO, 1996) identified clear cut criteria for biosphere reserves and their management, refined on the basis of experience. The biosphere reserve concept became in a sense was one of the significant testing ground for linking conservation with sustainable livelihood needs of local communities in the short-term time frame and sustainable development of the region as part of a long-term strategy. Meanwhile there was a different shift in ecological paradigm from a situation where ecosystem research kept out of the humans, emphasized on biophysical aspects only, to a new situation where humans were looked at as an integral component of a socio-ecological ecosystem.

Management and Protection

The core and buffer areas of biosphere reserves must be delineated and have protected status under the legislation of the country concerned in order to ensure their longer-term protection. The transition area is usually undelineated and depends on the degree of cooperation and involvement of the different managers and landowners concerned (Vernes, 1992). The creation of protected areas has often been top-down, based on elitist concepts of land use and surrounded by restrictive legislation. Many protected areas in India, as in other countries, have existed only on paper. The guidelines for their control are not viable and they lack management plans. Intervention in development and conservation activities in and around reserves/protected areas particularly in developing countries are on the increase. Arguments for involving rural communities in the management of reserves use the concept of buffer areas and are based on the following assumptions that:

- The management of legally designated protected areas is made more effective and efficient if inhabitants of buffer areas are involved.
- Resource users with secure rights protect their resources, and

- Conflicts between all the different stakeholders can be resolved.

In more and more cases, biosphere reserves are being established by creating a new protected area and not adding on to an existing one. New mechanisms are being explored to cooperate the administrations of the different legal entities which make up the biosphere reserve. Currently, studies are underway to explore how countries can strengthen the legal status of individual sites for better management and protection.

International Biosphere Reserve Network

In 1983, UNESCO and the United Nations Environment Programme (UNEP) jointly convened the first International Biosphere Reserve Congress in Minsk (Belarus) in cooperation with the Food and Agriculture Organisation (FAO) and the World Conservation Union (IUCN). During this congress it was estimated that there were 226 biosphere reserves located in 62 countries around the World, both in developing and developed nations. At the second World Congress on Biosphere Reserves held in Seville in March, 1995 about 324 biosphere reserves in 82 countries were reported.

Current Status of Indian Biosphere Reserve Network

In India MAB committee in 1979 has identified a network of 12 representative ecosystems to be designated as biosphere reserves. Subsequently the State governments/experts and expert groups suggested a number of potential sites to be designated as biosphere reserves. The name of the existing biosphere reserves, date of their notification (revised notification and location are given in Table 1. The other proposed and identified potential sites are listed in Tables 2.

How Biosphere Reserves are Designated and Managed in India

At the initiative of the central/state governments, detailed study is carried out and a project report is prepared following the criteria adopted by the central government. The land and forest being state concerns, the respective state governments have to agree to designate the identified area as biosphere reserve and provides financial assistance for management and research activities.

Table 1. Present status of biosphere reserves in India

S.N.	*Name of the BR*	*State(s)/U.T.*	*Date of notification*	*Area under reserve (km^2)*
1.	Nanda Devi	Uttarakhand (Chamoli, Pithoragarh and Bageshwar districts)	18/01/1988 (revised in 07/01/2000)	5860.69 (out of which 624.62 + 87.5 is core zone)
2.	Nokrek	Meghalaya (Garo Hills)	01/09/1988	820 (out of which 520 is core zone)
3.	Manas	Assam (Kokrajhar, Bongaigaon, Barpeta, Nalbari, Kamprup and Darang districts)	14/03/1989	2837 (out of which 520 is core zone)
4.	Sunderbans	West Bengal (Delta of Ganges and Brahamaputra river systems)	29/03/1989	9630 (out of which 1700 is core zone)
5.	Gulf of Manar	Tamil Nadu (Indian part of Gult between India and Sri Lanka)	18/02/1989	10,500
6.	Nilgiri	Tamil Nadu, Keral and Karnataka (Wynad, Nagarhole–NP, Bandipur–NP and Madumalai, Nilambur, Silent valley–NP, Mukuruthi–NP, New Amarambalam and Sivuvani hills)	01/08/1986	5520 (out of which 1240 is core zone)
7.	Great Nicobar	Andaman & Nicobar Islands (Southern most islands of A & N islands)	06/01/1989	885 (out of which 520 + 185 is core zone)
8.	Similipal	Orissa (Mayurbhanj district)	21/06/1994	4374 (out of which 845 is core zone)
9.	Dibru – Saikhowa	Assam (Dibrugarh and Tinsukia districts)	28/07/1997	765 (out of which 340 is core zone)
10.	Dehang Debang	Arunachal Pradesh (East Siang, West Siang and Debag valley districts)	02/09/1998	5111.5 (out of which 4094 is core zone)
11.	Pachmarchi	Madhya Pradesh (Parts of Betul, Hoshangabad and Chindwara districts)	03/03/1999	4926.28 (out of which 524.37 is core zone)
12.	Kanchanjunga	Sikkim (Parts of North and West Sikkim)	07/02/2000	2619.92 (out of which 1784 is core zone)

Management of Biosphere Reserves is the responsibility of the concerned state with necessary technical input and training facilities provided by the central government. The programme is guided by a national level committee constituted by the central government which oversees the implementation of management action plans and policy issues. Another expert group is constituted by the central government to recommend research projects in priority areas.

At the state level a high steering committee is constituted, usually under the chairmanship of chief secretary, to develop and recommend items of management and monitor its implementation in the Biosphere Reserve. A local committee is also constituted by the state government to ensure proper coordination among various departments responsible for different development schemes in biosphere reserves.

Table 2. Other potential biosphere reserve sites have been identified by Indian MAB Committee of the Ministry of Environment and Forests, Government of India and yet to be notified.

S.N.	*Name of proposed BR*	*State(s)/U.T.*
1.	Cold Desert	Jammu & Kashmir and Himachal Pradesh
2.	Namdapha	Arunachal Pradesh
3.	Kaziranga	Assam
4.	Thar Desert	Rajasthan
5.	Kanha	Madhya Pradesh
6.	Abujmarh	Chhatisgarh
7.	Little Rann of Kuch	Gujarat
8.	Amarkanthak	Madhya Pradesh
9.	Seshachalam	Andra Pradesh
10.	Chintapalli	Andra Pradesh
11.	Sahyadri Hills	Goo, Karnataka and Maharashtra
12.	Agasthyamalai	Kerala and Tamil Nadu
13.	Lakshadweep Islands	Lakshadweep
14.	North Islands of Andamans	Andaman & Nicobar Islands

The guiding principle of development and implementation of management plans is participation of local in planning, implementation and evaluation of conservation schemes. Their perception of ground conditions, traditional wisdom and skills as well as their committed concerns are essential for successful execution of any development project.

Presently responsibility of management of biosphere reserve is with the forest departments. Gradually other line departments and most importantly the local persons have to be brought into the routine management of biosphere reserve, something which has not been in practice but all government agencies and, in particular, the forest departments now consider a necessary element.

Acknowledgements: Authors are thankful to the Director, G. B. Pant Institute of Himalayan Environment and Development, Kosi-Katarmal, Almora, Uttarakhand for providing necessary facilities.

References

UNESCO (1994). *Biodiversity Science, Conservation and Sustainable Use*, No. 7, 16 p.

UNESCO (1995). Seville Strategy for Biosphere Reserve. *Nature and Resources*, 31: 2-10.

Vernes, J.R. (1992). Biosphere Reserves: Relations with Natural World Heritage Site. *Parks*, 3: 29-34.

12

ECOLOGICAL CONCERN AND POSTERITY

Dr. Kanchan Saxena

It is widely known that man's attitudes toward nature and technology have led to the environment crises. It is one of such problems which though involves the knowledge of scientific and technical aspects, but can not be addressed without involving society, its socio-economic conditions and guiding moral principles. This means to say that environmental degradation in terms of pollution, deforestations and natural resource exploitations can not be resolved without molding the attitude and behavior of human beings. The reason behind this is that all the environmental havocs are the result of misuse of techno-scientific knowledge and unrestricted exploitation of resources by the human beings.

Sometimes, it is contended that every person does have a right to a livable/clean environment precisely because a livable environment is a necessary condition of fulfilling human capacities. But, as we all know that being the relative terms the concept of right necessarily involves the concept of duty. Consequently, it can be said that **the well-being of the existing human community, or alternatively, every existing person's right to a clean environment may be considered the grounds of a prima-facie moral obligation, not to pollute the environment**. This prima-facie duty may be understood as being based on the needs and interests of the existing human community, though one may wish to argue that it is based on the needs and interests of future generations as well.

Environmental decay poses serious problems for contemporary society-problem which did not arise for our ancestors. Before the advent of industrial technology and its mixed blessings, drinkable water and breathable air were thought to be virtually limitless. Before the consumption habits underlying our standard of living had taken root, such natural resources as coal and oil were thought to be inexhaustible. It is now widely accepted that such beliefs however defensible in their own time, are no longer defensible in the contemporary world. As a result, we find ourselves confronted with ethical questions in regards to environmental conservation.

The central ethical question in regard to ecological concern might be phrased as follows: **"To what extent, if at all, we are morally obliged to end present practices, which in effect serve to pollute the environment and/or to decimate its resources"?** In attempting to answer this question, we shall have to take note not only of the needs and interests of the present human community but also of the needs and interests of the posterity.

In any discussion related to the ecological concern and posterity, the conservation of natural resources may be taken as the central concern. Thus, we should widen our ethical frame of reference and should pose the question, **"To what extent if at all, do we have a duty to future generations to conserve natural resources?**

As a response to this important question, we find two distinguished approaches:

(a) Approaches minimizing the duty to future generations:

Supporters of this argument say that science and technology will develop to the point that future generations will easily find substitute for natural resources, that we find essential. At any rate the needs of posterity are so uncertain and unforceable that we ought not to bother about conservation at all. This optimistic, interpretation of the situation comes especially from economists and from nuclear physicists....If these scientists, these economists are right, simply there is no problem of conservation.

(b) Approaches maximizing the duty to future generations:

Advocates of this argument contend that, despite inevitable uncertainties about the needs of future generations, we are relatively certain about some of these needs. At any rate, we must act responsibly on the facts as we see them. Thus it is our duty to posterity to conserve the planet's natural resources, to cut excess consumption, and to recycle as effectively as possible.

Let us examine both the approaches critically. As we have seen that the conservation of natural resources is the main concern in any debate on environmental control and future generations. This conservationist programme confronts us with a fundamental moral issue: **ought we to pay any attention to the needs of posterity?** This question may be answered in both the ways i.e. **positively** and **negatively**. Those who give negative response, put themselves in the category of first group i.e. approaches minimizing the duty to future generations. They argue that posterity can safely be left to look after itself, provided only that science and technology continue to flourish. The argument involves three basic assumptions. **Firstly** that science and technology will provide the substitutes of natural resources for the posterity, **secondly** that our environment and its resources are infinite and **lastly** the needs of posterity are so uncertain that we need not to bother about conservation of natural resources. If we accept the first assumption, we will find that the argument involves the fallacy of circularity. Development of science and technology is one of the root cause of ecological crisis. Although it can not be denied that the advancements of science and technology have provided us comfort and quality of life. Moreover technologies use resources, create further wastes and always use up energy and release heat. Further new inventions are likely to be utilized for the purposes of particular industrial interest. Much of the air and water pollutions has been created by the industries furnished with technological advancements, sometimes, it is said that technology is inherently destructive of both environmental and human values.

Now, if technology will provide the substitute of resources, and in return produce much pollution then further new technologies will be required to get release from pollution and it will continue in future, which means to say that pollution will exist altogether with new technologies and posterity will never be in a position to exercise a right to clean/ livable environment.

As far as the second assumption is concerned, I would like to say that our environment and its resources are finite. However, most considerations of the world's future tend to loose sight of this fact. Thus, it will be worthwhile to spend some time discussing the physical limitations of the earth-especially because it is not generally recognized that we are already quite close to several physical limitations which define the carrying capacity of our globe. Further, the denial of the problem of conservation means to deny that our society would be a better one-morally better-if it were to half the rate at which it is at present exhausting its resources. Or it is to deny this, at least in so far as the arguments in favour of slowing down are purely conservationist in character–ignoring for the moment, that is, such facts as that the lowering of the consumption rate is one way of reducing the incidence of pollution and that a high rate of consumption of metals and fossil-fuels makes it impossible to preserve untouched the wildernesses in which they are so often located.

The argument of uncertainty with of the needs of posterity can not be fully overlooked or ignored. This is true, no doubt, that the interest and needs of future generation are uncertain but even then it looks very unreasonable that we should consume all the resources and left posterity with empty hands.

A close observation of the second approach i.e. maximizing the duty to posterity shows that it also involves **three** fundamental assumptions: **Firstly,** it is our pious duty to conserve our natural resources for the posterity. **Secondly**, we should cut down excess consumption habits and **lastly,** we should try to recycle waste materials as effectively as possible. Here, it is to be noted that the followers of this approach although have accepted the uncertainty thesis but even then they are committed to save the interests of posterity.

John Passmore a famous western thinker reviews the question of the extent to which we can be certain that our successors will need certain natural resources. He concluded that uncertainties in this regards are difficult to eradicate. Yet he argues, to the extent that there is a reasonable certainty that our successors will need certain resources, we are obliged not to waste them. According to him, we ought to be prepared to sacrifice certain forms of enjoyment for the sake of conservation, but we ought not to sacrifice the continued development of our cultural heritage. He wrote in his famous book **entitled "Man's responsibility for nature'** that "We are called upon not to waste those resources our successors will certainly need. But we ought not to act, out of concern for posterity's survival, in ways which are likely to destroy the civilized ideals we hope posterity will share with us. We should try so to act that our successors will not be wholly without electricity, but we need not, should not, close down our civilization merely in the hope that a remote posterity will have some hope of surviving."

Joel Feinberg, another famous thinker has discussed the problem of conservation from a different perspective. Feinberg provided a detailed analysis of the concept of right. He undertakes such an analysis for the proximate purpose of showing that it is conceptually possible to ascribe rights to unborn generations and for the ultimate purpose of providing support for the view that unborn generations have rights against us-rights which entail the moral demand that those of us now living should protect the environment. With regard to unborn generations he contends, it is clear that they will have interests when they eventually come to exist. Feinberg argues that the rights of unborn generations are contingent. According to him it is in our power now to make the world a much less pleasant place for descendants than the world we inherited from our ancestors. We can continue to proliferate in ever greater number using up fertile soil at an ever greater rate, dumping our wastes into rivers, lakes, and oceans cutting down our forest and polluting the atmosphere with noxious gases. All thoughtful people agree that we ought not to do these things. Most of us would say that we have a duty not to do these things, meaning not merely that conservation is morally required, but also that it is something due to our descendents, something to be done for their sakes. Surely we owe it to future generations to pass on a world that is not a used up garbage heap. Our remote descendents are not yet present to claim a livable world as their right but there are plenty of proxies to speak now on their behalf. These spokesmen far from being mere custodians, are genuine representatives of future interests.

The whole debate on the issue of environmental protection or conservation of natural resources to my mind is based upon three things.

(a) Limitations of natural resources.

(b) Growth of science and technology.

(c) Man's attitude towards nature and posterity.

If we are supposed to think that the resources of nature are infinite and our patterns of resource consumption can continue even over the next century, we are certainly making a blunder. Our environment–the earth–is finite, growth of human population and industrialization can not continue indefinitely. This is a simple and obvious fact, but its consequences pose an unpreceedental challenge to mankind. The challenge lies in deciding on the ethical basis for making the trade-offs which will comfront us in the near future-trade offs which arise because in a limited world we can not maximize everything for everyone.

The belief that growth of science and technology is beyond question and it will provide substitutes for our major resources, is a matter of debate. The possibility, that substitutes will be discovered introduces a note of uncertainty into the whole discussion, an uncertainty which can not be simply set aside as irrelevant to our moral and political decisions about conservation, which inevitably and properly influences. Men can learn to substitute one source of energy or one metallic alloy for another, the more plentiful for less plentiful. But that is the most they can do. They can not harness energy without machines, without radiating heat, without creating wastes. Nor can they safely presume that no source of energy, no metal is indispensable; there is nothing either in the structure of nature or in the structure of human intelligence to ensure that new resources will always be available to replace old resources.

Given the crises of our environment there must be certain

fundamental changes in attitudes towards nature, man's use of nature, posterity and man himself. Given that crises we can no longer look upon water and air as free commodities to be exploited at will. In other words, the environmental crisis is forcing us to change our attitude. What we would be called upon to do at this level, is to reduce the consumption of certain goods–those which depend on raw materials which can not effectively recycled and to recycle wherever that is possible even although the costs of doing so would involve the sacrifice of other goods. Men should learn to live in harmony with nature. Men should feel concern for posterity and ought to be prepared to sacrifice certain forms of enjoyment for the sake of conservation. We should adopt ecological attitude, which forces one to reconsider a host of values which have been held dear in the past, and it forces one to reconsider the appropriateness of the social systems which embodied and implemented those values.

It can be better understood from the above discussion that man has a prima-face duty towards nature as well as for posterity. Not to pollute environment is the duty towards nature and control over the consumption, or over harvesting nature, is the duty towards posterity.

Another interesting point here to be noted is that both the approaches towards posterity accept the uncertainty thesis but one is ready to sacrifice some of its good for the sake of future generation while other think it to be needless. I would like to end the discussion with the words that we ought not to pollute the environment and should conserve our environmental inheritance for our descendants, because the act of pollution is itself a wrong and ethically unacceptable action.

References

1. William T. Blackstone; "Ethics and ecology University of Georgia Press" 1974.
2. John Passmore, "Man's responsibility for nature, 1974.
3. Joel Feinberg "Philosophy and environmental crisis" University of Georgia Press.

4. William L. Thomas, (Ed.) "Man's role in changing the face of the earth", Vol. I & II. The University of Chicago Press.
5. W. Norman Richardson; Evolution, Human ecology and society Thomas H. Stubbs, Macmillan publishing Co. New York.
6. Thomas A. Mappes and Jame S. Zembaty Social Ethics: Mcgraw Hill book company.
7. Lan G. Barbour;' Western man and environmental ethics, Wesley publishing company London.

13

BALANCE BETWEEN ENVIRONMENTAL PROTECTION AND ECONOMIC GROWTH

Dr. Indoo Pandey Khanduri

Whenever we think or talk about environmental issues in terms of danger and deterioration, it is generally felt that excessive use of harmful technology and scientific ventures made for rapid development and economic growth is one of the most important factors responsible for the catastrophe we are bound to face today. Rapid economic growth at regional level has also invited activities like rapid forest cutting leading towards deforestation, construction of small and big dams leading to vulnerability and fragility of areas and tempering the natural water ways resulting in some devastating results of floods. It appears that environmental protection and economic growth are contradictory to each other and attempt for one has to meet the challenges of the other one. But at the same time we require both in the present scenario for economic growth is necessary to meet the challenges projected by the global competitive market and we can not afford to risk the life and livelihood of ourselves and future generation so we have to protect the environment. Thus the fundamental requirement of the era is to maintain a balance between conducive and least polluted environment-air and water and efforts made for economic growth.

The present paper is an attempt to search the moral ways to maintain the balance between the two through the guidelines of environmental ethics. For the above purpose, this paper has been divided in three parts. The first part will try to answer the question whether economic growth is detrimental to environmental cause? It will also try to present the brief description of environmental deterioration, attempts to check it, obstruction seems to be grasped at the fronts of economic growth and the connections and relations between the two could be underlined. In the second part we shall try to see consequences of economic values preference with reference to environmental cause and in third part of the present paper we shall try to discuss the Indian and Western ways of sustainable development to maintain a balance between the two. In the concluding remarks we shall try to examine the moral strategies meant for maintaining balance between the economic growth and environmental protection that are suitable for the present scenario.

Is Economic Growth Detrimental to Environmental Concern?

The economic growth and concern for the environment seems to be having ethically opposite value rather contradicting each other. Peter Singer[1] has explained it through examples implied in the favor of building a dam which tempers and blocks the natural flow of water. The benefits listed for favoring dams construction enlist mainly economic growth and energy use of unutilized water resource for more economic growth in terms of directly providing employment for three to five years for thousands, longer term employment for twenty to thirty, establishment of energy needs for more than a decades and consequently it would encourage the establishment of energy intensive industry thus further contributing to the employment and economic growth.

But the cost of the anticipated economic growth is more than it has anticipated. The natural flow of the river itself attracts the more daring white water rafters, deep in the shelter valleys, there is a home of rare species and vegetation, it is the home of many endangered species that has seldom been found outside the valley, there may be other plants and animals as well but no one knows, for scientist are yet to investigate the region fully. The views of

Peter Singer have been reflected by Baskhtanovsky, William James and Erich Fromm.

The rapid economic growth is considered hammering the concern for environmental protection and many have accused that human beings' greed to acquire more and more material comforts has put threat to entire humanity as it has been reflected by Baskhtanovsky, "*Man's efforts to change the environment have inevitably led to destructive consequences. Today, when the population and the volume of production are growing at the unprecedented rates and sciences and technology are making rapid strides, the destructive impact is especially significant. Society is facing a task of major importance from nature but to reproduce it in a way that will guarantee mankind's further progress. The state of the environment is incorporated into the sphere of society's priorities. Remaining a means, it also becomes a goal. Thus society's attitude to the nature acquires a moral meaning.*"[2]

This particular feelings about the practical uses and implications of scientific inventions otherwise inspired by purely intellectual motives invites the moral attentions, has been clearly expressed by William James in the following words; "*...the scientific tendency in critical thought, tho' inspired at first purely intellectual motives, has opened an entirely unexpected range of practical utilities to our astonishing view. Galileo gave us accurate clocks and accurate artillery practice*" he further says, "*...the scope of practical control of nature newly put into our hand by scientific ways of thinking vastly exceed the scope of old control grounded in the common sense. The rate of increase accelerates so that no one can trace the limit; one may even fear that being of man may be crushed by his own power that his fixed nature as an organism may not prove to stand the train of the ever increasingly tremendous function. He may draw in his wealth like a child in a bath tub who has turned on the water and who cannot turn it off.*"[3]

The above two philosophers have projected their views that human being while attempting for the economic growth which may be designated as improving financial conditions and material comforts have taken the help of fast growing technology and science to mold and control the nature and its entities, but undue interference with nature has invited several disaster for his existence. Human being as an ambitious and rational unit of this cosmos has been in the pursuit of unlimited desires, which continued to increase in the shadow of the techno-scientific and industrial world. But he is hardly aware of his own wishes. Erich Fromm narrates this position and its consequences in beautiful words, "*...yet, modern man feels uneasy and more and more bewildered. He works and strives, but he is dimly aware of a sense of futility with regards to his activities. While his power over matter grows, he feels powerless in his individual life and in society.*"[4] He further said, "*While becoming the master of the nature, he has become the slave of the machine which his own hands built.*"[5]

Erich Fromm is absolutely right in his assertion but the consequences have been reflected in a more serious and distorted forms. This is so because, in his pursuit of uncontrolled desires, human being had concentrated on his self interest and overlooked his moral responsibilities towards the non-human world or nature and environment as whole. As a result, his self – centered attitude has dragged him to exploit the nature up to the prohibited level and the outcome has been the environmental crisis of the present era and it has been intensified up the extent of creating a threat for human being itself. The mad persuasion of human being after unbridled desires, are now being proved to be threat to his own existence. Although, apparently self-interest leading towards threats for self-existence seems to be paradoxical but if one attempts to understand the intricate connection of man, nature and the whole cosmos, its mystical channelized circle and cycle, than only the factual truth could be realized.

No doubt the primacy of individual and his desires has continued to encroach exponentially, in the shadow of scientific and industrial world. In this reference, two questions need to be answered, one how one can deny people of their rights to self fulfillment? Yet, how can one survive on the planet of ten billion points of infinite greed?

The above views project that human desire for material comforts and things has been a real challenge for the protection of virgin form of natural entities. This may be explained in the other words that nature has its definite resources, but human beings population is increasing at the unprecedented rate. In order to meet the needs of the growing population nature has to be exploited and in such scenario the very standards of economic growth that per capita income of the individual is bound to project threat for the environment. A slightly advance view also has been presented in the following word:.. in India regarding environmental degradation and pollution is either due to over exploitation or unscientific exploitation of natural resources in order to accelerate the pace of development. It may be emphasized that both the aspects of human society viz. quality and quantity of human population are equally important in degrading the natural environment world ever. The high quality population with greater skill and advanced technology of the industrialized western world has used more than 80 percentage of world natural resource and has caused more than 80 percentage damage to the environment. On the other hand, the high quantity population i.e. more than 70 percentage of the world population with lesser skill and inferior technology in the developing countries have also stressed the environment by their greater demands of natural resources mainly for food and fuel.[6]

Questions of Value Freference

Human being needs both existence as well as prosperity, thus he needs to aspire for more economic gain and at the same time care and concern for environmental entities, even if not for valuing the intrinsic worth of it, it is must for survival and appropriate holistic development which involves security, survival and social security at the same time. But the blind race for the economic growth of human beings has invited only short term gains as Peter Singer writes; ' *The gains made from cutting the forest employment, profits for business, export earnings and cheaper cardboard and paper for packaging- are short term benefits. Even if the forest is not cut, but drowned to build a dam to create electricity, it is likely that the benefits will last for only a generation or two; after that new technology will render such methods of generating power obsolete. Once if the forest is cut or drowned, however the link with the past has gone for ever."*[7]

Apart from long term benefits of preserving nature and healthy environment, the cost of short term benefits is going to harm and will be born by the every generation that will follow later on. It is the reason why environmentalist has designated the virginity and wilderness as the World- heritage. It is some thing that we have inherited from our forefathers and that we must preserve for our coming generations. But this is true that our modern political and cultural ethos has great difficulty in recognizing long term value. This is so because they value the income growth from the short term perspectives like economist who, "... *have been taught to apply a discount rate to all future goods. In other words, a million dollars in twenty years is not worth a million dollar today, even when we go for inflation. Economist will discount the value of million dollars by a certain percentage, usually corresponding to the real long term interest rates*"[8]

Is it possible to apply the economic pattern of counting benefits to environmental and natural treasures we have today as it has been pointed out in the following words; "*This makes economic sense, because if I had thousand dollars today, I could invest it so that it would be worth more, in real terms, in twenty years. But the use of a discount rate means that values gained one hundred years hence rank very low, in comparison with values gained today; and value gained one thousand years in the future scarcely count at all. But from this standpoint of the priceless and timeless values of wilderness however, applying a discount rate gives us the wrong answer.*"[9]

Apart from counting the economic growth, one must take into account that if at the cost of environmental destruction, we are bound to invite several other disaster like ever increasing air pollution, contamination of drinking water, green house effect, specific species extinction, disappearance of the rain forest and so forth as it has been explained; '*...by depleting the ozone layers and increasing the amount of Carbon-dioxide in the atmosphere, we have already brought about the change...Thereby we have deprived nature of its dependence and that is fatal to the meaning. Nature's dependence in its meaning, without it there is nothing but us.*"[10] Thus the economic growth as predicted by the economic value preference is going to be adversely affected by the crisis of daily needs like food, water, fuel and shelter. The beautiful predicted dictum is that the next world war is going to be for water. If the agricultural lands are converted into buildings the agro-items are bound to be matter of conflicts and price of cost of these items are going to be high. If a person is planning to high income at the cost of creating the deteriorating conditions for physical and mental health the basic purpose of acquiring high income is lost. Anybody wants more money and more income for the material comforts and enjoyment, but if he is not mentally and physically fit to enjoy the comforts it would be better to improve the surrounding conditions so that the earned money could be enjoyed at least. In the same way if a nation is planning to increase per capita income at the cost of creating a wider and unbridgeable gap between rich and poor. And, in the long run, this attitude will be creating crisis for the even economic fronts by increasing the cost of food, water, fodder and consequently deteriorating health conditions of the mass. As it has been pointed out in the following words; "*Since in the past hundred years many plants and animal species have begun to disappear and our planet's genetic resources are being exhausted with growing rapidity, the need has arisen to protect flora and fauna.*"[11]

The above analysis shows a kind of value conflicts of short term and long term benefits. The acceptance of the intrinsic value is behavior of high moral standard. But even if one goes for economic concern the misuse and exploitation of natural resources are bound to create disaster at the economic fronts and health hazards. Keeping the above picture in mind that mad persuasion for economic growth at the cost of environmental disaster will lead to a more destruction of human beings. At the same time looking at cut throat global competition at the economic fronts, it would not be practical option to remain as we are in the name of environmental protection and go on worshiping nature as it has been taught by the Indian tradition.

Balancing Strategies of Sustainable Development

The core concepts and objectives used in the environmental ethics are sustainable development, planning and growth and management of environmental disaster are basically action oriented and again requires techno-scientific knowledge to move in the ventures. But this again overlooks the fundamental moral insights for taking decision what to do and what not to do. And more or less sustainability of development could be ensured only through the way suggested by the ethics in general and environmental ethics in particular, as it has been given in the following words: "*Today most of the people agree that one must establish good strategies for securing sustainable development. The teaching of ethics can play a decisive role in the work for sustainability. Ethical values are the principal factor in the social cohesion and, at the same time, the most effective agent of change and transformation. In considering the ethics of sustainability, our moral responsibility towards the future generations is of prime importance. In living up to this responsibility, we must strive to achieve balance and continuity between meeting the needs of today and the challenges of the future.*"[12]

It is for the above reason the need for ethical studies are intensified now. The increasing impact on environment and its adverse consequences has compelled the study of environmental ethics as the discipline which could not be fulfilled by pure ethics or ecology, as it was expressed; " *As the magnitude of man's impact on the environment is increasing, mainly through over-exploitation of resources and through pollution, our environment is deteriorating fast and there is growing concern that something must be done, that development must be sustainable and the precautionary principals must be applied wherever one deals with complex systems whose behavior is difficult to predict.* "[13]

Not only for dealing with complex behavior of human being but also for determining the approach in the conceptual analysis of development, hazards management, economic use of resources and explaining the very concept of sustainability could be taken up rationally by philosophical analysis through its branch of environmental ethics and it decides the nature of sustainability to be opted, as self- interest oriented notion of sustainability would not be useful for long term as it has been expressed in the following words; "*The root of the idea of sustainability seem to be in something like Hobbes' notion that we begin moral philosophy by thinking of individual interest, and only arrive at any more generous notions than that by extension and analogy from individual case.*"[14] He calls it reductive notion of sustainability as just the continued meeting of our present need grows out of egoist tradition which leads another kind of chaos and danger to disturb the sense implied here. The analysis of vital concept useful for environmental issues could be provided only by environmental ethics.

The Indian way of the sustainable development could be traced from Vedic period agro culture in general and the concept of Rit particularly as it has been described by Radhakrishan when he says; "Rta literally means the course of things."[15] It stands for law in general and the immanence of justice.; "... Rta denotes the order of the things. Everything that is ordered in the universe has Rta for its principles."[16] The early Indian way of looking at relationship between man and nature is that of mutual respect, exchanging culture, equal concerns for preservation and conservation of traditional ritual. Another peculiar feature of early Indian attitude towards nature is far from any controversy and contradiction persisting in the modern ethical theories in the field of environmental ethic i.e. Anthropocentric and eco-centric approaches. On the contrary to Indian tradition, the western tradition goes for the option that each and every entities of the nature is meant for the use of human beings as picking the views of Aristotle, Peter Singer writes; Plants exist for the sake of animals, and brute beasts for the sake of man's domestic animals for his use and flood, wild ones (or at any rate most of them) for food and other accessories of life, such as clothing and other various tools"[17]

The above quotation implies three points; first the natural world exists for the human beings. Secondly the creator of this world has allowed human beings' dominion over the natural world without any concern how the treatment is going to be. Thirdly human beings are the only morally important numbers of the world. Nature, itself is of intrinsic value and the destruction of plants and animals cannot be sinful, unless by the destruction we harm human beings. While talking about the moral strategies of the sustainable development, we have to keep in the mind the present resources, requirements and future impacts as well as needs. And, a balance needs to be maintained between the above. The Indian tradition makes us God in terms being caring, giver and good to all creatures on the earth while western tradition prompt us theoretically to go for demon approach which etymologically demanding and destroying in its temperament. None of approach is acceptable for Indian tradition is too idealistic and western one too insensitive to not only nature but even future generation of human being itself. So again we need a balance between the two approaches and that is going to contribute our concluding remarks.

Concluding Remarks

Human beings having temptations and emotions apart from rationality cannot follow the path of Divinity i.e. goodness for the goodness sake. At the same time he cannot be categorized to be following the path of demon absolutely for he has feelings of care and concern for natural entities as we feel for badly hurt people and bird, we feel the emptiness in the absence of tree and vegetation which has been in our habit to be with them. Of course human beings are the creature in between the Deity and Demon and for pragmatic strategies for the sustainable development he should be thinking about his needs and interests and decide judicially up to what extent the interference, use and modification of the nature is required to meet the need but not greed of any particular person. At the same time, for rest of natural entities and environment should be following the divine care and concern. This will ensure the objective of sustainable development in a pragmatic way for taking care of the needs, resources, environmental protection though in name of the taking care of the future generation. And this is what has been reflected in the following words; "What is needed is creating environmental awareness or consciousness and inculcation of the spirit of responsibility and accountability in our relation with nature. A sustainable development leading to more and more perfection stands in need of the environmental stewardship implies a sense of mutual care to be spearheaded by the human beings only. If we care for nature and nature will care for us."[18]

References

1. Peter Singer: Practical Ethics: Cambridge University Press, USA, 1993, p. 264.
2. Baskhtanovsky, V & et. al *'Ethics'*, Progress Publishers 1989, trans. Belskaya, Natalia, p. 218.
3. James, William; *Pragmatism and Four Essays from the Meaning of Truth*, Eurasia Publishing House, New Delhi, Indian reprint of original version of 1907, p. 123.
4. Eric Fromm: *Man for Himself*, Fawcett Premiere, New York, 1975 p. 14.
5. *Ibid.*
6. Savindra Singh & et. al. *Environment, Resources and Development* in Central Himalayan Environment and Development; Potential Actions and Challenges. ed. MSS Rawat, Vol. 1 Transmedia, Srinagar (Garhwal) 2003, p. 25.
7. Ref. no. 1, p. 270.
8. *Ibid.*
9. *Ibid.*
10. *Ibid.*
11. Ref. no. 2 p. 218.
12. COMEST: (The World Commission on the Ethics of Scientific Knowledge and Technology) recommendations on *The Teaching of Ethics,* submitted on August 27, 2003, p. 2.
13. *Ibid.*, p. 4.
14. Chappell, TDJ. Ed. *The Philosophy of the Environment,* Edinburgh University Press, 1996, p. 8.
15. S. Radhakrishan: *Indian Philosophy*. Vol. I Oxford University Press, Reprint 1999, pp. 69-70.
16. *Ibid.*
17. Ref. no 1, p. 269.
18. Bhatt, SR, *Applied Philosophy and Professional Ethics*, Applied Philosophy Series; 1 ICPR Publication, New Delhi 2003, p. 19.

14

ENVIRONMENTAL CRISIS AND INDEGENOUS COMMUNITIES: INTELLECTUAL DILEMMAS CONFRONTING SUSTAINABLE FUTURE

Bina Saklani

In the past two centuries, humanity had struggled hard to win human- rights and socio economic and political freedoms, but today these freedoms are being undermined and have become subservient to the demands of market which in turn wants unfettered freedom to earn money and profits and calls it economic liberalization and globalization.

Most of the States, world over are giving priority to economic development, relegating their welfare agenda to background. Governments everywhere are embracing the free-market gospel. (Chomsky, 1999, Pg. 66). "Today, legitimacy of government is subordinated to sovereignty of the market." (Koshy, 2002, Pg. i). Market democracy is challenging the traditional democracy, based on the principles of liberty, equality and welfare state. Democratic freedom under the market ideology is being interpreted as freedom of investment, freedom to consume and freedom of exploiting natural resources to grow.

However, the current global economic recession, symbolized by the free- fall of free market has given a huge jolt to global capitalism and multi- nationalism. Worshippers of laissez- faire are running for cover under new protectionism and new economic orthodoxy. Wreck less consumption has put the very existence of earth and humanity at stake through the dangers of climate change and environmental crisis. It has given serious urgency to the issue and intellectuals have a opportunity to pause and ponder over the issue of sustainable future.

One of the biggest dilemma before civil society today is to reconcile the contesting demands of unfettered consumption with the sustainable economic development in future. In a world dominated by the neo-liberalist credo, the considerations of ethics, politics and social desirability are being re-negotiated. Select scholars were cautioning the society for many years that profits are ruling over people. (Chomasky,1999) In the name of globalization, profits and money need a free- market which has promoted unfettered exploitation of natural resources. New ethics are being created in the marketplace to suit money power and promote consumption. The economic model of global production and global market and consumption has further endangered the survival and existences of 'small communities'. They were never before so fragile, weak, poor and helpless.

Researches among indigenous and tribal communities have shown that these cultures have unique systems of concept of thoughts evolved from experience and its surrounding environment. (Claude Levi-Straus, Ref. in Jha. M, Pg. 190). Their deep intellectual engagement and abstract reasoning, understanding of nature and its intricacies is different from but in no way 'inferior to that evolved in cultivated structured systematic thoughts'. Since post industrial revolution era the modes of production associated with these communities like food gathering, slash and burn farming, hunting, pastoral –economy and fishing, even subsistence farming are systematically removed and forced to be discarded by the modern society. More- over, their identity and culture as a different category of human existence is threatened and in peril. Indigenous knowledge is ignored or expected to be discarded in favor of distant goals of capitalism and intellectual property rights are imposed on knowledge which is traditional.

With-in last few decades, there is a growing public awareness and growing corpus of scientific knowledge related to environmental crisis and its protection, population explosion and its control for sustainable development. Indiscriminate and over exploitation of natural resources, in pursuit of surplus production for fulfillment of constantly burgeoning human needs and greed in the name of development and consumerism are fast depleting natural resource reserves and causing environmental hazards with serious implication for humanity. Due to over exploitation and affects of modern industrial development, marketing and commercial agriculture, humanity has become aware of ecological imbalance and environmental crisis. Unfortunately, even in the discourses associated with the threats of climate change and globalization, indigenous and small communities are neglected and treated as marginal curiosities.

The Indigenous People, their Natural Habitat and World

Indigenous people's lives have depended from time immemorial upon natural resource base of their local environment. These are the people who have strongly resisted global economy. They belong to sustainable economies, and have survived in cultures which are direct expressions of ecological niches which has been their habitat. Societies of indigenous people may be scarred by natural catastrophe, like drought, cyclone, flood, but they rarely over used their own habitat beyond its carrying capacity. Peasant and tribes are affected more by vagaries of nature then by the poverty.

Discourses on globalization assume that populations living away from market economy rely on free exchange of environmental services for sustenance, and it is gross under-utilization or wastage of precious resources. 'But they forget, even under the market economy most basic human values are available free of cost like generosity, good will, clean air and mothers love, creativity, inventions, software available in public- domain, all are given through a non- monetary exchanges. This makes our lives rich beyond anything that can be bought in the market'. (Ninan, K. p. 48)

Indigenous people who produce their own food and build their own homes are less dependent on the market. However, markets play a functional but important role in local communities.[6] In money driven rich societies the market dominates as all 'needs' are 'bought' and not 'provided by' the family unit or local producers or available freely from habitat. On the contrary traditional societies have subsisted for centuries on non-monetary exchanges which makes their life style a model of sustainability.' (Ninan, K. p. 49)

Concept of Common Property vs. Private Property

Tribal and farming Communities subsist in consonance with their natural environment and culture. The developed world has lost such communities in the process of development and change. The indigenous knowledge, culture and technology of such communities need to be rediscovered and acknowledged (Seabrook. pg 51), as they hold the cultural wisdom of the people to live life in a sustainable manner. Such indigenous technologies are evolved to sustain life in harmony with nature without creating imbalances in the order of nature. Thus they maintain a symbiotic inter- relationship within the community and the environment.

Urban life is different from rural life as urban life is totally dependent on money. Today ideology of development envisages development as converting rural economy and exchanges into an urban economy and monetary exchanges. Growing usage of industrial inputs like chemical fertilizers, pesticides, and agricultural machinery has undermined the roots of rural self sufficiency, exposing them to onslaught of market forces. "The poor migrate to seek security: they wind up chasing wealth. But wealth is more agile than they are. It is better fed, it is healthier, and it is more mobile. (Seabrook. Pg. 90-91). In this arena of wealth driven global market, small tribal communities need deeper and closer look as they falter in the race of survival of the fittest.

Natural Resources as Common Property

At least 80% of India's natural resources were common property and only 20% were privately utilized till the end of the 19th century. This extensive common property, available, free to all, was the resource base for a non-cash, non-market economy in the past. All kinds of natural resources were available, free, to the people, such as, fuel for cooking and heating, material for making houses, animal fodder, and a number of vegetables, fruit and roots as food (Chattrapati Singh. pg. 46). In a pre-capitalist scheme of things, Tribes were free from the notions of personal ownership and nature was for community use, it was a common property of the community or a tribe and no part of nature was owned as personal, Tribes have always contested for and claimed territorial influence, but nature was never personally owned. It was meant for community use.

The concept of private property and ownership over anything available in nature was beyond the comprehension and understanding of the tribal world view. Human entry and presence in forests was regulated by the colonial rule and regulations and even petty offences like collecting domestic fuel and cutting grass for fodder became punishable offence. The restrictions on free use of forests resources was an atrocity and injustice by the logic of villagers and tribal forest dwellers. Imperial heavy boots marched over and trampled upon the common property rights, they encroached and displaced the tribal population from their ancestral lands. The alienation of tribal rights over land, forests, hunting and fishing, and the resultant changes in the traditional subsistence base had converted a self sufficient community of people, into poverty struck dependents and laborers, now living on the mercies and largesse of the others and the government.

Bhoxa -A Tribe in Crisis: A Case Study

The primitive tribe of Bhoxa in Uttarakhand had to face this tragic past and still the future holds little hope. The Bhoxas are a primitive tribal group inhabiting the foothills of central Himalayan region of northern India. This tribal group cohabits the Himalayan foothills and its malaria infested jungles along with the Tharu tribe in Indian Himalayas, whereas Tharus are well spread from India to Nepal. The Bhoxa tribe has a history of origin-believing in the / migration to this habitat dating back to Muslim occupation of northern India in medieval period.

This group is listed as one among 76 primitive tribal groups in India and is on the Government list of priorities for upliftment and welfare of their lot. Somehow, efforts of Govt. and its schemes to ameliorate the lot of this tribe are modest and marginal in effect for the tribe.Bhoxas population is distributed over the commissionaires of Kumaun and Garhwal in the province of Uttarakhand and also in the district of Bullandshahar in Uttarpradesh .

Mr. Amir Hasan, a liberal Government official observed that "till very recently the Bhoxa were masters of all that they surveyed. Few dared to settle in inhospitable marshy tracts of the bhoxa lands at that time, which was full of elephant grass and reeds and infested with mosquitoes and elephants. Unmindful, the Bhoxa carried on their shifting cultivation and helped the State in exploiting forest produce. With the development of the foothills and the Terai, eradication of malaria, construction of all-weather roads and modernization of agriculture, a large number of adventurers, free booters and tough guys from neighbouring states have muscled in to usurp the benefits of development. Resulting in the original settlers being pushed into the interior. Much simpler than the Tharu, the Bhoxa of Nainital were easily overrun by Rai Sikh hordes and other who now control large chunks of their land, often employing the original master as labour. Such is the irony of fate." The Bhoxas in Garhwal are largely immune from the Rai - Sikh menace but there is no peace-the more prosperous and numerous highlanders, the Garhwali and Kumaoni and Jaunsari have been able to purchased or occupy large tribal areas by fair or foul means.

Immigration of Outsiders

Because of the immigration of outsiders, the native population of Bhoxa tribe is getting marginalized and they remain almost untouched by the development and economic prosperity that is taking place around them. Except for few exceptions Bhoxa community in general suffer from sense of marginalization, depletion and insecurity for their subsistence and survival. The socio-economic condition of Bhoxa in many parameters of development is worse than local schedule caste population. (Saklani Bina, 2005. pg. 20.)

Tribes, Market and Uttarakhand

Threats of market economy in this age of globalization is a serious issue for Uttarakhand Himalayas and more so for Bhoxas. This tribe is showing signs of deep distress and panic in a fast changing world where they feel incapable of coping with changing times, feel insecure to survive and protect their identity and culture. Their fear is that 'we will not last long as a tribe and be lost for ever by next generation'. The traditional mode of give and take for fulfillment of daily needs is a exchange in kind, and a changed form of barter system exists even today in the Bhoxa villages. Earlier it used to be mutual, now it is between the baniya and Bhoxas who have opened shops in the Bhoxa villages. Bhoxas take whatever they need from these shops whatever they require in exchange for grain or cash for small needs, and by mortgaging land for a pittance, which they are not able to get back because of inability to pay back loans and the non-bhoxa person gets it registered in his name with complicity of various, agencies and middlemen. There is large scale land alienation and the owners at one time now work on their own land for wages, increasing poverty and indebtedness. The major economic issue of land alienation at the hands of new migrants after Indian independence, and now due to the pressures of new industrial economy, growing urbanization, in Uttarakhand has increased and compounded new stresses related to their survival, growth and development.

Three Phases of Eroding Subsistence Base

Bhoxa in Uttarakhand is a prime example of showcasing the degeneration of indigenous communities, first through colonial rule and now of globalization. Their economic degradation could be seen in three phases.

In the first phase, during the colonial rule, in late 19 th century onwards to pre – independence decades, they were systematically and forcefully evicted from their natural habitat and traditional modes of subsistence for the colonization of marshy foothill land for agriculture and human re-settlement. Main source of income during that period of colonial rulers was land revenue and to increase it forests were cleared for agriculture and after mid 19the century, with the introduction of railways, forest become precious commercial resource, as they supplied railway sleepers and teakwood for ship- construction. Increasing interest of colonial administration in forests became biggest man made disaster for communities living on forest resources. (Bisht S.S., 2008, pp.10-11) All Their traditional modes of subsistence like food gathering, hunting, fishing, slush and burn farming were prohibited..The forest protection act dissociated the Bhoxas from the traditional forest rights by curtailing their free entry into the forests on which they were traditionally dependent for their economic subsistence. The forests were the natural resource base for supplementing economic needs of the tribal, like herbs, fodder, fuel, foods, and game animals. The dissociation from nature occurred at two levels:

-At the level of loosing forest rights.

-At the level of loosing agricultural fields, i.e., land alienation.

Second phase of decay started in post independence decades, when these very fertile virgin agricultural land of Himalayan foothills were given to Punjabi Refugees and other settlers. They were traditional farmers and for them land was a coveted personal asset, where as for Bhoxa tribal- land was a common property and not a individual asset and were not emotionally and culturally attached to it. They had little sense of personal and private ownership and with little persuasion and inducement were ever ready to sell off or mortgage the land, consequently a major part of Bhoxa farmers were duped to sell off the lands. Soon a large part of their population became land less and started working as labourer in their own ancestral lands.

Tribal's indigenous knowledge used for generations to take care of their needs fell into disuse and decay, depriving them of using whatever means they knew of to earn their livelihood. Slowly their traditional knowledge was destroyed and in the absence of any other alternative modes of skill or livelihood their competence to survive has become a huge issue. They are held to ransom by modernization and social change. The market forces have swallowed up their traditional modes of subsistence, making them insecure in a system they do not understand and to which they are vulnerable. Due to breakdown and destruction of the traditional subsistence base most of them are now unemployed and have no traditional community skills to look after themselves. The unemployed youth, on a first available opportunity wants to sell off its ancestral land for his own marriage or children's marriage or even for drinking. The Rai-Sikhs, Bengali, Jaunsari, Garhwali, Muslims and Kumaoni, migrant farming settlers have snatched most of the Bhoxa land.

Third phase of their decay starts with the growing urbanization and Industrializations in and around their habitats. In a national economy which is growing at a annual pace of 7% to .9%, their poverty and backwardness is also growing with a same pace as they feel totally left behind from this consumption based prosperity. They were never so backward and poor as they feel today. Due to continuously declining purchasing power, they feel themselves to have become increasingly poorer. They are continuously faltering and lagging behind in consumerist consumption and the progress made all around them.

Unemployment

Our field studies show that these tribals suffer from a great sense of inferiority and backwardness from the inroads of other educationally better off, economically prosperous and politically powerful groups of Jaunsari and Tharu population, particularly around Dehradun, Udhamsingh and Nainital districts respectively. Most of the state sponsored benefits to schedule tribes are garnered by Jaunsari and Tharu tribes and Bhoxa remain empty-handed and helpless. 80-90 percent population of the area is dependent on daily wage labor, petty labor and field labor. Since this area is near to main roads, the pace of urbanization is relatively fast. After the formation of the Uttarakhand state this area is under the spell of fast pace of industrialization as many private and state sponsored industrial estates have been established and Bhoxa lands are first one to be swallowed by the property sharks. (Saklani, 2005, Pg. 23). The health condition is relatively dissatisfactory. Many of them suffer from chronic diseases. Drinking is a big social problem with the tribal families which is one of the main reasons for economic decay.

Bhoxa community in general is loosing even a semblance of their self motivation, and self initiative for taking charge of their own lives. Their sense of dependence on largesse of State sponsored welfare schemes has made contemporary state of Bhoxas pathetic. Their inert eternal wait for fall of manna from state coffers is leaving little margin for any self help on their part. A very hard working community is converted into hard drinking alcoholics who are averse to any manual work.

Declining Local Institutions: The Panchayats

Today Bhoxas are almost leaderless, and directionless as their traditional leadership is marginalized and discarded Most of the traditional Panchayats are in the process of decay and dis-integration on account of the statutory Panchayats set up by the State. In several Bhoxa village of Pauri Garhwal, Bijnor and Dehradun, these Panchayats have completely disappeared. (Saklani, bina, 2005, pg. 56) Even where they exist, they function only for ritualistic purposes, and they are hardly effective and are able to inflict only nominal punishment like asking the guilty to hold his ears, render a public apology or blacken the face. Young generation has little regard for this institution as they feel it more profitable to align with modern panchayats, political parties and its agents as through them they feel more empowered and useful for themselves. Even in a majority based democratic setup, numerically minor tribe like Bhoxa are not able to get any advantage of tribal reservations as all the advantages are garnered by the numerous, educated and prosperous tribes like Jaunsaries, Tharus and Bhotias. Due to the lack of numbers they are engulfed by more numerous neighbours, entire apparatus of local self governance is out of their reach. In a tribal community numbering 20 thousand only 13 are the Punchayat members. The intra- tribal competition may go out of hand in the hands of political provocateurs.

High Drop- Out Rate

The social awareness and backwardness of this community can be gauged from heavy drop out rate of nearly 80% in the primary education. In order to minimize the Psychology of Dependence on Government jobs after receiving the basic education, there is no technical hands on skill trainings available, so that Bhoxa youths may be trained and readied for the open market requirements and private sector needs. (Saklani Bina, 2005, pg. 21)

Some of the better off students showed total aversion to attend the schools as they had to face racial taunts and humiliations at the hands of other communities and more powerful tribal groups. In order to motivate other Bhoxa students for continuing the education and act as role models, in every Bhoxa village school, at least one Bhoxa youth be employed as teacher. In every Anganwari of Bhoxa villages, Bhoxa girls should be given appointment. At least one post should be reserved in each village.

Suggestions for Economic Parity

Most serious problem confronted by this tribe is problem of land alienation. Land alienation also leads to alienation of the surrounding livelihood resources which the tribal depend on. For any procured land for industrial, developmental or business purposes, it should be converted to share value along with payment of market price. Rentals should be given for any land used for setting up high tension towers, electrical poles, irrigation canal, and construction of embankments of river sides on denudated or barren tribal land. Industrialists win all arguments as they give more profit and revenue to State, and pauperization of a individual or community rarely get any considerations. Here many freedoms are compromised and many small mutinies are quelled by the state in support of the market and money powers.

Identity Crisis

Identity crisis has generated feeling of self depreciation and low self esteem due to their feelings of failing, and incapability to adjust with the fast changing times. Sense of dejection and apathy towards manual work has accentuated habits of drinking, which has emerged as a major cause of degeneration of the tribe as a whole. Low self confidence in their capacity and culture has become real cause of concern. There is a sense of panic looming in their eyes as they find themselves helpless and incapable in coping with dominant culture and new economy which is engulfing and riding rough shod over their traditional modes of subsistence and way of life.

Conclusions: Philosophy of Profit or Co-existence

Under the spell of globalized economy the tribal land and natural resources are vulnerable as they seem to be easy and cheap pickings for market forces. A public debate may be initiated to safeguard the natural resources and stopping of the land alienation of tribal communities. It should be ensured that the Tribal lands should not be procured by the state for Industrial activity or for developmental projects. Since land is one time sale, they are to be paid urban market rates and not the subsidized Government rates. The tribal land is an inherited ancestral heritage and should be treated as share money which could also be handed over to next generation. This land should be made a investment in public or private enterprise along with payment on current market rates.

Many indigenous technologies, skills and processes that are still part and parcel of tribal life and are appropriate for sustainable development had harmony with the nature. These communities are still able to provide themselves, based on their own ecological niche. These subsistence systems are less dependent on global market network, must be saved from being swallowed up by modernization. Modern economic activity draws people to consume products which are produced by market economy. Those who have less dependence and less use of the market economy are termed as backward. Even though they have the capacity and satisfaction to provide themselves through their own local resource base. This paradigm of development forces people' into the pursuit of MORE instead of the search for ENOUGH which poor people WANT.'(Seabrook, pg 45- 47.)

Economic and industrial growth has threatened to replace traditional cultures with the global values and have almost driven out environment to the brink of collapse. This trend has to reverse. The present economic recession is indicative of the fact that the new world order, based on-globalization- is finally loosing momentum. The philosophy of coexistence and parallelism will replace it in future. It has to make space for the "multitude of small scale communities in which people live traditional, self- providing, sustainable healthy life styles." To day, if poor are taught ways to get sustainable livelihood then better off class must also be trained and be sensitized to live a sustainable lifestyle. Dilemma generated by demands of globalization and sustainability of human civilization due to environmental crisis and its ultimate destiny is one of the basic intellectual poser and philosophical challenge before the civilization.

Once upon a time, primary aim and objective of intellectual life was Brahma- Gyana and today it is Profit- Gyana. Powerful and rich need a new- Gyana to secure a sustainable future.

Bibliography

Bisht Surendra Singh, 2007: *Himalaya mein Upniveshvad Aur Paryavaran,* Trans Media, Srinagar (Garhwal).

Chomsky Noam, 1999: *Profit over people: Neoliberalism and Global Order.* Madhyam Books, Delhi, India.

Jha Makhan, 1963 :: *Anthropolcgical Thoughts,* Vikas Publishing House, U.P. India, Khor Martin, 1999: International Journal of Rural Studies, Vol. 6, No 2, Penang, Malaysia.

Koshy, Ninan, 2002: *Globalisation, The Imperial Thrust of Modernity.* Vikas Adhyayan Kendra. Malad West, Mumbai 4000 064.

Saklani Bina, 2005: *Baseline Survey of Bhoxa Tribe: A Primitive Tribal Group of Uttarakhand:* Ministry of Social Welfare, Government of Uttaranchal Dehradun and Ministry of Tribal Affairs, Govt. of India, New Delhi.

Seabrook Jeremy, 2006: *World Poverty.* Rawat Publication, Jaipur, India. Singh Chattrapati,1985: *Common Property and Common Poverty,* Oxford University Publishing, New Delhi.

15

ETHICAL PERSPECTIVES ON ENVIRONMENTALISM IN INDIAN TRADITION

Dr. Nitish Dubey

Modern society is facing a lot of emotional and other psychological strains besides a number of socio-economic and political challenges. But more terrifying are the ecological degradation and disequilibrium which are haunting us with their prospect of irreparable damage to nature as a whole and threatening the very existence of entire race of *homo sapiens*. The situation ensued discussion on environmental ethics, some important problems of which are environmental degradation, deforestation air, water and sound pollution, or destruction of ecological balance. One of the under currents in most of these discussions is the utilitarian approach. This is evident in the works of Sen and Williams[1] and Smart and Williams.[2]

In order to provide proper perspective thinkers like Arne Naess[3] (who advocated the idea of deep ecology) and Johnson[4] focus upon a different approach towards environment. According to Johnson's holistic approach, the ecosystem as a whole is to be regarded as a great organic whole comprising of all organic and non-organic systems. In the realm of cosmos, each and every system animals, plants or other things have a place and value. Destruction or degradation artificially brought about, starts a chain reaction, which disturbs the equilibrium of the ecosystem as a whole: It is not only things on the earth, but total atmosphere above and around it, which form the ecosystem. The present threat to human race is evidently due to 'means' i.e. entire human instrumental set up-created with the help of scientific technological skills to achieve more and more, luxury and comfort for us without corresponding increase in wisdom to maintain the environmental equilibrium. When the natural surrounding is exploited by knowledge divorced from wisdom, the resultant condition is one of sorrow.

The dominant ethical tradition in the western world has been human centered. Growth and evolution of biotic species is determined by their living interface with environment though, the biotic species are different from inanimate. Object as they possess consciousness and feelings, but their actions are subject to laws of biological determinism. Human existence is value centric. The awareness to norms of social behavior consists in giving back, what is obtained after judging it, right or wrong, desirable or undesirable, from the yard stick of social value pattern.

Right and duty are two faces of moral behavior. Right of one is duty of other and vice-versa. Naturally, the question arises whether in the light of environmental ethics; humans have any duty or moral obligation in relation to biotic species, vegetable life and natural environment consisting of the forests, lakes, oceans, rivers and mountains.

The believers of human centred ethical tradition deny moral right to non-humans in relation to human beings on the ground that man, being the most evolved creature, his interest is more important. The interest of non-humans is ubiquitous. As the non-humans have no duty, so they cannot have a right. The duty of humans follows from the right of non- humans to live and grow. The ontological justification draws our attention to certain realities in nature which require protection of non-human existents. The state of nature is one of absolute harmony and mutual dependence; humans inhale oxygen and exhale carbon dioxide. The moon stimulates the growth of tiny plants on the surface of the ocean. Except the humans, the rest of the created evolutes live in consonance with law of nature.

It is only humans who on account of greater intelligence act against the laws of nature and disturb the equilibrium of the state of nature. Every part of the creation must co-exist in equilibrium with every other part to maintain the harmony. Any harm to a part creates a far reaching ripple and results in the disorder of whole. Likewise the existence and growth of one is dependent on the other from the utilitarian view also a protection of environment is necessary in the interest of humans, as nature being the habitat of man, it is to be preserved not only in our interest but also in the interest of our successors. The earth has limited resources like coal, diesels, minerals etc. So they have to be sparingly used, with an eye to future.

The interest of biotic species should be treated at par with the interest of humans as they are connected with well being of man. Actually man is more dependent on the non- humans than the humans on them. If by chance human species completely vanish from earth. The plants and animals will continue to survive. On the contrary if flora and fauna do not exist, the humans can hardly survive.

Thus key concept of interdependence leads away from anthropocentric to cosmocentric value stance. The survival of anything in the universe is a matter of the vital dependence on other things, including the whole system. It is evident that humans are dependent not only on each other but on non-human surroundings of the world also. We are as much supported by he forces of nature as the other creatures. We are fully enmeshed in nature in cosmic order. What goes for us also, goes for other creatures available in universe. This is cosmic inter-dependence of all beings in the ecosphere.

Naess has termed this togetherness or unity with nature as a matter of becoming part of "the great self". This concept of Great self or vision of ultimate unity of everything is quite clear in Indian philosophical visions. The Indian philosophical tradition provides a solid foundation for adequate concern and deep respect for nature's things, biosphere and ecosphere included. In the Vedas, Bhagwadgita, Samkhya, Advaita Vedanta and Upanisadas, this vision is intended to regulate our conduct in tune with cosmic order. The principle of interdependence is manifestly present in the philosophy of Buddhism especially in the doctrine of dependent origination or *pratityasamutpada*. This doctrine reveals our place in the universe and the value of system we are to interpret and accept in our conduct in this universe.

The Indian philosophical thinkers see the nature as root of all the existence. Nature is considered as an entity from which everything has evolved. So human beings are a part of nature. Nature is not considered merely a physical world which is separate from humans. Human are also not considered as essentially spiritual and alien to nature.

According to Samkhya Darshan, *Prakriti* is material cause of everything. It is the vital source of every being. Human beings as conscious beings are conditioned by the natural world. The interaction between physical world and human beings is a logical necessity. *Prakriti* is necessary for manifestation of consciousness. The *mool prakriti* is constituted of three *gunas*, the *sattva, rajas* and *tamas* and is source of entire process of evolution. These *gunas* pervade the whole beings. They evolve into this creation full of diversities because of the reflection of cosmic consciousness the (*purusa*) unity thus evolves into diversity. Like rest of the creation the human beings are one of the evolutes. So the creation full of diversities is contained in *mool Prakriti.* Every things or being is constituted of three *gunas.* The only difference between the objects can be of degree of *gunas*.

Vedas, the oldest text of Ancient India are a source of rich heritage of ancient Indian philosophers on environmental ethics. The philosophical speculations found in the Vedas and the Upnishads, the concluding part of the Vedas have reached their culmination in the philosophy of Vedanta. There are many hymns of Rig-Veda which consist of the praises of the different personified powers of nature at deities or *devas,* such as *Agni, Marut, Varun, Indra, Savita, Upas* and even plants, and sacrifices were offered to all these *Devas*. In Rig-Veda, it has been prayed that medicinal plants may prosper with many leaves, flowers and fruits for the benefit of the sick.[5] *Devas* were regarded as the realities underlying and governing the different departments of nature. The 16th Chapter of Yajurveda (*Neel Sukta*) is devoted to a number of *Rudras,* each responsible for prosperity of particular class of creation such as cattle, trees, herbs, water resources, land, hills and mountains and also natural calamities.

Though the nature was peopled with different deities, it was thought that it was subject to some basic law, which governed the whole world of objects, living and non-living. This basic law is called *Rta.* It denotes the order of the world. Regularity of movements of sun, moon, stars the atterations of day and night and of the seasons. They all follow the path of Rta, the right path. They never overstep the regions. The whole universe is founded on Rta and moves in it.

The conception of God is one who gives to man. God is God because he gives the whole world. The learned man who imparts knowledge is also a God. The sun, the moon and the sky are God because they give light to all creation. Father, mother and spiritual guides are also Gods.

The conception of gods in the Vedas shows a process of development, firstly there is polytheism i.e. belief of many gods. Secondly there is henotheism (a term coined by Maxmullar) which extols for the time being one of the Gods as supreme God. Thirdly monotheism which is belief in one God or ultimate reality. Thus vadic thought developed from polytheism to monotheism. According to Dr. Radhakrishnan, in "Philosophy of India" the concept of deities evolved from naturalism. He says, "We may begin with the identification of the Vedic gods in some of their aspects with certain forces of nature and point out how they were gradually raised to moral super human beings. The Earliest seers of Vedic hymns delighted in sights of nature in their own simple unconscious way being essentially of poetic temperaments, they saw the things of nature with such intensity of feeling and force of imagination that the things suffused with souls. They knew what it was to love the nature, and be lost in the wonders of dawn and sunrise, those mysterious processes which affect the meeting of soul and nature. To them nature was a living presence with which they could hold communication............The moon, the stars, the sea and sky, the dawn and the night fall were regarded as divine, the worship of nature as such is the earliest form of Vedic religion".[6]

But even these hymns which refer to many gods, make it clearly stated that all these Gods are the various manifestations of the one supreme deity. Not only the Vedas refer to the many gods as being the various manifestations of the one and same supreme God., they also clearly point out that the whole Universe is the manifestation of this supreme God. In the famous '*Purusa Sukta*' the Vedic seer visualizes one great (*purus)* who pervades the world and remains beyond it. The whole creation whether in past, present or future is Purush.[7] The creation has evolved from Purush.[8] All the existence, earth, heavens, plants, gods, living things and non- living things are conceived this Sukta as the part of this person. In another hymn known as Nasawdiya Sukta we see the Vedic conception of the impersonal absolute which under lies all the existence, but which defies all description. The Chhandogya Upanishad describes the Absolute as '*Tajjalam*' meaning the absolute from which every thing springs, in which every thing abides and to which everything returns after dissolution. Brahadaranyka Upanisad describes this Absolute as Reality. In Upnisads, this Reality is sometimes Brahman, sometimes *Atma* and sometimes a Sat, Chandogya Upnishad says "*Atma-eva idam sarvam*"

(Sri, Sri Paramhans Yoganand sees the thought power of God as the cause of cosmic creation. In his lecture "A new look at the origin and nature of cosmic creation" He says that when that supreme intelligence began to muse "Long have I remained thus, alone, very peaceful, absorbed in my own bliss, consciousness and wisdom, but now I am going to dream a cosmos"). The cosmos is manifestation of ideas of God.[9]

Advaita Vedanta recognizes Brahman as the ultimate reality, pure cosmic consciousness. Everything in the world has evolved from Brahman by operation of law of duality; Brahman expresses itself in the form of manifold particular "Akohaman bahu bhavishayamah". He is not creator of many, but has become many. The whole world is pervaded with Brahman. The first verse of 40th chapter of Yajurveda i.e. Ishavasyopanisad says, "The entire creation is pervaded with God, regardless of visible or invisible, even a trace of creation 'Sarvam khalu idam Brahman' There is essential unity of all existence. Diversity is only phenomenal, unity is real. As divine is all pervasive. So every being in universe should get equal respect and we should not have a feeling of mastery over other species of universe. It precludes the idea that other things and being only have instrumental value for human being. The ideal ethical code expounded in the second part of this verse is that true enjoyment consists in renunciation and not in acquisition. The only plausible inference in the light of above outlook is that man is a part of nature and governed by basic laws of nature.

Bhagwadgita is a text of pragmatic ethics. It preaches the art of living in this world happily, peacefully and free of tension. Chapter-3 termed the world without any pain or sorrow of leaving it. Karma yoga verses 8-15 elucidate the code of conduct in relation to other humans, highly evolved and less evolved beings of the creatlon.

The 8th verse says "Perform those actions that are obligatory, for action is better than inactivity, even simple maintenance of body would be impossible due to inaction". This verse sets a foundation for our actions. It is not merely action itself that is purifying and uplifting, but dutiful actions. To improve one's self is to help society by the example of virtue.

In the 9th verse, Krishna tells Arjun to work unattached in the spirit of *Yajna,* offering actions as oblations. The formal rite in India of pouring ghee and oblation into the fire is symbolical of unifying life energy with cosmic energy Swami Yoganand Paramhans in his comments on Gita has defined *yajna* with reference to this verse as all duties which quicken ones evolution towards soul freedom may be termed as *Yajna*. He says "The word *yajna* has many meanings. It refers not only to the act of ritualistic worship, but to the sacrifice or oblation offered into sacred fire. It is also the fire itself, and the deity (Vishnu) to whom the offering is made."

Five *yajnas* namely *(i) Pitri yajna (ii) Nri yajna (iii) Bhut yajna (iv) Dev yajna (v) Brahman yajna,* mentioned in Hindu scriptures have been detailed as under by Paramhans ji *Pitra yajna*-offering oblation to ancestors i.e. the past essence of whose wisdom illumines man today.

Nri Yajna

Offering food to hungry i.e. the present responsibilities of man, his duties to contemporaries.

Bhut Yajna

Offering food to the animal kingdom i.e. man's oblations to less evolved forms of creation, instinctively tied to body identification (a dilution that affects man also) but lacking in that quality of liberating reasons which is peculiar to humanity. Thus the ceremony of *bhut yajna* symbolizes man's readiness to succor the weak, as a man in turn is comforted by countless solicitude of higher unseen beings. Humanity is also under bond of rejuvenating gifts of nature her self, prodigal in earth, sea and sky. The evolutionary barrier of incommunicability among nature, animals, man, astral angles is thus over come by offices of silent love.

Deva Yajna

Offering of life current from the senses, as sacrifice to soul sight.

Brahma Yajna

Offering the soul on the altar of all pervading spirit. This finality is attainable only after faithful performance of the preceding four ceremonies, which inwardly as well as out worldly acknowledge man's debt to (i) Past (ii) Present (iii) Worlds of lower being and (iv) Worlds of higher being. Thus providing his fidelity to creation, man is fit to touch the hem of the creator's rope."

According to verse 10, 11 and 12 Prajapati created mankind along with yajna and directed them to propagate and fulfill their desires and strengthen the Devas by yajna and Devas may uplift the mankind. The Devas communed with by yajna will grant them craved for gifts. He who enjoys benefactions of the universal deities without due offerings to them is indeed a thief.

Paramhans Yoganand has described Devas as astral forces, angles devine soul who as God's Cosmic Agents are instrumental in governing the worlds. Devas respond favorably to those in harmony with exacting laws of nature. He comments. "Among the customs of all ancient people's were nature rules whose purpose was to acknowledge man's dependence on the natural forces and the bounty of environment. Instinctively, they recognized the debt and reverence owed to a higher intelligence working with in the circumambient wonders. It is no coincidence that the godliness prevalent in the modern age has spawned a civilization out of touch with the beneficence of nature. The God given role of guardianship of the earth did not confer on man absolute sovereignty his wanton domination is destructive of the very conditions necessary for his existence."[10]

According to verse 14 and 15 the creatures are sustained from food, food is product of rains, a rains are caused by yajna, yajna is born of Karma, Karma originated from Vedas and Vedas originated from Brahman. So by performing yajna, we work according to the will of God.

To conclude, the Indian scriptures teach the innate relation and the attitude of human race with nature and its forces. Among the customs of all ancient people were nature rites whose purpose was to acknowledge man's dependence on the natural forces and bounty of his environment. In ancient people adored and worshiped the natural powers due to a feeling of allegation, they felt kinship without being akin to nature. It is no coincidence that the utilitarian attitude prevailing in the modern age has spawned a civilization out of touch with the beneficence of nature. The God given role of guardianship of the earth did not confer on man absolute sovereignty. His wanton domination is destructive for the very conditions necessary for his existence. The only way in the present circumstances is to thrive on our old sentimental legacy, increase our awareness and broaden the frontiers of empathy. This is possible only by increasing rationality, so that human mind may be trained to feel more identified with the rest of the creation. Love and be loved should be the very creed of humanity.

References

1. Sen and Williams (eds) utilitarianism and beyond Cambridge, 1982.
2. Smart and Willams (eds), utilitarianism for and against, Cambridge 1973.
3. Naess, A "Deep Ecology and ultimate premises society and nature" Vol. I No. 1992: Deep Ecology in Good conceptual Health, the Trampeter, fall 1986.
4. Johnson, LE A morally Deep world.
5. Rig-veda (1, 17, 3-5).
6. (Indian Philosophy, Part-1, p. 73 Dr. Radhakrishnan).
7. Second Richa Purus Sukta.
8. 3rd Richa Purus Sukta.
9. The devine Romance, p. 18.

   Paramhans Yoganand Page 352 (Bhagwad Geeta by Chapter- II Verse- II).

16

REVISITING BUDDHIST ECOLOGY OF HUMAN FLOURISHING

Dr. D.C. Srivastava

Buddhism considers the intrinsic value of both humans and nature as providing a more meaningful way of living. This is in contrast to extrinsic value, the economic valuation of nature for resource exploitation for the market economy. An individual should limit personal use of natural resources to obtaining optimal satisfaction of basic needs. Instead of the use of nature, the Buddhist is more concerned with the contemplation of nature, especially through meditation. All life forms have a natural right to existence as functional components of the ecosystem; thus the Buddhist should avoid the use of pesticides and other unnecessary destruction of life. Thich Nhat Hanh (1988:41) writes: We should deal with nature the way we should deal with ourselves! We should not harm ourselves; we should not harm nature. Harming nature is harming ourselves, and vice versa. If we knew how to deal with our self and with our fellow human beings, we would know how to deal with nature. Human beings and nature are inseparable. Therefore, by not caring properly for any one of these, we harm them all.

Buddhism is eco-centric rather than anthropocentric since it views humans as an integral part of nature. As Kaza (1990) explains, Buddhism focuses on the interaction of mind and nature through the three practices of direct knowing, discriminating awareness, and deep compassion: By cultivating these three practices, one's actions in relation to the environment come to be based in relationship and interconnectedness, rather than in dualistic subject-object modes of separation. Through this approach, one's orientation to the world is fundamentally altered from dominant species to member of a community, from part to process (Ibid, p. 22). With interdependence as a core understanding, an environmental ethic becomes a practice in recognizing and supporting relationships with all beings (Ibid, p. 24).

We know that mankind has failed to take account of the intimate connections within the ecosystem, between himself and the world, arrogantly charging in with new found technological powers, destabilizing intricate systems of ecological organization, the complexity of which we are only just beginning to realize. We know that subtle strands of influence link our shopping habits and the economies of the developing world; that the chemicals we use in our homes and industries have a pervasive effect throughout the oceans and the skies; that our relative affluence and luxury are inextricably bound up with the poverty and toil of others.

If we are to exist in a way which no longer perpetuates the damage done so far, and begins to heal some of the ecological and social wounds we have created, we must appreciate more and more our own interconnectedness and the intimate relations which exist between things in the world around us. To achieve this, scholars have begun to interrogate religious traditions as a possible resource for the development of an environmental ethic. At one end of the spectrum are apologists who see the world's religions as a key resource in addressing the environmental crisis; at the other, critics point to religion as redounding to the crisis. In his controversial 1967 article on Christianity and the environment, Lynn White commends Buddhism for its holistic, egalitarian worldview, and an environmentally friendly style of life in contrast to the Biblical worldview and mainstream Christianity that White sees as promoting human dominance over nature and, hence, contributing to the environmental crisis (White 1967: 1203-1207).[1] White's positive evaluation of Buddhism's eco-friendly worldview has been promoted by Buddhists and scholars of Buddhism in Asia and the West.

My purpose in this paper is to assess and evaluate a selection of contributions to the field of Buddhism and ecology. My analysis here is intended to highlight what I construe as four sometimes overlapping positions regarding Buddhism and the environment. I have labeled this four-fold taxonomy: *eco-apologists, eco-critics, eco-constructivists, and eco-ethicists*. I hasten to add that these categories are intended to be suggestive rather than definitive, and that I intend them primarily for heuristic purposes.

The first position holds that Buddhist environmentalism is a natural extension of the Buddhist worldview; the second that the Buddhist worldview is not compatible with an environmental ethic; the third that a Buddhist environmental ethic, while not *co-terminus* with the Buddhist worldview, can be constructed from Buddhist texts and doctrinal tenets; and the fourth, that a viable Buddhist environmental ethic should be evaluated in terms of Buddhist ethics rather than inferred from the Buddhist worldview.

Mindful living in Buddhism cultivates a view of human beings, nature, and their relationship that is fundamentally ecological. Awareness opens our perception to the interdependence and fragility of all life, and our indebtedness to countless beings, living and dead, past and present. If we have any real identity at all in Buddhism, it is the ecology itself—a massive interdependent, self-causing dynamic energy-event against a backdrop of ceaseless change (Badiner 1990: xiv-xv). The majority of the writings on Buddhist ecology promotes the normative position that the Buddhist worldview is inherently eco-friendly and attuned to the natural environment. Three anthologies in the field—*Dharma Gaia: A Harvest of Essays in Buddhism and Ecology*, ed. Allan Hunt Badiner, (1990), *Buddhism and Ecology*, ed. Martine Batchelor and Kerr Brown (1992), and *Dharma Rain: Sources of Buddhist Environmentalism*, ed. Stephanie Kaza and Kenneth Kraft (2000)—explicate and justify this position using a wide ambit of texts that range from the *Mahratnakuta Sutra* to Thich Nhat Hanh and the Dalai Lama.

The *Avatamsaka Sutra* (Flower Ornament Sutra) is one of the most often cited classical Indian Mahayana texts to which an ecological significance is ascribed. This important scripture and the metaphor of the Jewel Net of Indra are offered as evidence that Buddhism, in particular, the Hua Yen tradition, views the cosmos as an infinitely repeated interrelationship among all the members of the cosmos, likened by Francis Cook to a cosmic ecology: "Each individual is at once the cause for the whole and is caused by the whole, and what is called existence is a vast body made up of an infinity of individuals all sustaining each other and defining each other" (Cook 1989: 215). Since the majority of sources in these anthologies are contemporary rather than classical texts, the eco-apologist position has been identified with Engaged Buddhism.

Eco-apologists find in the personal example of the Buddha and Buddhist monks a model of environmentally sensitive behavior. Stephanie Kaza observes, "The courage and inspiration of the Buddha and the *bodhisattvas*...are helpful to me in examining the spiritual dimension of the environmental crisis" (Kaza 1993: 137). Eco-apologists appeal to the simple lifestyle of Buddhist monks as providing an example of how to live non-acquisitively, and point out that *vinaya* rules prohibit monks from cutting down trees, from eating ten kinds of meat of wild animals, and they are forbidden to contaminate water. As proof of the importance of trees and forests in early Buddhism it is pointed out that the Buddha was born, achieved his awakening, and died under trees, and that forest dwelling was prized as an ideal environment in which to practice the religious life. Beyond appealing to particular texts and the exemplary life of the Buddha and *arahant* monks, eco-apologists ascribe an ecological significance to seminal Buddhist doctrines, in particular, *paticca samuppida* (interdependent co-arising), *anatta* (not-self), *sunnati* (emptiness), *tath igatagarbha* (the womb of suchness).

They make the general claim that these teachings represent a non-dualistic, nonhierarchical, holistic worldview in which all sentient beings—humans and animals- and insentient nature are conjoined. In the resonant prose of the late Thai monk, Buddhadasa Bhikkhu, "The entire cosmos is a cooperative. The sun, moon, and stars live together as a cooperative. The same is true for humans and animals, trees, and the earth. When we realize that the world is a mutual, interdependent, cooperative enterprise...then we can build a noble environment." (Buddhadasa 1990: 35)

Harris characterizes attempts to find an environmental ethic in Buddhism (*i.e.*, "eco-Buddhism") as a modern American initiative to articulate an authentically Buddhist response to current environmental problems, a response that grew out of the American environmental movement of the 1960s dominated by educated liberal elites and inter-religious environmental dialogues with a liberal socio-political agenda (Harris 1995b:173). Building on insights from Antony Gidden's The Consequences of Modernity (1990), Harris sees Buddhist environmentalism as an expression of a type of globalization that promotes an erosion of culture-specific boundaries and a homogenization or uniformity of attitude that overrides significant differences in doctrine and practice: "It is the impact of modernity and of globalization, in particular, that has tended to encourage traditional religions, such as Christianity and Buddhism, to move to a closer intellectual and emotional harmony the more they move away from the geographical locations that have given them their specific cultural and historical forms" (Harris 1995b: 175).

Harris finds a shared utopianism among the representatives of this collective eco-religiosity, namely, an effort to reestablish an original purity of nature, a biospheric community, a soteric this-worldly eco-activism that has become a virtual religion in and of itself. Harris contends that supporters of a Buddhist environmental ethic, in particular, have been indifferent to the history and complexity of the Buddhist tradition; they have uncritically appropriated modern globalized discourse and in doing so have departed from the critical spirit that has played a major role in the history of Buddhism to the modern period. Furthermore, even a cursory examination of the languages, doctrines, and historical permutations of Buddhism debunks any notion of a Buddhist environmental ethic as such, just as there is no Buddhism as such. Nevertheless, Harris is sympathetic with the aim of the eco-apologists. While he sees this position as representing a significant departure from the traditional Buddhist worldview he acknowledges that all traditions must change if they are to adapt and flourish. Therefore, to reject an eco-Buddhism as a sham, supermarket religion is problematic from a broad, historical perspective: "Consideration of the genesis of eco-Buddhism and of its activist programme suggests that it shouldn't be characterized as a deviation from traditional norms but that it should be seen as an example of a vigorous tradition engaged in a healthy process of reflexive apologetics" (Harris 1995b: 207).

The critics of Buddhist eco-apologists contend that today's ecological concerns are quintessentially modern and that, consequentially, Buddhist foundational documents lack any explicit discussion of what today we would label environmental ethics (Harris 2000: 113). While the eco-critics may sympathize with the intention behind the eco-apologists' project, they judge it to be a serious distortion of normative Buddhist teachings and historical traditions. They focus their critique on what they consider to be a misreading of early Indian Buddhism, in particular, although they cite misrepresentations of East Asian Buddhist traditions as well, e.g., Noriaka Hakamaya's attack on the concepts of Buddha-nature, *tathat i* (suchness), and non-dualism. They argue that the soteriological focus of [early] Buddhism based on a negative assessment of the realm of sense experience including "nature" as fundamentally unsatisfactory (*dukkha*) and subject to change (*anicca*), does not provide the grounds for an environmental ethic. Furthermore, they charge that the tradition is primarily anthropocentric, not bio-centric, in its focus on spiritual liberation. At best, the non-human environment occupies a role as the context for the pursuit of trans-mundane ends. Eco-apologists, in response, object to the narrowness of this criticism, contending that from the outset the way of the Buddha was broader than a narrowly construed quest for Nirvi ,a without regard for other sentient beings and natural surroundings.

Stating the traditional Buddhist Attitudes of not injuring (*ahims i*), benevolence (*metta/maitr*) and compassion (*karu,i*) to entail an 'ecological' behaviour is surely justified in so far as these attitudes are not limited to human beings as their object but include also other living beings, especially animals. Still, it should be clear that neither of these attitudes has, primarily, an 'ecological' purport.

(Schmidthausen 1991: 32) Eco-constructivists adopt a critical stance toward the formation of a Buddhist environmental ethic based on a normative commitment rather than the tools of critical scholarship. Nevertheless, using these tools they seek to uncover ecologically positive elements in Buddhist textual and historical traditions on which to build an environmental ethic.

Eco-constructivists such as Lambert Schmidthausen contend that a viable Buddhist environmental ethic depends on ascribing a positive value to nature and to natural diversity but in such a way that the essentials of the tradition are not lost. In his analysis, the soteriological focus of early Indian Buddhism has, at best, only a "passive" ecological significance although later forms of Mahayana offer more promise. He shares with eco-critics the view that early Buddhism did not ascribe an inherent value to nature. In his view, early Buddhism does not seem to confer any value on nature, neither on life as such nor on species nor on eco-systems. The ultimate value of early Buddhism is not in nature or in culture. Ultimately the issue is not preserving, restoring, transforming or subjugating nature but only for liberation (*vimutti*) for all constituents of existence. (Schmidthausen 1997:11) Even so, the soteriological orientation of early Indian Buddhism can be construed to have ecological consequences in that the person who has attained liberation is motivated by sympathy and compassion to act on behalf of other sentient beings. These virtues, highlighted in the Mahayana *bodhisattva* ideal, are primarily ethical rather than ecological terms. The same is true for the concept of interdependent co-arising (*paticca samuppida)*, the knowledge of which leads to the overcoming of ignorance and desire. It is primarily psychological, ethical, and spiritual in nature. In Schmidthausen's view, "This analysis of the presuppositions of individual bondage and liberation could [not] without a radical reinterpretation, provide a basis for ecological ethics based on an intrinsic value of natural diversity and beauty" (Schmidthausen 1997: 12-13).

The doctrine of rebirth which posits that animal forms may have been or be one's relatives seems to be closer to an ecological sense of interconnectedness even though it is anthropocentric in its intent.

In Hua Yen Buddhism, however, the principle of universal interdependence assumes more resemblance to the structural principle of scientific ecology. In terms of Buddhist ethics, although the emphasis on overcoming desire and greed is framed in terms of spiritual practice and ascetic virtues and does not ascribe a positive value to nature as such, they do have environmental consequences and are ecologically beneficial. More pertinent to an ecological ethic are the values of non-killing, loving-kindness, sympathy, and compassion.

Although the principal of *ahims i* began as protection against the vengeance of injured animals in the world beyond, and loving-kindness and compassion are associated with states of consciousness attained in meditation, these virtues have ethical significance beyond one's own spiritual benefit. To construe them as constituting an ecological ethic that promotes the protection of species or as an *apologia* for biodiversity distorts the historical tradition; however, they are not without ecological import.

Both the eco-constructivist and the eco-critic hold that early Buddhism's focus on the achievement of a soteriological goal problematizes an environmental reading of the tradition. However, an eco-constructivist such as Schmidthausen believes that, nonetheless, selected teachings of the tradition are not without positive ecological consequences. The distinguished Thai scholar monk, P. A. Payutto, echoes the eco-constructivist effort to derive environmentally salient lessons from texts and historical traditions without sacrificing the essentials of the tradition. He finds the potential for promoting a positive, beneficial attitude toward the environment in three moral virtues—gratitude (*katannu*), loving-kindness (*metta*), and happiness (*sukha).* Payutto sees an environmental lesson in the following passage from the *Khuddaka Nikaya*, "A person who sits or sleeps in the shade of a tree should not cut off a tree branch. One who injures such a friend is evil "observing". This maxim reminds us that the shade of a tree we enjoy is enjoyed by others as well. A tree is like a friend that we have no reason to injure. To injure a tree is like hurting a friend.

Such a virtuous attitude toward nature will prevent us from destructive behavior, on the one hand, and will prompt helpful actions, on the other" (Payutto 1994: 22-23). In an even broader sense Payutto links human happiness to the natural environment. Citing the historical example of forest dwelling monks, he contends that throughout the history of Buddhism in Thailand the forest was seen as a teacher of mind and spirit and that living within a natural environment engenders a greater sense of happiness and wellbeing (Payutto 1994: 33). Payutto does not derive an ecological ethic based on the inherent value of the nature from such examples taken from text and tradition but he does discover teachings pertinent to what Schmidthausen would characterize as an "authentic" Buddhist environmental ethic.

The interests and concerns of religion and ecology are closely linked to an ethic of moderation, the Buddhist "Middle Way" (*majjhima patipat i*), as promoting a less environmental harmful life style. In the words of the popular bumper sticker, "Live simply so that others many simply live!" Over forty years ago, E.F. Schumacher's *Small is Beautiful* advocated a non-exploitative "Buddhist economics" lifestyle of simplicity, nonviolence, and moderate consumption: "The teaching of the Buddha...enjoins a reverent and non-violent attitude not only to all sentient beings but also... to trees" (Schumacher 1973: 56). Inspired by Schumacher's vision, Buddhist social activists and environmentalists have become vociferous critics of the consumerist values associated with economic globalization. Much of this literature is provocative, insightful, and inspiring. From a philosophical perspective, however, equally if not more interesting has been the effort to view Buddhist environmental ethics from the perspective of virtue theory. Recent studies of Theravada Buddhism have proposed an analogical relationship between Buddhist ethics and the tradition of virtue ethics in the West, e.g. the Stoics, Epicureans, Aristotle. Damien Keown, for example, observes that despite differences in social and cultural contexts there are formal parallels between the ideal of human perfection as taught by the Buddha and Aristotle (Keown 1993: 193), and James Whitehill sees the cultivation of the *piramit* is ("awakened virtue") as the heart of Buddhist ethics (2000: 24-26).

Whitehall characterizes the *piramit* is as biocentric and ecological based on what he considers to be the relational and processional nature of the self-concept in Buddhism, but he does not develop this notion in the direction of an environmental ethic. However, such a project on different grounds has been undertaken by two British scholars at the University of Durham, David E. Cooper and Simon P. James (2005). It is their case for the relationship between the cultivation of virtue and environmental ethics to which I shall refer in arguing that in the construction of a Buddhist environmental ethic preference be given to the Buddhist vision of human flourishing over and above reconstructing seminal teachings from the Buddhist worldview, e.g. *paticca-samuppida, anatta, sunnat i, tathat /garbha,* from an ecological perspective.

In general terms, moreover, I am of the opinion that the most compelling contribution to environmental discourse that can be made by the world's religions is in the area of what I have termed "ecology of human flourishing" (Swearer 2001: 231). Cooper and James challenge the dichotomy between intrinsic and instrumental value made by environmental ethicists who claim intrinsic value to be the *sine qua non* of environmental ethics. In defining environmental ethics as "philosophical reflection on how human beings should relate to and act toward non-human life in natural environments" they shift the focus to human agency (Cooper and James 2004: 3). Furthermore, by focusing on those traits and dispositions of character essential to a good and realized human life they problematize the dichotomy in ethical theory between deontological and consequentialist ethics, namely, whether the rightness or wrongness of an action should be judged in terms of principles of obligation and duty, or whether or not they produce desirable results (ibid: 7). Buddhist environmental ethics, then, is most properly generated by "an account of the virtues and their implications for treatment of the natural world" rather than consideration of rights or utility (ibid: 108).

Eco-ethicists agree with eco-critics and eco-constructivists in rejecting ecological holists who claim that human beings and nature are inseparable. Cooper and James assert that the canonical teachings of *paticca samuppida, anatta,* and *sunnati* on which claims of inseparability are made are "no more than a gesture at the form which explanations of natural processes would take," and that such asseverations "provide a very fragile basis on which to erect any substantial account of the empirical relationship between human beings and the rest of the living world" (ibid., 110). Furthermore, eco-apologists who espouse the view of inseparability do not convincingly demonstrate how ecological holism yields an enlightened environmental ethic or, as Cooper and James put it, "Recitation of the doctrines of conditioned co-arising and not-self is, by itself, quite incapable of showing that 'we should not harm nature' rather than exploit it whatever ways 'maximize' and 'fitness' of human genetic material (ibid., 112).

In contrast to an eco-critic such as Ian Harris who attacks eco-Buddhist apologists for fabricating what he considers to be an inauthentic Buddhist environmentalism, the eco-ethicist holds that a Buddhist environmental ethic can be read as a natural extension of Buddhist virtue ethics. Such a move is a construction of a "Buddhist environmental ethic on the basis *both* of a wider philosophy *and* explicit remarks found in the texts on environmental matters (ibid. 118). In the tradition of Western virtue ethics, Cooper and James divide their analysis into an ethic of self and other-regard. Self-regarding virtues are humility, self-mastery, and equanimity—components in the process of self cultivation by which one attains "*nirvanic* felicity" (ibid. 118). As elements of an environmental ethic they examine the implications of these virtues for a proper way to regard and treat animals and plants as a moral resource of the cultivation of these virtues. Other-regarding virtues discussed by Cooper and James as antidotes to environmental vices are solicitude, non-violence, and 'responsible-ness,' the latter being an antidote to overwhelming despair in the face of global environmental degradation (ibid., 127). Eco-ethicists shares the eco-constructivist's respect for the integrity of the Buddhist tradition and suspicion of the eco-holism; however, they shift the focus of Buddhism and ecology from an evaluation of the ecological saliency of the Buddhist world view to a Buddhist environmental ethic firmly grounded in the received tradition of virtue with its strong emphasis on character transformation.

To conclude, this paper is an effort to describe its diversity in terms of a four fold scheme of classification. The question of whether there is such a thing as an "authentic" Buddhist ecological ethic begs the question of what constitutes "authentic" Buddhism. As is true of all historic religions, Buddhism has evolved and changed over time and place. Today if the Buddhist tradition is to remain a living tradition, it has to supply answers to new vital questions and accommodate its heritage to a new situation by means of explication, re-interpretation, re-organization or change. One of these questions is doubtless whether or not an ecological ethics is required. Many of those involved in the ecology movement have found inspiration and valuable parallels within the Buddhist tradition and many Buddhists themselves have begun to draw out the ecological implications of their tradition. The fundamental Buddhist teachings around interconnectedness, non-violence and conditionality all contribute to both a practice and understanding that augments and honors the ecological paradigms now arising. The application of Buddhist insights to our current ecological and social ills constitutes one of Buddhism's most creative and dynamic responses to the contemporary context.

References

1. Buddhadasa, Bhikkhu. (1990) *Phutasasanik Kap Kan Anurak Thamachat* (Buddhists and the Care of Nature). Bangkok: Komol Thimthong Foundation.
2. Cook, Francis, H. (1989) "The Jewel Net of Indra," in *Nature in Asian Traditions of Thought*, Albany: State University of New York Press: 213-230.
3. Cooper, David E. and James, Simon P. (2005) *Buddhism, Virtue and Environment*, Aldershot, England: Ashgate.
4. De Silva, Lily. (2000) "Early Buddhist Attitudes toward Nature," in Stephanie Kaza and Kenneth Kraft (ed.) *Dharma Rain: Sources of Buddhist Environmentalism*, Boston: Shambala Publications: 91-104.
5. Giddens, Anthony (1990) *The Consequences of Modernity*, Stanford University Press.
6. Harris, Ian (1995b) "Getting to Grips with Buddhist Environmentalism: A Provisional Typology." *Journal of Buddhist Ethics*: 173-190.

7. Harris, Ian. (2000) "Buddhism and Ecology." In *Contemporary Buddhist Ethics.* Richmond, Surrey: Curzon Press: 113-135.
8. Kaza, Stephanie (1990) "Towards a Buddhist Environmental Ethic," Buddhism at the Crossroads Fall 1990:22-25.
9. Kaza, Stephanie (1993). "Planting Seeds of Joy," in Fritz Hull (ed.) *Earth and Spirit*, New York: Contnuum: 137-148.
10. Keown, Damien (1993). *The Nature of Buddhist Ethics.* New York: St. Martins Press.
11. Payutto, P.A. (1994). *Khon Thai Kap Pa* (Thais and the Forest). Bangkok: Association for Agriculture and Biology.
12. Schmithausen, Lambert. (1991) *Buddhism and Nature.* Tokyo: International Institute for Buddhist Studies.
13. Schmithausen, Lambert. (1991) *The Problem of Sentience of Plants in Earliest Buddhism.* Tokyo: The International Institute for Buddhist Studies.
14. Schmithausen, Lambert. (1997) "The Early Buddhist Tradition and Ecological Ethics," *Journal of Buddhist Ethics* 4: 1-74.
15. Schumacher (1973) *Small is Beautiful*, New York: Harper & Row Publications.
16. Swearer, Donald K. (2001). "Principles and Poetry, Places and Stories: The Resources of Buddhist Ecology." *Daedalus* 130, no. 4 (Fall 2001): 225-241.
17. Thich Nhat Hanh (1988). "The Individual, Society, and Nature," in Fred Eppsteiner, (ed.) The Path of Compassion: Writings on Socially Engaged Buddhism, Berkeley, CA: Parallax Press: 40-46.
18. White, Lynn Jr. (1967). "The Historical Roots of Our Ecologic Crisis," *Science* 15 (10 March,1967): 1203-1207.
19. Whitehill, James (2000) "Buddhism and the Virtues" in Keown, Damien (ed.) *Contemporary Buddhist Ethics*, and Rutledge: 17-36.

Footnotes

1. White's essay created a storm of controversy. For example, see Elspeth Whitney, "Lynn White, Eco-theology, and History," *Environmental Ethics* 15 1993): 151-69.

17

A COMPARATIVE ANALYSIS OF DEEP ECOLOGY AND COSMO-CENTRIC ETHICS

Dr. Shiva Bhanu Singh

The display of marvelous remarkable technological Knowledge and the achievement of splendid means for bringing about spectacular changes in our living environment have been the hallmark of the last century's human image on this planet. Ironically however, it is with utmost alarming consciousness that the same humanity has experienced, in the same century the imminent dangers of an environment massively misused and exploited by the most knowledgeable race on earth. The rising awareness and movement of Environmentalism and eco-friendliness are direct reflections of our candid confession of eco-insensitivity. It is very unfortunate that the most intelligent species on earth live such an eco-unfriendly life on it and it is necessarily a glaring example of human folly. Bertrand Russell, once said that knowledge is power, but it is power for evil just as much as for good. Unless men increase in wisdom as much as in knowledge, increase of knowledge will be increase in sorrow. He warned that given knowledge and competence combined with folly, there can be no certainty of human survival. In the later half of the 20th century, environmental awareness and eco-sensitivity seems to be the belated awareness of environmental wisdom.

It has been a debated question in contemporary Philosophy as to which beings have and which do not have a claim to be considered morally important in their own right. Modern western ethical theory has been anthropocentric or human centered because it does not give importance to non-human beings. It does not establish any moral relation with the natural environment and non-living beings. The contemporary moralists have advocated for a new ethics i.e. 'Environmental Ethics', that extends the range of morally considerable cases beyond human beings and includes in it non-human beings, animals, plants and other living beings by accepting their moral worthiness and establishing their independent moral status. The environmental ethics, later known as deep ecology is concerned with the question should we value non-human being, living as well as non living only because of their utility to human being or they are valuable in themselves. Here we can adopt two standpoints. According to one standpoint, the non-human beings are morally valuable and important because they are relative to human interest. This idea has been called as narrow scope view. The second view may be that non-human beings and entire eco-system are morally important and valuable in themselves, irrespective of any relation to human interest. This second view can be called as wide-scope view.

Ecology is the science of Environment which is the sum of all conditions, agencies and influences that affect the development, growth, life and death of an organism, species or race. Ecology has been defined as the study of organisms in relation to their environment. It is the pattern and balance of relationships between plants, animals, people and their environment. Human ecology is at present in crisis almost everywhere in the modern world because man seems to be unable to adjust to the change in the environment and the mode of life which he himself has created. The prime purpose of human ecology is to find through research into interaction between man and his environment, the optional conditions necessary for man to survive and develop his physical, mental and spiritual ability.

The ecological imbalance and environmental crisis are the result of western attitude towards nature. According to the dominant western tradition, the natural world exists for the benefit of human beings. God does not care how we treat it. Human beings are the only morally important members of this world. Nature itself is of no intrinsic value, and the destruction of plants and animals cannot be sinful, unless by this destruction we harm human beings.

In the later half of the 20th century a changed attitude towards nature evolved and reverence for life was advised. More than forty years ago the American ecologist Aldo Leopold wrote that there was a need for a new ethic, an ethic dealing with man's relation to land and to animals and plants which grow upon it. His proposed "Land ethic" would enlarge the boundaries of the community to include soils, water, plants, and animals, or collectively, the land". Another Norwegian philosopher Arne Naess wrote a brief but influential article distinguishing between "shallow" and 'deep' strands in the ecological movement. Shallow ecological thinking was limited to the traditional moral framework.[1] Deep ecologists, on the other hand, wanted to preserve the integrity of the biosphere for its own sake, irrespective of the possible benefits to humans that might flow from so doing. In a paper published in 1984, Arne Naess and George Sessions, American philosophers involved in the deep ecology movement, set out several principles for a deep ecological ethics, beginning with the following;

1. The well-being and flourishing of human and non-human life on Earth have value in them selves (intrinsic value). These values are independent of the usefulness of the non-human world.
2. Richness and diversity of life forms contribute to the realization of these values and are also value in them.
3. Human have no right to reduce this richness and diversity except to satisfy vital needs.[2]

Two Austrians working at the deep end of environmental ethics, Richard Sylvan and Val Plum Wood also extend their ethics beyond living things including in it an obligation not to jeopardize the well being of natural objects or systems without good reason. In Deep Ecology Bill Deval and George Sessions defend a form of 'bio-centric' egalitarianism.[3] The intuition of bio-centric equality is that all things in the biosphere have an equal right to live and blossom and to reach their own individual form of unfolding and self realization. This basic intuition is that all organisms and entities in the ecosphere as parts of the interrelated whole, are in intrinsic worth.

In order to cope with the environmental crisis a contemporary environmental ethics is developing. Such an ethics would regard every action that is harmful to the environmental as ethically dubious and those that are unnecessarily harmful as plainly wrong. An environmental ethic would find virtue in saving and recycling resources, and vice in extravagance and unnecessary consumption. We may illustrate an example from the perspective of an environmental ethic. Our choice of recreation is not ethically neutral. At present we see the choice between motor car racing and cycling, between water skiing or wind surfing as merely a matter of taste yet there is an essential difference; Motor car racing and water skiing require the consumption of fossil fuels and the discharge of carbon dioxide into the atmosphere. Cycling and wind surfing do not. Once we take the need to preserve our environment seriously, motor racing and water skiing will no more be acceptable form of entertainment than bear baiting is today.

A truly environmental ethics fosters consideration for the interest of all sentient creatures, including subsequent generation, stretching in to the far future. It is accompanied by an aesthetic of appreciation for wild places and unspoiled nature. An environmental ethic rejects the ideals of a materialistic society in which success is gauged by the numbers of consumer goods one can accumulate. Instead it judges success in terms of the development of one's abilities and the achievement of real fulfillment and satisfaction. It promotes frugality, in so far as it is necessary for minimizing pollution and ensuring that everything that can be reused is reused. Carelessly to throw out material that can be recycled is a form of vandalism or the theft of our common property in the resources of the world.Thus the various green consumer guides books, about things we can do to save our planet recycling what we use and buying the most environment friendly products available are part of new ethic that is required. Thus we see that new environmental ethic will promote frugality and simple life.

Reverence for nature, the principle of sanctity of life, bio-centric equality and cosmo-centric attitude can be very easily found in Hindu tradition from ancient times. Hindu tradition believes only God has absolute sovereignty over all creatures including man, thus man had no dominion over his own life or non-human life. Hindu scholars do not accept absolute superiority of man over nature. The idea of the Divine being as the one underlying power of unity is beautifully expressed in Yajurveda. The sacredness of God's creation means no damage may be incurred on other species without adequate justification. Therefore, all lives human and non-human are of equal value and all have the same right to existence. According to Atharvaveda, the earth is not for human beings alone, but for other creatures as well.

The Hindu Rishis of the Vedic and the upanishdic era perceived the values of maintaining a harmonious relationship between the need of man and spectacular diversity of the universe. They believed that nature was not only the mother that sustained their life; it was the abode of diversity. They never supported the exploitation of nature for fulfilling the selfish purpose of man. Only God has absolute sovereignty over all creatures including man. Thus man had no dominion over his own life, man has not being allowed to act as the viceroy of God over the planet, nor assigns degree of relative worth to other species. The religion provides no sense of absolute superiority of man over nature. Hindu tradition gives respect to whole natural world including the flora and fauna of the earth and creatures in the sky and under the sea. It is believed that all that exist has been created by the Supreme Being which is an adequate basis for the veneration of natural world in which man find himself. The history of human survival stands as a good example of the interdependence, cooperative living and close association which exists among the forces of human and non-human nature.

From the above observation of Hindu tradition, it is obvious that Hindu culture in ancient and medieval times provided a system of moral guidelines towards environmental preservation and conservation. Environmental ethics, as propounded by ancient Hindu scriptures and seers, was practiced not only by common man, but even by rulers and kings.

In Indian tradition, we find in place of man opposing nature and nature opposing mankind, antic identity between them, the identity of microcosm and macrocosm and entire creation is being governed by extraordinary moral cosmic order Rta. In Yajurveda, it is prayed that sky, atmosphere, earth, water and plants be peaceful. May all the learned persons, God and Veda be peaceful. May peace itself be peaceful and let peace come unto me.

Thus it becomes very obvious that the concept of deep ecology environmental ethics or known as land ethics is quite similar to Cosmo-centric view of Indian tradition. Both lay stress on harmonious relationship between man and nature; both lay emphasis on preservation of nature and other non-living beings. The difference between western and Indian view lies in the fact that western approach seems to be belated realization of human folly and therefore suggests for increasing environmental wisdom. The deep ecologist now recognized the intrinsic value of non -living beings and wanted to preserve the integrity of the biosphere for its own sake, irrespective of the possible benefits to humans that might flow from so doing. As far as Indian view is concerned it believes in sanctity of life, reverence for nature and divine origin of all living and non-living beings, thus establishing metaphysical unity of all beings. Conclusively we can say that ecology and cosmo-centric morality are bio-centric and eco-centric.

After presenting the expositions of deep ecologists and proponents of Cosmo-centric ethics, I would like to reflect critically on these two stands of environmental theories. At first stance eco-centrism appears attractive because it regards that the whole eco-system comprising both the biotic and a biotic parts of nature deserves moral worth but critical reflection shows the inherent unavoidable difficulties in it. Eco-centrism has been considered as egalitarian anti-anthropocentric tendency of ecological holism. This theory maintains that all eco-system and species have equal right to live and blossom, and we have to acknowledge it if this is admitted, then bacteria and humans have to be considered equal and have to be protected equally. But such egalitarian outlook can hardly be accepted in practice because it seems to go against the modus-operandi of the nature. The critics say that egalitarianism which posits that every form of being has an absolutely equal right is not a rational statement. Morality, being a matter of choice human should be given some sort of priority in value distribution, some form of anthropocentric is inalienable in moral discourse. If we disregard this and are guided by the so called egalitarianism, then there might come up a demand of returning back to the original nature condition of hunter gathering society. Critics further allege that then we will have to eliminate 80% of the world population, will it not be a systematic genocide? As a matter of fact, this would amount to eco-fascism[4], and that can never be admitted or supported. K.A. Parker has rightly remarked, "Blind anthropocentrism has deplorable consequences for non-human world, but a blindly misanthropic eco-centrism is no less deplorable."[5]

The critics of egalitarianism argue that undoubtedly human chauvinism is condemnable, but we should at least acknowledge human experience as the measure of all things. It is logically possible for us to decide that a world without humans has a value, yet it is we who are making this decision. Our point is that in order to determine our goal, and to go forward with environmentalism, this inalienable element of anthropocentricity is to be acknowledged. As long as the one who values is a human being, it is impossible for being radically non-anthropocentric in environmental matters.

But the admission of this element of anthropocentricity does not mean the unavoidability of human Chauvinism or speciesism. What is unavoidability of human? We have no alternative but to make use of human yardstick in making any type of value judgment. Human valuers find that in all consistency they must give priority to the basic needs of human over the non-basic trivial needs of humans. But the Chauvinist, on the other hand, holds that the interest of humans must always be accorded priority. It is to be noted that the Chauvinist does not take human values as reference point, as he admits no comparison between humans and non-humans. He values human interest because they are humans and such stand point is highly objectionable. But, what is being emphasized is that it is beyond debate that the element of humanness makes any ethics possible. It is human being who could develop an ethic to include others interests in to his concern. In such a way eco-centric morality can only be developed by human beings only. This, indeed is the non-contingent but, substantive limitation. On any attempt to develop totally eco-centric ethics.[6]

Some critics have argued that the conclusions of deep-ecologist that the nature has intrinsic value involves naturalistic fallacy. According to them ecology and ethics are separate disciplines. Ecology is the study of facts (nature), where as ethics is the study of values. As an 'ought' is not simply derivable from an 'is', how can the eco-centric values be derive from the ecological facts? To step from fact to value is to fall in the trap of naturalistic fallacy. In Principia Ethica, Moore has raised this problem. This fallacy consists in the attempt of drawing a value conclusion from some premises of fact. In order to respond to this objection, it is said that contemporary investigations of science have shown us that the natural environment is also a community to which we belong. We human beings want to survive meaningfully, and so feel obliged to preserve the eco-sphere.[7]

In another way to work around the naturalistic fallacy, it is advocated that nature has intrinsic value independent of human concern. This independent value commits no fantasy as no value as it is axiomatic) is derived from ecological facts.[8]

In group of deep-ecologist have suggested a non-naturalistic theory of intrinsic value. They maintain that the nature has intrinsic value contradicts deep-ecologist's is own conception of them as pasts of a single whole. If it is worth, it will imply, again, that human and nature are separate.[9]

In order to overcome the above difficulties and dualistic position we are required to embrace the Vedanta *seen* and point where all duality is seen to be dissolved with cosmic self-realization. For an acceptable version of eco-centricism, we have to put emphasis not only on the thesis of intrinsic value, but also on a form of human say realization, which spring out of ecological consciousness. And it is interesting to note that Naess has ultimately invoked[10] the Bhagwatgita to emphasize on this self-realization; "He where self is harmonized by Yoga sees. The self-adding in all being and all beings in self, everywhere he sees the same."

The Hindu scriptures like Vedas, Upnishads, great epics and Puranas have advocated a respect for nature and the concept of environmental harmony and conservation. These scriptures perceived the value of maintaining harmonious relationship between the needs of man and the *spectacular* diversity of the nature. To them, nature was not only the mother that sustained their life, it was abode of divinity. They did not believe that man's role on earth was to exploit nature nor they supported those the end of man was essentially to dominate and control nature by all possible means. On the contrary sanctity of life to them included not only the effort to see salvation, but to seek it by developing a sacred attitude towards the spiritual significance of nature.

It has been commentated that if such has been the tradition, Philosophy and ideology of Hinduism, what then is the reason behind the present state of environmental crisis? It has generally been observed that our ethical and moral believes and our values influence our behaviour towards others, including our relationship with all creatures and plant life. Here we can say that due to different external factors like cultural invasion, and other factors, religious and spiritual values which provide basis for environmental protection do not retain a higher priority because people have to worry about life and freedom, respect for nature was replaced by the worship of ideals and others supposedly supernatural powers. It seems that what happen in India during foreign cultural domination. Due to these reasons, Hinduism was enable to protect and preserve the ancient values which encourage respect and due regard to Gods' creation, again in 20th century, impact of naturalism and consumerism, compiled man to be aggressive and possessive and was led to adopt exploitative tendencies.

Coming to conclude this discussion we can say it will not be a prudent step or the present time to reverse the process of modernization to preserve the environment. What we can emphasize that in order to build a national environmental conscience and ecological wisdom, we have to draw upon those religious, ethical and spiritual values and beliefs which have been proven time less and eternal. Such tendency and attitude will be of great help in transforming society from its current pre- occupation with materialism and consumerism to a conserver society. Various laws enacted for environmental protection can be strengthened by a moral and spiritual awakening.

References

1. Peter Singer, practical Ethics, Cambridge University press, 1993, p. 280.
2. A Naess and G. Session, Basic Principles of Deep Ecology Eco-philosophy Vol. 6, 1984.
3. W. Devall and G. Sessions, Deep Ecology: Living as If Nature Mattered (Salt lake city) 1985.
4. Cf. S. Suvvarac, Ethics of Ecology and Environment Rajat Publication, New Delhi, 2001, p. 146.
5. Kelley A. Parker, Pragmatism and Environmental Thought in Andrew Light and Eric Katz (eds), Environmental Pragmatism, Routledge, London, 1998, p. 33.
6. Tom Hayward, Political Theory and Ecological Value Policy Press, Cambridge, 1998, p. 52.
7. J.B. Callicott, Hume's Is/Ought Dictionary and its Relation to Land Ethic, Environmental Ethics, Vol. 4, 1982, p. 163.
8. Holmes Rolson III, Is There an Ecological Ethics, Vol. 85, 1974, pp. 93-103, as stated by Alexander Gillespie, *op. cit.*, p. 164.
9. David Pepper, Modern Environmentalism, Routledge, London, 1996, p. 50.
10. Arnae Naess, Identification as a source of Deep Ecological Attitudes in Tobias, Deep Ecology, San Diego, Avant Books, 1985, page 260, as stated by Freya Mathews in his paper, Value in Nature and Meaning in Life, in Robert Elliot, Environmental Ethics, Oxford University Press, Newyork, 1998, p. 142.

18

PARTICIPATION OF WOMEN IN CONSERVATION OF HIMALAYAN ENVIRONMENT

Dr. Kiran Dangwal

The Himalaya is known as the source of inspiration since time immemorial for the man kind. The rivers coming out from the Himalaya have been the life stream of the country and source of prosperity and happiness of the people. The forest here had been the place of peace, learning writing, meditation and worship. The Himalayan forest are known as the birth place of the Upanishadas and the cradle bed of civilization. Its nestling beauty always attracted the people from all over the world. Its forest cover has given glory to the Himalaya. The forest of Himalaya has vital role in influencing the climate of the region. The forests in the catchments of the rivers have given perennial stability to their out flow through water conservation. They have been powerful factor in preventing depletion of the glaciers by maintaining proper temperature and providing stability to soil by checking erosion and land slides.[1]

Now-a-days, the man is playing with the nature in such a manner which has destroyed the forests, polluted the rivers, changed their natural flow, stopped and hold them in a number of dams. The river in Himalayan region are now given new name as **tunnel vahini** (flowing) due to construction of a series of dams and converting the flow of river through tunnels. It has polluted and disturbed the biosphere for the name of scientific development, specifically in the field of atomic development. Industrial development is one of the another major factors which has also affected the natural balance of the environment. The rapidly increasing population and efforts to meet their requirements put pressure on the environment. We are cutting the trees in large number which has reduced the water observing power of the land causing big floods and land slides.

The fertilizer, we are using in big quantity are damaging to the fertility of the land as a result big areas of the fertile land have been converted in to non-fertile land. Thus, not only the soil, water, and air pollution but noise pollution too have polluted the environment. This is why, the environmental balance is facing a big problem of disorder which has alarmed the people all over the world. No doubt, on the one hand the forest cover has diminished alarmingly due to modernization and industrialization while on the another hand a number of wild species are no more and many are struggling for their existence. Water and noise pollutions are rapidly increasing day by day. In such circumstances we depend more on forests rather than on others. If the forests are saved, the man kind is saved and if there are no forest there will be no man kind.

One of the greatest tragedies of the last century was destruction of Himalayan forests for the satisfaction of the carnal greed of the man. Denudation of the forests has rendered once luxuriantly glorious ranges completely bald. The valleys have been turned into stony bed of sand and gravel. The flow of water into river has become erratic and they have been causing disastrous floods year after year. Extensive land slides have endangered the lives of local inhabitants. The fauna is fast becoming extinct. The rise of temperature has caused fast depletion of the glacial snow fields.

The benefits of modern civilization is a favourite debating subject on university platforms and at erudite seminars, is a matter of life and death for thousands of hill people in the Western Himalayas. In the early 1960s the hitherto neglected region was opened up by a wide network to roads, largely for strategic reasons, and the people had welcomed the convenience but the extensive blasting and deforestation required led to increasing erosion, disintegrating hill sides and sinking mountains. Living by the roadsides has become precarious. Pilgrims to the many religious shrines and tourists have poured in; more trees have been cut for fuel. Worse still, instead of "development" the roads have brought in wealthy businessmen exploiting the rich forest resources through contract on nominal payments. The number of trees actually felled, to fashion expensive sports goods and furniture to meet the timber industries needs often exceed those marked. Besides every year thousands of trees are damaged through unauthorized cuts for resin. Large logs rolled down the hillside have caused top soil erosion and landslides. The villagers too, have been guilty of over grazing pasture lands.[2]

Former Prime Minister, Morarji Desai expressing his views pertaining to the then circumstances pointed out that the mountains that today presented such bare and bleak look were once green and thickly forested but man thought he will subdue and control nature. Climbing of Everest is described as the 'conquest' of Everest. The idea seemed to be to conquer, to subdue, to control both the surrounding and the people. So long as this attitude is not changed, things will remain as they were. There is no mountain system as massive as the Himalayas whether in extent or in height. God has endowed India with three mountain systems : the Himalayas, the Vindhyas and the coastal ranges. These three together influenced our climatic conditions. If the forests remain green, our country will prosper. Rainfall will be plentiful. Wealth will multiply. Otherwise, the desert will conquer our land. the denudation of Himalayas meant be denudation of the entire country.

For the last more than one century the reserved forests in Himalaya have been used for commercial exploitation of raw materials while the private and community forests have been used for local needs of fire wood and fodder. Rest of the land was put to the agriculture. This classification had a basic defect instead of harmonizing the need of man with the nature of land, it resulted in the heartless exploitation of land. Water and soil observing Oak trees covering the hills were sacrificed for expansion of commercial timber yielding conifers.

Women involvement in the forest movement is due to the role of forests in supplying fuel, fodder and drinking water, which is a primary concern for hill–women. When the women of the Himalayan region met the Prime Minister, Sri Morarji Desai, in July 1977, he conveyed his admiration for the heroic role they played in the Prohibition Movement. The request of the women to the Prime Minister was "Make your plans for the Himalaya in such a manner as will provide us fuel, fodder, and drinking water near our villages." Deforestation, construction of big dams in sensitive zones, illegal and without proper mining and construction of roads, exploitation of medicinal plants at large scale, and migration of men from hills in large number have become serious dangers for the Himalayas. On one side where the men are in making attempts to leave his environment, on another side the women are struggling hard among the environmental problems of hills. This is why, that the rural women of the hill areas are very much well aware about the importance of the forests because they know that the forests play important role in the catering the needs of their daily life. The women in hill areas are axis of families. They are mainly responsible for arranging fuel, fodder and water which are directly related with trees or forests.[3]

No doubt, the women in rural areas of Himalayan region without being aware with the scientific definition of the environment or its meaning, have been attracted towards saving the trees and plantation or conservation of the forests due to the fear of crisis of their daily needs related to the plants or forests – fuel, fodder and water. They know that if the forest are rich, there will be no crisis of these products. They knew the importance of the forests directly through their needs. Massive floods and land slides inspired them towards other natural issues. They are aware about the soil erosion and know very well the importance of the trees in preventing it. They too, know that where on the hills the Oak forests are rich, water is there but where there are no forests there is no water or have much less water.

By this way the rural women apart from knowing the meaning or definition of forest conservation are playing vital role in environmental conservation. What is all around them, they understand it very well and their relationship with human beings. They too, experience the total requirements of their conservation and thus are associated in this direction. Thus by this way the women of the Himalayan region are very well dedicated to the movements in saving and expansion or planting of the forests which is their participation in conservation of Himalayan environment.

The participation of women in Himalayan environmental conservation was recognized world-wide and got separate identity after the birth of Chipako Movement. On 26th March, 1974 when male members of village Raini of Chamoli district were out of village, a group of tree fellers and workers of Simon Company – a sports goods manufacturer with personnel of the Forest Department reached to the village forest for cutting the trees. As they moved forward for felling the trees the women of Raini village under the strong leadership of Smt. Gaura Devi opposed the tree fellers and other workers from cutting the trees. They said they will not allow to cut the trees and came forward in front of their axes. Finally they hugged the trees and announced that: "axe us not the trees"[4]. Thus they did not care for their lives in saving the trees. When all efforts of tree fellers failed, they returned keeping in view of strong determination of the women. The action of hugging the trees of the women was spontaneous as when they did not find any way out to save the trees, they hugged the trees. This action of the women was highly appreciated. It got wide publicity through media and became all over the world. A-Smt. Gaura Devi also became popular after the event of Chipko at Raini. Her abled leadership and dedication to save the trees at any cost, even at the cost of sacrifice herself, and her motivation to other women got high appreciation. After this particular event, she become popular as the Mother of Chiplo.[5]

After Chipako Movement of Raini, the women have launched the Chipako movement at Gopeshwar to save trees.. further, they saved the trees in Bhyundar valley in January 1978 which were to be felling for Badrinath temple. On February 25th, 1978, the auction of the trees of Damargarh was stopped due to the threat of Chipko by women. Similarly, the marking of the trees in three places of the Chamoli district was stopped on 25th January, 1979. It was 12 th August,1979 the Bhotiyas of Parsari village saved the trees of their village from felling by taking the help of Chipako movement.

After this Chipako movement or threat of such movements saved the trees. Women of Dungari–Paintoli threatened Horticulture department to launch Chipako movement to save their forest and were successful. B-Within a small span of time the Chipko became a powerful weapon to fight against the tree fellers or those who intended to cut the trees. The Government in March, 1980 in view of the recommendations of the high power committee put the ban on cutting the forests. Later on, the Chipako movement also covered other aspects related to forest conservation.

The women have also shown their active participation in other environmental movement like Maiti, Save the Seeds, Save the Ganga, Anti Dams and other movements. Mahila Mangal Dal have also been actively participating in the movements related to the issues of environmental conservation and awareness. The hill women also have taken up the issues related to make a healthy social environment. They have been actively not only participating but also leading such movements.

C-The mother of Chipko-Smt. Gaura Devi was an illiterate village women but she was very practical. She was very well known with importance of forests for the mankind and their relationship. Her feelings for forests were that: "Jungal is our Mayaka (maternal home) and trees are Rish. If forests are removed, our agriculture land, houses with plain fields would be no more. If forests are saved, we are saved. Forest is our employment. These feelings are not only limited to forests but convey a wide message for environmental conservation in an emotional way to all.

References

1. Negi, Dhoom Singh : Parvatiya Navjeevan Mandal, Silyara Silyara.
2. ....: Denuding Mountains, The Hindustan Times, New Delhi, 15th January, 1978.
3. Bahuguna Sundaer Lal : From a paper presented in the National Seminar on "The People and Forest", New Delhi, 21-22, 1977.
4. Aggarwal, Anil : Gandhi's Ghost Saves the Himalyan Trees, and Shefard, Mark : North India's Tree Huggers, Chipako Experience, D.G.S.M., Gopeshwar, June 1988.
5. Dangwal, Dr. Kiran : Chipako Andolan Aur Nari Shakti, Binsar Publishing Company, Pauri, 1998.

19

HUMAN FREEDOM AND ECOLOGICAL CONCERNS

Dr. Abha Singh

Right from the earliest known and historically recorded times, the search for freedom has been the perennial problem of philosophy. It has been an irresistible inner urge and the master passion of person's life. Naturally, down the ages it has attracted the attention of savants from every corner of the globe. They tried to examine and re-examine the nature and possibility of freedom in man's life. This, in turn, revealed its baffling nature and provided further stimulation to thinkers to resolve its snag. Freedom, in general, consists in overcoming the various determinism which hinders man's progress – may it be political, economic, religious, social, ethical, and spiritual and so on. If the individual overrides these obstacles, he regains his intellectual, emotional and sensuous potentialities and, thereby, realizes perfection in life.

The essential condition of freedom is that the individual should be able to fulfill his desire. To desire is to feel dissatisfaction as long as a certain object, which is the object of one's desire, is not realized. This can be illustrated with the help of an example. If I now desire to listen to music, I feel dissatisfied so long as my wish for music is not fulfilled; and it is this feeling of dissatisfaction that seems to drive me into a course of activity directed towards the realization of the object of my desire. Desire, then, appears as a development of impulse. The individual, to feel impelled, need not closely foresee what he feels impelled to do; but he feels impelled to do something he is not doing yet because what he is actually doing fails to yield him complete satisfaction. When, however, the individual foresees what he is going to do in order to relieve himself of his present dissatisfaction, he may not only feel impelled to do but also the desire to do. He now seems to be determined not merely by his present dissatisfaction that impels, but by his idea which attracts.

If desire is viewed as a development of impulse, both desire and impulse may be viewed as a development of behavior processes. The diverse organs of our body act in various specific ways until they reach certain states which serve to complete the specific activity. What we observe is simply the continuation of a process until it reaches a certain state. Here we can refer to the Freudians, who suggest that our actions are of the nature of compromise formations, a result not merely of our desires, but of our various impulses and of our various organic processes of which we are not even conscious. But whatever our action may express, it is necessary that it should express our desire if we are capable of feeling free.

Being conscious, at least partly, of the operation of the laws of nature and culture, man is in a position to assimilate what is given and anticipate what is not yet given. His power of anticipation works in respect of both facts and values. And this power itself, to a great extent, is native to his nature – a legacy of evolution and environment. Strictly speaking, it is only as an integral part of a given segment of nature and a particular society that man understands himself, intends and acts to fulfill certain needs. In other words, man does not understand, intend or act as an abstract or unrelated self. In order to vindicate the immutable character of values, some thinkers, taking their clue of thought from Plato and Kant, have conceived the solitude of man as the paradigm of freedom. The unrelated man is, in a sense free, but that freedom does not enable him to tell what is good and right for others, other persons and places. Unless the "free" man is found to be free and cognitively competent enough to speak unerringly of other's values, to legislate for and on behalf of others, his freedom, by definition turns out to be a sham.[1]

The fear of nature, either because of its "tooth-and-claw" (Neitzsche) or because of its "casually determined" character (Kant)[2], is responsible for the definitions of freedom in terms of unrelatedness or solitude, withdrawal from nature and culture. Interestingly enough "the defenders of these notions of freedom ascribe to the withdrawn, i.e. free, man the competence to tell us which values are universal and necessary, i.e. not related to and conditioned by the considerations of particular persons and places. The said fear of nature rests on a serious misunderstanding of the relation between man and nature, an untenable dualism."[3]

Actually to speak in terms of dualism of life and environment, or of man and nature is itself a mistake. Here everything is related, directly or indirectly, proximately or remotely, to everything else. As so, one may say, and quite rightly so, that everything is an environment of everything else. There are no separate causes and separate effects. Everything is, at once, a cause and an effect in an extremely intricate relationship. Considered anthropocentrically, man's environment consists of other men, animals, plants, birds, bacteria, earth, water, fire and air, all of which are affected by one another. This totality is also in relation to the other heavenly bodies in the vast, apparently largely empty space. All these things are affecting one another in an extremely complicated manner, which is not within the possibilities of human comprehension. The cosmos inclusive of man forms an incomprehensible unitary existence.[4]

As so, one can presumably say that human freedom is the corollary of ecological sustainability. Humanity is a potentially thinking, conscious and creative part of an organic whoie. Human society exists in metabolic relation with the world that sustains us, and we shape and reshape society and ecosystems with our labour. Much human labour today is organized directly for capitalist profit which is a necessarily wasteful, chaotic and morbid motive force with regard to the environment and human life.

Nevertheless man and environment have been in close interaction all the time. Hence, mankind has always been conscious of environmental impact and influence. Over four hundred years ago, Queen Elizabeth I, the last ruler of Tudor dynasty (1485 – 1603) in

Britain, often kept out of London because she was "unable to stand the smoke of sea coal and other stinks" in her capital, and she was greatly concerned about the river Thames being "a vast sewer which spread disease and death around"[5], quite alike we, in India, have been lately concerned about the Ganges river. However, Tagore had characterized modern civilization as being 'masculine' since it is aggressive and insensitive. This thesis comes through in his symbolic drama *Rakta Karavi*, where he expounds the tragedy of a demonic civilization.[6] Again, rational philosopher Bertrand Russell, in his autobiography, expressed grave concern that modern man has been swayed with the misguided sense of an all-pervading "cosmic impiety".[7] Man has been so cruel and aggressive over the period that he has come to believe that he has every right to manipulate and to exploit non-renewable resources of mother earth for satisfaction of his unmitigated greed and consumerism.

In this age of information and technology the freedom of man knows no bound. Everything seems knowable to him. Man aspires himself to be truly invincible. George Beacon[8], through his explosive dictum "knowledge is power", has become father of modern man. Following the material boom and the euphoria generated by the unprecedented economic 'progress' in the 19th and the 20th centuries, the environmental and ecological awareness tended to recede into the background. Interestingly, the international organization between the World Wars, i.e. League of Nations – for its entire international agenda – was virtually unconcerned about these issues. Nor did they figure out as major concerns in the Charter or early programmes of the United Nations. But today – thanks to the Indian proposal for a Planet Protection Fund at the Belgrade NAM Submit and the Commonwealth Submit at Kuala Lumpur and some recent studies and experiences – the environmental and ecological issues have climbed to the very top of the global agenda. Hence, its various manifestations and implications – and the challenges arising from them – deserve fuller analysis.

It was the UN Conference on Human environment, held in Stockholm from 5-10 June 1972, which drew attention to environment and the related issues of population, ecological and resource depletion as matters of overwhelming global concern. And, as a first step to deal with these problems, it set up the United Nations Environmental Programme (UNEP).

Today's ecological crises are the result of an uncaring, consumerist society that likes to think that man is the centre of universe. Man has evolved himself as the sole 'subject' and the rest of the world has been relegated to mere 'objects'. Having been engrossed with the idea of an 'I-It' relationship, man has progressively estranged himself from nature and mother earth. As a result, he has also got alienated from his true self. It is the consequence of the deep-rooted psychological aberration of modern man, suffering from what is called 'cosmic paranoia' or enmity with the cosmos. The clash between nature and civilization reaches its most extreme form in the total transformation of the natural world that takes place in modern industrialized nations. Here human manipulation, exploitation and out-and-out destruction of what is given by nature are on so huge a scale that the entire physical and biological composition of our planet is profoundly affected. Given the rise of advanced technology, an economy dependent on as well as geared for high-level consumption and the human population explosion, what is left of the natural world is quickly disappearing. The more we take for ourselves, the less there is for other species.

Verily, in the present industrial and technological advancement some unforeseen consequences have taken place. With the greater control of the natural environment, man has so intervened in the natural processes that the original balance of nature has been lost and he has inadvertently given rise to the problem of environmental crisis which is indeed proving to be suicidal.

In the main, the environmental concern is a three-dimensional problem. The three dimensions are: (1) environmental pollution, (2) ecological decay or destruction, and (3) resource depletion. The greatest pollutant or "environmental killer" is radioactive fallout from nuclear testing, nuclear plants and the long-term storage of nuclear materials, disposal of nuclear wastes and occasional nuclear accidents.

Two other types of air pollution have been a matter of international concern as well. One, the increasing concentration of carbon dioxide in the atmosphere due to large-scale burning of fossil fuels (coal and petroleum) in the modern industry and transport system leading to a "greenhouse effect" and the flooding of coastal areas through the warming and melting of polar ice caps.

Apart from air pollution, land and water are being widely poisoned by the large-scale use of pesticides and chemical fertilizers in modern agriculture in developed countries generally, and in many developing countries (including India) in the effort to reach for the so-called "green revolution".

Environment and health have other convergent concerns for health too. Increased vehicular density in urban areas not only contributes to increased fossil fuel consumption and exhaust emissions, contributing to global warming, but also dumps toxic pollutants into the air we breathe, leading to respiratory diseases and cancers. Automated transport also reduces physical activity, contributing to hypertension, heart disease, diabetes, obesity, and some cancers. Yet we do not pause to ponder why our city planners only build more flyovers to accommodate many more cars, while pedestrian pathway shrink and protected cycle lanes disappear.[9]

A serious environmental and ecological problem has arisen from large-scale deforestation which, in turn, has led to increased floods (due to lack of absorption of rain precipitation by the forests), soil erosion, silting of river, contraction of agricultural production areas and eventual desertification and wide-spread food scarcity. The increased demand of farmland by large landed interests for growing 'cash crops' and the growing demand of wood by modern industry and for the "wasteful pattern of resource-use for conspicuous consumption by money elites" constitute the main cause of this reckless operation, especially in the Third World, - leading to deforestation to the extent of 11 million hectares every year.

According to the Brandt Commission Report this has (besides depriving thousands of people of their gainful job or work) led to large-scale flooding and soil damage most notably in Bangladesh, Nigeria and Panama. In India, these operations (especially in Kumaon and Garhwal regions) have generated the "Chipko"movement which has attracted worldwide attention. Needless to say that that the environmental issue is a matter of grave international concern.[10]

This entire malady was due to the arrogance of man in the pride of science and technology. But he soon realized that what he thought to be the conquering of nature is, in effect, proving to be otherwise. He has so damaged nature in the process of his technological control of it that it has led to his own strangulation and the consequent environmental suffocation of man and life. We are now awakened to the problem: Has man conquered nature or has nature in the end conquered him? In spite of his unprecedented knowledge of nature, what has gone through a stage of what could be described as explosion of knowledge, he has been discovering a sense of frustration, of having lost the battle.[11]

It would be tantamount to say that Man has intervened into the processes of nature, but nature, in its own way, has disturbed his smooth life. This has happened because he has not made any serious effort to understand his ecological relationship with nature, which is both within and without him. In fact he is a part and parcel of nature. He is a participant in the entire environmental system. But because of the possession of self consciousness and intelligence, he has designed a social system that is motivated by the anthropocentric selfish interests of raising the standard of life. For the sake of economic enrichment, man has indiscriminately exploited his environment to such a degree that he has proved himself to be a destroyer of his home of environment along with himself. Nature and man can live amicably by forming a unity, else man turning inimical to nature would destroy both man and nature.[12]

It is clear from what has been discussed above that man, in his endeavour to enjoy unbridled freedom, reached to somewhat perverse state of mind. His consciousness and action have been shaped by the commands and imperatives of how to manipulate nature to his advantage, often with disastrous consequences. Action without reflection is blind, while reflection without action is impotent. Unguided and un-illumined action frequently leads to destruction. On the other hand, one should also be aware that so much abstract thought consists of merely scholastic exercises, which help nobody and only exhaust the mind. What is needed today is to make a balance in thought and deed. Such balance one finds in the philosophy of ecology.

A deep study of the philosophy of ecology shows that it is reverence in action. It is a deep identification with the beauty of life pulsating through the universe until we become part of it. Its central spiritual tenet is that the human species is a part of the Earth and not separate from it. A process of self-realization would help an individual to intuitively gain an ecocentric perspective. The notion is based on the idea that the more we *expand the self* to identify with "others" (people, animals, ecosystems), the more we realize ourselves.

Many ancient cultures understood both the cosmos and life in it as sacred, special, and exquisite. This assumption is much more palatable to human reason than the assumption that the world is a senseless mechanistic aggregate of physical bits of matter. From the idea of the sacredness of world follows reverence of life as the main ethical imperative. If the world is sacred, the reverence for all that is there is an inevitable consequence. To put it in the words of Albert Schweitzer:

> Ethics thus consists in this, that I experience the necessity of practicing the same reverence for life toward all will-to-live, as toward my own. Therein I have the needed fundamental principle of morality. It is good to maintain and cherish life; it is *evil* to destroy and to check life... A man is really ethical only when he obeys the constraint laid on him to help all life which he is able to succor, and when he goes out of his way to avoid injuring anything living. He does not ask how far this or that life deserves sympathy as valuable in itself, nor how far it is capable of feeling. To him life as such is sacred.[13]

From the reverence of life naturally follows responsibility. The responsibility for one's own life, for the well being of nature, for future generations and for everything that is there. Responsibility is reverence in action. One cannot be truly reverential unless one exercises one's responsibility for everything there is in it. This sense of responsibility is empowering. It gives us wing and an enormous mandate for the future. It reminds us that we are here as the custodians, responsible guardians for all the heritage of life.

From responsibility follows the third ecological value – frugality. Frugality can be defined as grace without waste, as doing more with less, as treading gently on the earth. In other words, responsibility must be translated into appropriate life-styles, life-styles that are gentle and unharmful to nature and other beings. Frugality is both an ethical imperative and a political one. If our life-styles cause stress and injustices to other parts of the world, then obviously we are not being responsible, nor are we reverential to all life on earth. As Peter Singer rightly suggests:

> An environmental ethic rejects the ideals of a materialist society in which success is gauged by the number of consumer goods one can accumulate. Instead it judges success in terms of the development of one's abilities and the achievement of real fulfillment and satisfaction. It promotes frugality, in so far as that is necessary for minimizing pollution and ensuring that everything that can be re-used is re-used. Carelessly to throw out material that can be recycled is a form of vandalism or the theft of our common property in the resources of the world.[14]

We need to have the courage of our mind in elucidating and expressing the things which we feel and know in our instincts. This new perspective of the ecological world-view, spells out a new freedom for man. Man is doomed to freedom. We have the mandate for the freedom to take to the air. But we must do so in control. Therefore, it necessitates a limitation on freedom of action in the struggle of existence. Such is our destiny. This requires courage and, also, the strong sense of belonging to this world as well as the will to participate in the fascinating cosmic journey. The bottom-line lies in the tendency of interdependent individuals or groups to evolve modes of co-operation. It is a symbiosis in the language of an ecologist.

References

1. D. P. Chattopadhyaya, *Environment Evolution and Values* (Studies in *Man, Society and Science)* (New Delhi and Mardras: South Asian Publishers Pvt. Ltd.), p. 274.

2. Chattopadhyaya, p. 274.
3. Chattopadhyaya, p. 275.
4. A.G.Javadekar, "Philosophical Ecology", in *Problems of Indian Philosophy*, ed. S.P.Dubey (New Delhi: Indian Council of Philosophical Research, 1996), Vol. III, p. 314-15.
5. S.C.Ganga, "Mankind and Environment", *The Hindustan Times* (Patna edition), 27th November 1999.
6. Tagore, cited in Arup Kumar Majumdar, 'Think Cosmic and you can save the world', *Times of India* (Patna edition), 15th November 2003.
7. Burtrand Russell, cited in Majumdar's article, *Times of India* (Patna edition), 15th November 2003.
8. Majumdar's article, *Times of India* (Patna edition), 15th November 2003.
9. K. Srinath Reddy, "Pandemic threats: what is to be done", The *Hindu* (Delhi edition), editorial article, 13th May 2009. The author is Professor of Cardiology at All India Institute of Medical Sciences, N.D., and president of the Public Health Foundation of India.
10. Ganga's article, *The Hindustan Times* (Patna edition), 27th November 1999.
11. Javadekar, p. 313.
12. Javadekar, pp. 313-14.
13. Albert Schweitzer, "The Ethics of Reverence for Life", in Tom Regan and Peter Singer (eds.), *Animal Rights and Human Obligations* (New Jersey: Printice Hall, Englewood Cliffs, 1989), second edition, p. 33.
14. Peter Singer, *Practical Ethics* (Cambridge and New York: Cambridge University Press, 1993), p. 286.

20

MAN'S ATTITUDE TOWARDS NATURE IN HINDI POETRY

Dr. Suraj Bahadur Thapa

From the beginning of his life on this earth, man has found nature standing very closely to its various courses and stages of life for many centuries. In the long course of time, man understood it categorically that nature could survive without him but he could not survive without the blessings of nature. From the initial stage of food collector to food producer and even in this modern age of science, technology and industrialization, man has always been dependent on nature. The man of ancient and pre-industrial age had better understood the significant role of nature and environment in human life. This fact is quite evident from the vision and pattern of life of Indus valley civilization, Vedic Society and medieval historical ages of India. People of these periods built up a very divine, holy and eco-friendly relationship with nature and their environment. It does not mean that they did not take advantages of natural resources. Actually they practiced a lot of technologies to exploit them from nature. But there is a big difference in the attitude of modern industrial man and the man of those periods. The man of pre-industrial society felt nature as an integral and inevitable part of his life. That's why he considered earth as **'mata'** and moon as **'mama'**. There was a deep feeling of "**oneness**" and great emotional attachment with nature. But as the industrialization grew up by leaps and bounds, a great change evolved in the attitude of man. Scientific explorations and inventions revealed the truth regarding physical existence of nature and as a result it minimized the emotional attachment of man with nature. The feeling of oneness disappeared and nature was taken as **'other'**. The **'need'** converted into **'greed'** due to which an uncontrolled exploitation of natural resources and the dangerous process of environmental decay started simultaneously. Man wanted to conquer nature and he did so. He exercised his freedom arbitrarily and in return he is facing the menace of his existence on this planet. Things are getting worse and worse day by day. Even then man, the sole creator of pollution and unbalance in eco-system, is not yet ready to take proper lesson from his mischief and stop his aggressive attitude towards nature. As man has a vital role in the destruction of balance in eco-system, it is his responsibility to come forward to save earth and environment for the sake of his existence too. In Hindi literature we can find the depiction of almost all the above mentioned changing attitudes of man towards nature in the long course of civilizations. The main purpose of this article is to reveal and analyze that changing attitude of man and his relationship with nature as it is expressed in Hindi literature and poetry.

Hindi poetry exhibits that form of human thinking where man admits the inevitability of nature for human life and considering the whole environment an expression of the **All mighty** God, he wants to install an amicable relationship with it. This attitude of Hindi poetry is popularly known as **'Rahasyavad'**. **'Rahasyavad'** is different from **'Mysticism'** – that school of poetry which was led by English poet William Blake. Likewise the **'Rahasyavad'** of **'Chhayavadi'** poetry is also different from the poetry of **'Rahasyavad'** of medieval saint poet like Kabir because the former is empirical and emotional in character and is very close to nature while later is mostly dogmatic and metaphysical in its color. That's why here the focus will he on **'Chhayavadi'** poetry. Due to excessive depiction of the natural and environmental beauty, **'Chhayavad'** has been aptly defined as the poetry of nature. Like Romantic poets, the poets of **'Chhayavad'** have also adopted the art of personification of nature. For example, we can take the following piece of verse where the poet has described evening as a beautiful fairy landing on earth from the sky with all its sophisticated manners-

> Divasavasaan Ka samaya
> Meghamaya aasmaan se utar rahi
> Wah sandhya sundari pari si
> Dhire-Dhire.[1]

In this poem we can also find the great feeling of oneness of man and nature under the influence of philosophy of **'advaitvaad'.**

'Chhayavad' is also well known as the poetry of liberation. This liberation is meant for all fronts of life. We must be free from polical subjugation. We must liberate ourselves from all the old fashioned outdated visions of life, superstitions, prejudices, narrow and rigid social-moral-ethical values which create a lot of hindrances in way of building a progressive, broad minded, generous, moderate, developed and sublimed humanitrarian form of society. The poetry of **Chhayavad** chooses rivers, springs, ocean, wind, clouds, birds as its content because all these natural entities are the appropriate symbols of freedom. The famous poem of Kaviguru Rabindranath Tagore – **'Nirjharer swapna bhanga'** – containing the deep feeling of all kinds of above mentioned liberations is no doubt the inspiration of **Chhayavad** in this regard. In this way we can say that nature not only provides material sources of life to man but also teaches 'how to live'? Matthew Arnold says that the answer to the question **'how to live'?** is culture. So nature inspires man to chalkout a balanced and cultured path of life. In William Wordsworths' poem **'Three years she grew in sun and shower',** Nature says that **'I shall make a lady of my own'.** Actually this statement of Nature may be seen as a great endeavor of it to make a perfect human being without any artificiality. Many writers and critics like Aacharya Ram Chandra Sukla have felt that the isolation of man from nature makes him insensitive and spiritless.

Now let us discuss how man derives his moral, ethical and social values of life from the elements of nature. For centuries, man has keenly observed the behavior of various elements of nature and found a number of valuable and useful attributes for him. The following **'Doha'** of Kabir generates the conception of a true human being –

Vriksha Kabahu *nahi phal* bhakhai, Nadi na sanchaya neer
Parmaratha Ke Karane, Saadhu dhare shareer.

Kabir says that the tree and river never consume their fruits and water but always bestow these to others, likewise a '**Saadhu**' or a true man sacrifice all his life for the welfare of others. He lives for others not for himself. Here Kabir has taken the example of river and a tree to teach man how to be a man in real sense. Nature helps Kabir to set a role model for the human society. We can also see the following poem for another instance-

Parvat Kahata sheesh utha kar,
Tum bhi unche ban jao,
Saagar Kahata hai lahara kar,
Man mein gahrai lao,
Samajha rahe ho kya Kahati hai,
Utha utha gir gir taral tarang,
Bhar lo bhar lo apne man mein,
Mithi mithi mridul umang.
Prithvi Kahati dhairya na chhoro,
Chahe kitna bhi ho bhaar,
Nabha Kahata hai phailo itna,
Dhank lo tum sara sansaar.[2]

The poets says that mountain urges man to do such a great work so that he can achieve a height like it in his society. The ocean asks man to bring depth in his thinking and views of life. The earth suggests man to never quit from his huge responsibilities of life and the sky inspires him to develop his personality to such an extent that he can cover means influence the whole world. The waves of ocean teach him to be always enthusiastic. All the great personalities like Lord Buddha, Mahatma Gandhi etc. have succeeded to do this.

To build up a new society where **"nava gati, nava laya, taal chhanda nava, naval kantha nava, jalada mandra rava"** may prevail, the rebel poet **"Nirala"** has composed a series of **"Baadal**

Raga" which is aptly entitled as **"Bipalava Raga"** (The tune of rebellion) by the famous critic Bachchan Singh.

In this way we can find out a lot of illustrations in Hindi poetry where man's attitude towards nature seems to be very positive and constructive. This shows the feeling of oneness with nature. But with the advent of capitalism and fast growing industrialization, man's feeling of oneness with nature disappeared, Now with the power of science and technology man wanted to conquer nature considering it as **'other'**. As a result man and nature became two different entities and a destructive tension evolved in their relationship. Nirmal Verma, a famous Hindi fiction writer, has severely criticized this western view regarding nature.[3] Development hunger man's aggressive attitude towards nature caused a huge negative effect in human life and society. Man lost his sensibility and feeling of dignity for others life. Material gain and prosperity become the sole purpose of life. Man converted into a machine due to which he lost his liveliness and the whole scenario of life drastically changed. Hindi poetry catches all these curses of so-called development as well as man's destructive attitude towards nature. The veteran Hindi poet Kedarnath Singh aptly remarks -

> Mere Shahar Ke logon,
> Yah Kitna bhayanak hai,
> Ki shahar Kee sari sidhiyan milkar,
> Jis mahaan unchai tak jati hain,
> Vahan koi nahi rahata![4]

Yes, on the acme of development no human value exists. This is the real tragedy of anti-nature development that swallows the spirit of humanity. Man becomes a **"Selfish giant"** and heartless creature.

A question arises on the social concerns of the man. In this famous long poem **"Baagha"** Kedarnath Singh depicts the bad effect of the rivalry between man and nature. Baagh (The tiger) observes the continuous migration of people from villages to metro cities[5]. This incident deserts villages and Baagha gets puzzled because he knows that - "udhar se aati hai aadami ke hone ki gandh"[6]. Hence the co - existence of man and nature is most desirable in present time.

Ek jalati dophari mein
Baagha ne dekha ek adbhud drishya
Usne dekha ek vishal vatvriksha ke niche
Ek pakshi aur manusya
Apne daine aur kulhari
Agal bagal rakhakar
Nirbhay susta rahe hain[7]

One of the great modern Hindi poet Sachchidanand Hiranand Vatsyayan 'Ajneya' has depicted the tragedy of modern man's life due to his isolation from nature in his poem - "Savere utha to dhup khili thi". In this poem, the modern man wants to borrow warmth, sweetness, greenery, brightness, openness, sensation and limitlessness respectively from sunlight, bird, grass, Sankhapuspi flower, air, waves of water and the sky because in his opinion human life is consisted of all these natural ingredients and as a member of this so called developed world, he is far from these natural elements. He has forgotten the language of love which is the essence of life. The conscience of the modern man asks him -

Ek undekhe arup ne pukar kar mujha se pucha tha: kyon ji,
Tumahare is jivan ke
Itne vividha anubhava hain
Itne tum dhani ho,
To mujhe thora pyar doge udhaar, jise main
Saugune sood ke saatha lautaunga -
Aur wah bhi sau sau bar gin ke
Jab jab jaunga !
Maine kaha: pyaar ? udhaar ?
Swar achakachaya tha, Kyonki mere anubhava se pare tha aisa vyavahar.[8]

The life of modern man is no doubt full of material prosperity but it is hollow from the point of view of humanity. Development on what cost? This question now shakes the mind of rational man.

Patriotic poet **Ramdhari Singh 'Dinkar'** has cautioned man to keep proper balanced in his relationship with nature. In **'Kurukshetra'** he says that the attempt of man to over come nature will eventually cause a severe reaction and human world has to pay a heavy cost for it. Development is necessary but it must have certain limits. Man should not cross the **'Lakshaman rekha'** of eco-system. But inspite of this type of caution, man has been again and again repeating his harmful unjustified deeds. Some of contemporary Hindi poets have severely criticized this attitude of man. Let us take some glimpses of this criticism -

(a) Kis Vikaas ke Khul gaye, yaaro aaja Kiwaar
Dare dare hatprabha khare, jungle nadi, pahaar[9].

(b) Prithvi, Paani hava par, global yug ki maar.
Mausam ki yaha phaeley, mudra ke bazaar[10].

(c) Soot sarikhi Narmada, seencha rahi muskaan.
Ghayal hirni si nahar, hain vikaas ke baan[11].

(d) Ganga mein jab se pare, netaon ke paon.
Ganga maili ho gayee, huye visailey gaon[12].

In this way we can say that the Hindi poetry emphasizes on building a close, balanced and rational relationship between man and nature. Man must consider himself a part of nature and stop to see it as **'other'**. As he is the only creature, who causes pollution, this is his responsibility to take all necessary measures to save nature and earth for the sake of his existence.

References

1. **"Sandhya sundari"** – by Suryakant Tripathi 'Nirala'
2. **"Seekha"** – poem by Sohanlal Divedi.
3. **Patthar Aur bahata pani** - edited by Nand Kishore Aacharya, Vagdevi Publication, Bikaner.
4. Pritinidhi Kavitayen – Edited by Parmanand Srivastava, Raj Kamal Pub., New Delhi.
5. **Baagha – Unit 11,** Pratinidhi Kavitayen – Raj Kamal, New Delhi.
6. **Baagha – Unit 12,** Pratinidhi Kavitayen – Raj Kamal, New Delhi.
7. **Baagha – Unit 5,** Pratinidhi Kavitayen – Raj Kamal, New Delhi.

8. **"Kitni naon mein kitni bar"** by S.H.V. Ajneya.
9. **Doha by Ashok Ajnum** – Naya Jnanodaya – 13, March 2004, Bhartiya Jnanpeetha.
10. **Doha by Dinesh Sukla** – Naya Jnanodaya – 13, March 2004, Bhartiya Jnanpeetha.
11. **Doha by Kalika Tripathi** – Naya Jnanodaya – 13, March 2004, Bhartiya Jnanpeetha.
12. **Doha by Gopal Das 'Niraj'** – Naya Jnanodaya – 13, March 2004, Bhartiya Jnanpeetha.

21

SAVE ENVIRONMENT : MANDATORY NOT OBLIGATORY

Dr. Seema Srivastava,
Dr. Ambuj Srivastava

It is said that for every problem, there is a solution, but it is also true that unless and until we rise to a solution till then Seminars, Work shops, Conferences and Discussions will continue. The intellectual classes of society have to bear this responsibility. From the beginning of human history, problems did arise but there were solutions to it. But presently, in my opinion, there are two major problems that human beings face as:-

1. **Terrorism**
2. **Environmental Pollution/Ecological Imbalance**

In both these problems, there is a similarity. The similarity is that both these problems started from the 20th Century and in the 21st century, it has risen so much that it is causing a '**threat**' to our '**Human Race**' and '**Existence**'.

Due to their activities, thousand innocent lives are lost. People believe that Terrorism is a major problem because it causes a disturbance to the National Integrity of the whole nation as large. In my opinion, **Environmental Pollution and Ecological Imbalance** is more threatening than Terrorist Activities, because it is to pollute environment and create an imbalance to our Ecosystem. Many of us are involved directly or indirectly but where as for a terrorist activity, a small group is involved. There is more problem to the Environmental Pollution because we do things knowingly or unknowingly. The whole Human Race or Existence is gradually coming to an end, but whereas for a Terrorism the death is instant.

The summary of this is that in the point of number, the terrorists are less in number in comparison to **Environmental Pollution** where most of us are involved directly or indirectly. Whereas in the ultimate point of view, **Ecological Imbalance** is more dangerous because it involves every one of us one way or the other.

Historically, if we analyze this problem, in ancient time man was a slave to nature. He lived and worshipped nature. Everything he used was from nature itself. This phase of time, man was considered to be a spiritual or a natural person. As he was close to nature, he remembered God too. At that time, there was no problem of Environmental Pollution and Ecological Imbalance. Today too, in Indian Society, especially the Hindus worship trees like Tulsi and Peepal. But as time changed and man's needs and knowledge of nature increased, he started **exploiting nature** and **natural resources** for his gains. By doing this, man not only increased his products but also his life style changed. This phase of man is called **Physical Man**. Until this time, problem was not much serious, but in the 20th Century, man started doing things for his personal interest and thus he was thoughtless about his future generation. His aim was only to keep himself economically sound and that's how he started exploiting nature. That's the reason why he was called **Economic Man**. The natural exploitation increased so much that a problem arose in Environment. In the latter part of the 20th Century, this environmental problem became a Global problem in the form of Environmental Pollution and Ecological Imbalance.

Different Modes of This Problem Are As:-

1. Global Warming—"Green House" effect were first described in 1896 by Swedish Chemist named Svante Arrhenius. 'Green house gases in the Earth's atmosphere such as Carbon dioxide nitrous oxide, water vapour and methane help to trap heat and stop too much of it escaping into space. Without these gases the Earth would not be warm enough for us to live on. The problem is that more 'Green House' gas are being released into the atmosphere from human activities and too much heat is being trapped. The Earth became 0.5 Centigrade warmer during the 20th Century and a further rise of even a couple of degrees will damage its natural balance. Polar ice caps will melt, sea levels will rise and many areas will be flooded. Changing climates will also effect plants and animals which might not be able to adopt quickly enough new conditions, Carbon dioxide CO_2 and other gas in the atmosphere act like glass in a green house. Human activity such as human burning forests and running cars releases too much CO_2 into the air and may cause **'Global Warming'**.

2. Acid Rain—Acid Rain was identified in the year 19th Century. It is caused when Nitrogen Oxide, Sulphuric Oxide and other chemicals from volcanic eruptions and human resources combine with rain and fall as acid rain on land or into rivers and lakes. Gases that evict from different vehicles and factories, industries are responsible for Acid Rain Sulphuric Dioxide in the presence of sunlight and atmospheric moisture reacts and makes Sulphuric Acid and comes down to the earth in the form of water or ice. Like this oxide of Nitrogen makes Nitric Oxide. This Acid Rain too is dangerous and harmful to our Environment. The strength of acidity in rain varies but at its worst it can damage buildings, kill fish and harm trees and other plants too.

3. Ozone Depletion—In the stratosphere the ozone layer does exist. This absorbs the ultra violet rays of the sun and thus it saves plants and animals. The ozone layer shields the earth from dangerous radiation. The thin layer of ozone gas within the Stratosphere, protects us by absorbing harmful ultra violet rays from the sun, but builds up of man – made gases called Chloro fluro Carbons (CFC) has depleted the ozone layer and holes have started to appear in it.

4. Extinct of Different Species of Plants and Animals—Different species of plants and animals have been extinct and many more are in the process of extinction because of this there is an Imbalance in Eco-system.

5. Climatic Change—From the latter part of the 21st Century, most of the places on Earth are going through a rapid change in the climate. This is the reason why in the last two or three years the whole world is focusing on this issue and is a main part of discussion. This Environmental Pollution and Ecological Imbalance have caused grave danger to human existence. The whole world is involved in making an effort to solve this problem. On the latter half of the 20th Century, the world's largest Democratic Institutes like the U.N.O. had started making efforts in solving this problem because this has become Mandatory not obligatory.

Various efforts to solve this problem are as:-

In the year 1972, the U.N.O. organised a seminar at Stockhom, in which the problem was considered in its totality and it was desired to solve this problem a unified effort would be necessary. As a result, the **UNESCO** in its united Nation's **Education Programme** recommended including Environment as an education curriculum. Subjects dealing with Environment were made **compulsory**.

In 1975 in Belgrade, While recommending the Environmental education, it was emphaised that one third of the Earth should be reserved for forest.

In 1982, in Nairobi, the Stockhom's decisions were accepted and had to be quickly implemented. In 1987, in Montreal agreement CFC and other 'Green House' Gases had to be banned.

In 1992, Rio De Generio, the first Earth Summit was held in which a movement to **'Save Earth'** was started.

Then in 1997, Quoto Protocol, the suggestion to identify Green House Gases were required to be destroyed.

In the year 2002 at Johanesburg, during this summit a collective effort was made by the world leaders in an appeal to destroy the 'Green House Gases and **Save the Earth**, but there was a controversy between the Developed Countries and the Developing Countries. Being aware of this problem and the consequences none were ready to compromise for any agreement.

In Dec. 2007, under the supervision of the U.N.O., a summit was organised in Bali to decrease the 'Green House Gases. Ways were made in which the 'Green House Gases' could be reduced. A panel of top **Environmental Scientists** prepared a report in the year 2007. This report was called the **I.P.C.C.** Firstly man was only responsible for this situation but by the end of the 21st Century, it was stated the temperature of the Earth would increase approximately five to six degree, centigrade which would create great danger. Due to this, uncontrolled situations would rise thus would lead to **destruction** and **havoc.** In this situation and circumstances, it seems as if the Environmental and Ecological Imbalance and Technological Developments are contradictory because if we blindly rely on Technological Developments then **Human Existence** would disappear or be at **stake.** On the other hand, if we protect the Environment alone, the development of society would be hampered. Therefore any one of these could not be chosen alone at the cost of another. For this, we must find out a **middle** path in which both Human Existence as well as Technological Development can be maintained. A **middle path** is to find out so that, while the very existence of Human Being is safe guarded and at same time, the Technological Development is not affected.

Sustainable Development

Developments which were required to improve the Human Society had to be planned in such manner so that it could cope up to the needs of Human Being. For this purpose some vital points should be kept in mind. These points were as follows :-

1. Development should be restricted to the **extreme necessity** only. **Non-conventional** sources of energy should be given more attention. Harmful waste should be destroyed. Most important, a human approach should be applied to Nature. Human Being should have **Humanitarian approach** for nature. Love and affection be dealt with nature. Even on the destruction of Harmful Matter, there is a contradiction between the Developed Countries and the Developing Countries. In this dispute, the developed countries were determined to keep and maintain their status and thus were not in favour to destroy harmful matter. Where as the developing countries wanted more opportunities for development. So such efforts were not so much helpful as they were controversial, therefore nothing much could be done.

Under such circumstances, the question arose, what strategy could be evolved to find out the solution for these problems. In my opinion, **Ancient Indian Approach** could be helpful in this direction in which nature could be given her status as **Mother.**

In the Vedas :- Water, Earth, Fire, Air and Vanaspati, space Akash were kept in high view and these elements were worshipped as **God. Water** is considered to be the most important element as it gives life to every creature on Earth. All forms of life are dependant on water.

Rig Veda :- "apsu anth amritam apsu bheshjam 1:23:248.

'Water' is pure and has been described as nectar. It has a number of medicinal values too. Thus it should be kept clean and pure.

Air is a life giving power not only for Human Beings but also for plants and animals. Therefore, purity of air is necessary for a Favourable Environment. Air is also worshipped by Human Beings as God. People pray to it in order to keep all living things on earth healthy. We need air to breathe virtually every second of our lives.

Yajurveda

Syaham bhakhusa sarvani bhutani sameekshe 36:18.

In this Veda, all living creatures are treated as one Entity. We should be friendly to all living things on earth. No living thing exists in isolation. It interacts with other living things according to its physical surroundings. All plants and animals rely in, and influence, vital factory in their environment such as the supply of nutrients, food and water, Ecosystem does not always remain the same but may change overtime. People's action also changes the ecosystem and often the impact is so great that nature cannot repair the damage. The friendly thought towards all living creatures reflects on the concept of the ecosystem.

In the Rig Veda Fire has been described as **'Father'** the one who can take of us all. Burning out of control in forests or cities, a fire leaves a trail of destruction. Yet life without the benefits of fire is unimaginable. Flames of fire helped to hunt, clear land for forming and many useful purposes. No wonder some religions still worship fire as a hungry god.

"agni ! "sunave pita in nah svastya asachsva"

In the Rig veda 1:164:33. The Sun has been described as 'Father' Earth as mother, the sun's rays as Brother. All these should be respected equally.

In the Vedas, the Earth has been given an important status as a mother to protect all living creatures on it. The behaviour of Human Beings towards the earth has been described in this prayer.

"Vishnu patni namastuvhyam padsparsha kshamva me"

Oh! Mother earth we worship and salute you. Yet we are compelled to walk on you. Please forgive us. Since the Earth provides all the materials we need for living, from the food we eat and the water we drink, to the bricks we use for building it is called as our mother. Just as a mother nature and nourishes her children so also the Earth nourishes all human beings with food, fruits and flowers. The generosity of the Earth is unparallel to bear the weight of the hills, trees, forest. The earth develops in a manner that it causes the rain which is necessary for human beings. In Vedas, conserving the environment has been described as important philosophy for the development of healthy human life.

In the same manner, the later ancient epics such as **Upanishads, Mahabharat, Manusmiriti and Arthshashtra** had also been given importance of natural elements for e.g – Chandogya, Upanishad. These natural elements and human beings have been given the same status.

"Vayu bhutva dhumo bhavati"
dhumo bhutva abhram bhavati
abhram bhutava megho bhavati
megho bhutva pravarshati."

This means that air converts into smoke, smoke converts into fog, fog converts into clouds and then clouds into rain. Just as the air changes into different forms, so also all living things and all natural things are in different forms of the same absolute.

Similarly, in Bhrihdaranyak Upanishad, a comparison is made between a man and a tree. It is said that the hair of a human being is like the leaves of trees. Just as when a tree is cut down, it grows again from the roots, similarly Human Beings too after their, take a new life or rebirth. In Mahabharat, Shantiparv it is mentioned that atman yotri sanghtey sonyasya syat katham hitah ?

It means that for a good society and a friendly environment man has to keep his society in a healthy condition with **harmonius** relations with each other so that a healthy and a good environment can be developed. The environmental consciousness of the Manusmiriti can be understood from this quotation.

"antah sangyan bhavanti iti sukh dukh samanvitah"

This means that plants too have life. They also feel the sorrow and joy as humans do.

Kautilya, while preserving the importance of environmental elements in his Arthshastra specially mentions that the importance to protect forest, wild life and animals. Besides this the Indian Philosophical schools where moral values have been given special direction, this too has been taught in schools. Directions have been given to protect and conserve the environment.

Concentration, self control, patience, middle path, purgation of consciousness under which education is given to win over kama, krodh and lobh-moh hinsha and to ensure pity, generosity, non-violence, sacrifice, non-stealing (asteya) not being greedy (aprigraha). These qualities are developed among the Human Beings. These qualities teach us to behave equally with nature and to all creatures as well as Human Beings. This means as violence against human being is considered to be a sin. Similarly, violence against Humanism can ensure the protection and preservation of environmental pollution or Ecosystem or else we are facing mass destruction.

22

TRANSFORMATION OF MAN'S ATTITUDE TOWARDS NATURE IN PURSUIT OF LIBERATION

Dr. V.K. Tripathi

It cannot be the primary question, what obligations do we have concerning the natural environment? The question contains a heavy amount of anthropocentric primitivism. Rather, we may begin our inquisition with examining the conditions in which we really come to feel the actual moral crisis, a paucity of moral strategies towards environment- the nature, so to say. It is also not the issue that ethics should be extended beyond humanity and moral standing should be accorded to non-human natural world. The tension between anthropocentric and non-anthropocentric reasoning will lead to different account of moral standards. In the case, the crisis of determining obligations would remain unaddressed and unresolved. It would be more apposite to examine various treatment of nature that the human being is adapte to, so as to extract the nature and the cause of the apparent crisis *i.e.,* to apprehend the crisis in the schema of its origination. The different treatments of nature have their origin in different types of man's attitude towards nature *i.e.,* the crisis is fundamentally an attitudinal problem. There have been different attitudes predominant at the level of philosophical worldviews as well as at the level of the naive ways of our mundane interaction with nature which govern man's behavior. To take up a few, the following views may be mentioned:

1. The anthropocentric views that predominantly makes man a *measure of all things*. Man is a sentient being and endowed with moral sense. In a sense, ethics is possible only in terms of 'human-centeredness', as only the human being can reason about and reflect upon ethical matters. All ethical theories of 'good' and theories of 'right' have been developed presupposing their necessary reference to human judgment or, human rationality.

2. Non-anthropocentric views, which seems to be holistic in nature, as it talks of an extension of ethics ranging all possible entities which affect human life. In its enterprise of decentralizing, there is a scope for discourse on eco-philosophy, environmental ethics, and animal rights and so on. It is better to explore a 'holistic ethics' which grants moral standing to all individual living things. 'A thing is right when it tends to preserve the integrity, stability and beauty of the biotic community. It is wrong when it tends otherwise.'[1]

3. Evolutionistic views, which treat man as a product of nature, not radically different from nature per se. So, there cannot be a morally intelligible worldview based on a segmenting between man and nature. The very division has no basis *ipso facto* the term nature encompass all rational and non-rational, sentient and non-sentient beings. The goal of human life is where the evolution leads the human to.

4. Radical ecologists and deep ecologists firmly advocate that the extension of moral standings cannot be taken as sufficient to resolve the environmental crisis. A broader philosophical perspective is needed to change both our attitude and understanding of reality. We need to recognize the place of human being in the natural world. These views involve an ethical norm: 'self-realization', in which the self involves recognizing human beings, not isolated from nature, but are incorporated with it. It is also known as 'transpersonal ecology'. The radical ecologists' objection to the views like 2 is that the extension of moral standards is too human-centered and takes human being as paradigm example of entities.[2]

The very first view, as it puts man at the center of everything, entitles man to value nature in terms of its convertibility into human utility. It empirically entails that man can concur nature. This is a treatment of nature as an object- an object of human designing, exploitation, reconfiguration etc. Precisely, the nature is not taken as end in itself and it is the human wellbeing that deems nature a value. At the best, such views host ethics proper, because an ethical theory can best be developed on presupposition of a sentient and responsible being as agent. Human freedom is both presupposed and preserved. But, nature is always external to man, a peripheral entity, falling nowhere into the realm of human obligation.

The views like 2 emerge on experiencing or predicting the crisis of human survival. '*Save the environment*', '*Do no harm*', did not become a human cry unless a danger of human extinction was felt. If such a fear is the precursor of the paradigm shift – from anthropocentrism to non-anthropocentrism, the treatment of nature is no better than the view 1. Nature is condemned to be an object. The so-called non-anthropocentric venture is to serve the human ends in a concealed fashion. Even if it is taken to be the extension of human concern to the limits of his knowledge, those aspects of nature would have no value which have either nothing to contribute to human survival or out of the reach of human knowledge yet. Either of the cases entail that nature is not the end in itself. This is the basic attitudinal problem.

The non-anthropocentric views not only leave a possibility of extension of moral standings to the non-human entities, but also to the future generations. But, such envisage are no answer to the question whether what are our obligations to them. The difficulty is that we cannot extend the moral standing to future generations, because they are not yet present and lie outside our moral community and cannot act reciprocally.[3] So is the case with non-human entities. Derek Parfit calls it a non-identity problem.[4] It is difficult to decide just *what* obligations we have to them. Non-identity persists at both the levels – *what* obligations and to *whom*. This is another inner obscurity with the view. Further, if the criterion for moral standing is sentience - the capacity to feel pleasure and pain, the said obscurity will continue to exist. And in what sense we wish to extend the moral standings, precisely in the sense of rights – human rights, animal rights, plant rights, earth rights and so on.

This rights-based theory would again pose attitudinal problem, the conflicts of rights would continue. Besides, the 'holistic ethics' also is vague on how we are to flash out our moral obligations concerning the environment. We kill rats, because they harm crops. Can we kill men for the sake of a 'larger whole', as they harm environment. If not, then it is 'environmental fascism[5]' that prevails.

The views like 3 may be best based on scientific facts and be taken as an authentic interpretation of nature-man relation, far removed from conjectures and speculations, would project a determinism and hence the loss of human freedom. Human destiny and creativity would be determined by nature. The very aspect of human freedom is ignored as the human freedom is a conditioned freedom - conditioned by the laws of nature and, therefore, is no freedom. Discounting freedom is discounting *manhood.* The man, then, would become an object. Man would never like to be treated as a product. Thus, this view would minimize the scope of developing any authentic vision for or attitude towards nature. Such views can never resolve the conflict between human freedom and the glory of nature.

Views, as briefed in 4, fail to conceive one unified ultimate perspective and be free from religious and political allegiance. A claim is made to incorporate the *human* with nature, but the position is not radically different from the views like 2. It lacks the understanding of human freedom like the view in 3. The ideal of *ecosophy* is too hallucinating to offer any real guide for action. The ecosophy presupposes a transformation in man's attitude, rather serving as an instrument of transformation. At one hand it tends to incorporate human with nature and on the other, it moves to overhaul the entire societal-institutional set-up in the name of exploring new reality. The man at what juncture would be incorporated with nature – the man of the given world or, the man of an overhauled world; the position is obscure. And, therefore, the ecosophical self-realization is a hypothetical aspiration. The attitudinal problem with the view is that it necessitates a reconfiguration of the world; only in that world it would be possible to attain the ethical norms set by it.

To wind up the observation on the different views, it seems that the above mentioned crisis is founded in two facts, F_1: the very split between man and nature due to which there is a lack of authentic integral view. This split is a curse of Aristotelian split between rational and non-rational entities; and F_2: the human freedom is taken in terms of 'rights' presuming as if nature poses a challenge to it. Right is mistaken for freedom, so all theories pertaining to freedom are structured in the form of theories pertaining to rights. The freedom is of the nature of 'freedom to', entailing the justification of fulfillment of human needs, greed and lusts. F_1 is a kind of reason-centric attitudinal problem; F_2 can be taken as a kind of lust-centric or instinct-centric attitudinal problem. The anthropocentric views as mention earlier, of which all the varieties of non-anthropocentrism are mere extension, can be taken as ego-centric attitudinal problem, which is fundamental to rest of attitudinal problems.

How these attitudinal problems nourish the above mentioned crisis, can be seen from the following summarization:

(a) If nature is treated as an object (as in 1 and 2), human freedom is saved and there is a possibility of ethics. But, man has no obligation to nature as we cannot extend the moral standing to it.

(b) If man is treated as a product (as in 3), as an object, there would be no human freedom and no vision for nature possible as well.

(c) So called 'holistic ethics' (as in 4) fails to decide on *what* moral obligations do we have to nature. Ethics is impossible.

Before we assess the possibilities, we must take a note of the alternatives which are not available to us, these are:

Treatment of man as an object

Treatment of nature as an object

Discounting of man's freedom

Reduction of ethics

If we assess the possibilities, it is obvious that there is no scope for acceptance of (b), because the issue is not what scientific facts you furnish, but how you look at the facts. Evolutionistic views cannot emulate human freedom. Even (c) has less possibility for acceptance as one will never reach a juncture to draw a line for framing the obligations. With (a), it is required to re-look at the nature of human freedom, which is based on F_2 and contains attitudinal problem pertaining to it. But, (a) cannot be out rightly precluded, because at least freedom is possible therein. Further, the nature being an object is not a problem in itself, but the attitudinal difficulty is with its treatment as an object. Thus, at least there is a possibility of some scrutiny into (a) Such a scrutiny cannot begin in favor of treatment of nature as an object, because the basic question is why one treats nature as an object? It is because one has a wrong conviction about one's freedom. Therefore, human freedom has to be understood first.

It is, again, not the question what we mean by freedom or how to define it, but the question is, in what sense man is a freedom seeking being? Are we really seeking freedom? What we mean by freedom requires a great deal of inquiry, precisely because; we are often garbled by 'freedom as an idea' and 'freedom as a fact'. We are not dealing with the former here as it is obscure, vague and enigmatic and conceals the fact. If we look at freedom as a fact, we observe the following features about it:

It is not an atomic fact.

It refers to some instincts.

It is a-psychological.

It is an intellectual construct.

We require a meditative inquiry to see through the above features. What is that we generally call as freedom is a constitution of desires supported by intellect (justification and reasoning in favor of that) necessarily referring to some instinct. It is a-psychological as there is no such factor as freedom in human psyches other then instincts in favor of which we demand freedom viz. a guarantee or security for the fulfillment of the same. To assure the same we develop an idea of freedom which can easily be glorified and be established as an ideal, as a value. We equate it with 'rights'. It appears to be well justified. We seek bare objects, security, and satisfaction in the name of freedom. And, at certain moments when we are not seeking them viz. we reflect on them, there is awareness – we experience a 'freedom from'.

We are seeking some happiness, some kind of peace, a refuse. Why there is a seeking of these, because we want to be free from the given situations which we are put in. The given situation, the present condition is so miserable, so pain-filled. The psychology of possession is this much only (of which exploitation of nature and conflict of rights are mere types). We opine that there will be freedom in the altered situation, and that is impossible. This is our misunderstanding, the complete misunderstanding about the very structure of freedom. 'Seeking of something with a hope of seeking pleasure or happiness is not a seeking of transformation. It is avoiding of transformation[6].' The views as in 4 are guilty of professing an alteration in the situation and creating a 'new reality' in the name of wholeness. Transformation cannot begin with the gross, with the external- with creating a new social order. Rather, a realization of reality is required, not alteration of it as it will create a new disorder. Such realization is a seeing of reality, seeing the truth. 'Seeing of truth liberates.[7]' Freedom and order in the world are not different things; they are not opposite to each other. One is not free if one has to struggle for what one wants, to fight with oneself, that at maximum brutality of it expresses in the form of conflict of rights. Then we develop theories of rights to manage it somehow. All such theories are condemned to be failed as they lack understanding of the very freedom within. We seek freedom outside; it is a chaos- a disorder. And then, we feel that by managing the world outside or creating a new social order we can bring about freedom. One has to bring it about within oneself. Experiencing freedom is a dissociated understanding of reality, not the lustful involvement into that. 'As long as we are thinking in terms of gaining something, there is no freedom. Freedom cannot be taken in **terms of** utility'.[8] The experience of freedom must spring forth from the very experiencing of reality, from the nature of reality itself. We cannot live in a utopia of self-projected freedom.

If we, now, look back to the previous question if man is a freedom seeking being, it becomes easy to peep into why our gains do not give us freedom and we do not get satisfied with them. We start seeking a new gain and the unrest goes on and on. The further requirement of seeking gains is an indication that what we are seeking we are not getting through it: we are seeking freedom in the second sense (a 'freedom from' that is discussed in the recent paragraph).

Let us look at how far we are able to get out of the difficulties which are presaged in different views, their limitations and the attitudnal problems pertaining to them. Being a seeker of freedom in the second sense, we can successfully save human freedom at maximum of its glory which brings about a transformation in attitude and, to the seeker there is no object, no other – no further mistreatment possible. Man is free from the 'thing-hood'. Pursuing of a thing is an indication of treatment of something as an object. Freedom is lost into that. Why there is an occasion of treatment of something as 'other' at all? Because, we solely depend on the sensory experience, as if there is no other mode of knowing available to human being. Freedom as awareness opens up a new mode of reflecting upon things and upon the entanglement of mind into them. The reflection helps in coming out of self-centricity, and only then the treatment of something as other is avoided.

There is no possibility of the split as mentioned in F_1, for a free mind has nothing to differentiate as it experiences affinity with nature. In fact, it is a state away from all considerations of *self* – the 'I'. So, the possibility of ego-centric attitudinal problem is also precluded. With reference to (a), of course, we do not extend the moral standing to all entities, but anything untoward or undesirable is safely avoided. It is the freedom which needs to be holistic, not the ethics. Such a freedom is neither a subjective way of experiencing reality, nor a retiring state of consciousness. It is the universal schema of freedom, a realization of which can bring a transformation about.

References

1. Leopold, Aldo, *A Sand County Almanac: And Sketches Here and There*, Oxford: Oxford Univ. Press, Spl. Commemoration Ed., 1949/ 1989; pp. 218-225

2. None of the radical ecologists confine themselves solely to the realm of ethics. Their conviction is that fundamental changes in society and in its institutions are also required. It requires a radical change in governance policies. As Arne Naess projects his deep ecology out rightly criticizing the modern industrial society. Naess, Arne, "The Shallow and Deep, Long-Range Ecology Movement: A Summary", *Inquiry* 16 (1973): 95-100.

3. Golding, Mark, "Obligations to Future Generations", *Monist*, 56 (1972): 85-99.

4. Parfit, Derek, *Reasons and Persons*, Oxford: Clarendon Press, 1984, ch. 16.

5. Regan, Tom, *The Case for Animal Rights*, Barkeley: Univ. of California Press, 2nd ed., 1983/2004, p. 362.

6. Krishnamurty, J, "On Transformation", *First and Last Freedom*, Ojai, California: Krishnamurty Foundation of America, 2003, 2006, cp. 38, pp. 262-63.

7. *Ibid.*, p. 263.

8. Krishnamurty, J, "On Freedom and Order", *Krishnamurty on Education*, Ojai, California: Krishnamurty Foundation of America, 2000, 2002, 2003, cp. 4, pp. 32-3.

23

SUSTAINABILITY AND ECONOMIC GROWTH: ARE THEY COMPATIBLE?

Dr. Alok Tondan

It is generally assumed that sustainable development and economic growth are compatible objectives. Since no attempt has been made to specify this assumption, the debate on sustainability and growth remains vague and confusing. What is required is not only to clarify the interrelations of the two concepts, but also to analyze the contexts of the frame of reference of the two concepts. Only then we can understand as to what extent, under given preconditions, economic growth and sustainability are compatible. Our problem is that the notion of sustainable development is being proposed as the solution to the environmental problems that have resulted from our modern frame of reference which is diagnosed as inherently destructive to the environment. The ambiguity arises because the notion of sustainable development is being made to fit in to the same destructive framework to make it operational. Such treatment of the issue of sustainable development as a technical problem prevents critical reflection upon the frame of reference in which the problem originates. In this paper, we explore the normative and conceptual context of modern framework in order to determine whether the concept of sustainability fits in to freedom dominated framework. We take in to consideration both versions of sustainability conservative and radical – for the purpose. Finally we conclude that only a radical version of sustainability, having a strong normative dimension, has the capacity to relieve what is acute tension in modern frame of reference and to reconcile individual autonomy with the wider social and ecological good. But this represents a challenge to liberal democracy and its understanding of individual and collective goods. These problems can only be addressed by radical social transformations.

I

Now it is generally agreed that since there are biophysical limits to humankind's productive prowess, the utilization of world's material resources must be pursued without compromising the life chances of either present or future generations. Sustainable development is proposed as a way to combine economic growth with ecological health, in which, on the one hand the continued potential to meet human needs is to be safeguarded, while on the other hand, environmental limits are to be acknowledged. The common thread running through all political documents/definitions propagating such strategy is to focus on the preservation of the capacity to fulfill (current and future) human needs and the limitations to (economic) activities which are to be observed in order to achieve this objective. However, the concepts of needs and limitations, and in their wake other interrelated concepts, need to be if these definitions are to have any content at all. Otherwise, sustainable development becomes a convenient phrase for rallying support, rather than an agent for forcing environmental change.

Two variations of sustainability- weak and strong can be distinguished on the basis of restrictions they propose on the process of economic growth. It centers on the degree to which substitutions between natural and physical capital is deemed permissible. The week version conceives both forms of capital as complementary, with unlimited possibilities for substitution, and contends that the requirement of sustainability is met by means of the maintenance of enlargement of the sum of both capital flows. Though it allows for spending of the natural capital stock but it should be offset by a corresponding increase in physical capital stock, so that only the composition but not the total amount of capital stock, so changes. That, such version grants the overall capacity to reproduce the same standard of living to the future generations compared to the present one. Clearly, it is compatible with economic growth and even requires growth to offset environmental damage.

Since many relevant factors such as future consumption preferences, increases in populations and technological progress can not be predicted, we always remain in doubt about the required increases in capital stock to offset environmental degradation or to sustain the same level of well-being. Therefore, a strong version of sustainability is suggested, which acknowledges the supplementary character of both physical and natural capital stock aiming at a separate maintenance of both stock of capital assets. Accordingly, future generations should not just be as well off as we are, but should be endowed with at least the same amount of particular goods, such as environmental assets. Such a virsion makes the assumption of compatibility of growth and sustainability questionable. Growth that threatens nonrenewable environmental assets is not permissible.

The concept of sustainable development and growth may be said to be compatible if the conceptual and normative interpretations of their constituent concepts of needs and limitations are identical for the two concepts, thus we need to review the concepts of economic growth and sustainability in conjunction with related concepts and their implicit interrelations to determine whether they can fit together with in modern framework. While economic growth is grounded in the belief that the unhampered process. If redefinition and expansion of needs creates the incentives and opportunities for initiative and gain, which by including economic activity, are the best guarantee of fulfillment of essential needs, the concept of sustainable development suggest a different conceptual and normative content of needs, a distinction between needs and desires as well as the idea that constraints are to be placed upon desires in order to safeguard the fulfillment of essential needs implies that the idea of humanistic solidarity is part and parcel of sustainable development, not an appendage to the concept of liberty. The framework in which economic growth is given priority, freedom of choice and self-determination takes precedence over solidarity, whereas the concept of sustainable development assigns a role to solidarity on an equal plane with freedom. As such, a notion of sustainability that functions within the dominant framework bears a stronger imprint on growth, and thereby sets different requirements for sustainable growth because it is subordinate to the main idea of freedom. Thus, the interpretations of the concept of needs, limitations, liberty and solidarity in relation to the notion of sustainability differ from such interpretations in relation to the notion of growth and therefore, sustainability and economic growth can not be simply assumed to be conceptually and normatically compatible.

Both, the weak and strong notion of sustainability may be said to present a consistent view of the compatibility of economic growth and sustainability achieved by accommodating the analytic context of one or the other concept. While the strong version implies a plea for a through revision of the existing conceptual network to accommodate the notion of sustainability, the weak version smothers the innovative implication of the same concept in a way that it is made operational with in this framework. The fundamental difference in the evaluation of the basic values of freedom and solidarity and their mutual positioning implied in the conceptual network of the notion of economic growth and sustainability respectively, require that the ideal foundations of our society be brought in to the discussion in order to escape from the confusion that surround the debate on sustainable development. Only a radical understanding of sustainable development can uphold sustainability as much more than mere a compromise between the natural environment and the pursuit of economic growth. For the purpose, we need to examine as to which notions of human wellbeing and autonomy reconcile well with the concept of sustainable development.

II

If sustainability is to be the goal of human activity, wellbeing must be rethought with respect to a different set of goods for the making of good human lives. The market ethic dominant in modern liberal democracies presupposes a narrow conception of human wellbeing, equated with material comfort. Environmental problems engendered by the market stem in part, from the self understanding it develops. Such limited self understanding creates a delusory culture. If self-interest that stunts the development of human capacities and blends the modern individual to another in an instrumental kind of relationship. No inner need is felt to develop one's capacities to live an ethical life, the best of one's capacity. Moreover, because technological progress is a self-reinforcing process, the positive feedback affects of technological success not only compound the accumulating side effects, but they also tend to reinforce aspects of the lower human self, that is, the utilization, making/doing , self-interested, egoistic aspect at the expense of the ethical, altruistic, transparent self. This leads to a poverty of the higher self.

In the present context, when future of all life has become problematic, we not only need to recover the earlier Aristotelian understanding of a flourishing human life, but to broaden it to include promoting flourishing of other individual living things and biological collectives as an end in itself, simply because the flourishing of non-human nature in constitutive of human flourishing. The best of human life is one that includes an awareness of and practical concern with the goods and entities in the non-human world. Additionally in the light of recent insight in evolutionary biology, competition is not the dominant strategy in nature. Many organisms establish symbiotic relationship to further their chances of survival.

Replacement of the ethically limited understanding by a broader and more satisfying understanding of the good life goes well with the radical interpretation of sustainability, with its recognition that quality of life issues are intimately connected to environmental protection. The implications of such an expanded view of the good life for the social, political and economic institution of modern societies are quite profound. Ecological matters can not be left to the spontaneous order of market. Public policy must provide for the inclusion of the moral relevance of the other species and of future generation at a more profound level than the level of rhetoric.

In modern societies, the human nature relationship has assumed a state of imbalance with human liberty now being opposed to the freedom of nature. The question of interdependence of human freedom and the freedom of nature must be faced and dealt with if sustainable development is to be the ethic that recognizes and promotes the mutuality of ecological and social values in concrete living communities. Human being need to respect nature if they are to survive and preserve the existential ground on which to assert their freedom. Therefore, there can be no ultimate incompatibility between demands of nature and the exigencies of human freedom. Things have gone wrong not because human held an anthropocentric view of the universe (they could not do otherwise) but because they erred in defining the value content of their own development and freedom. The mistake lies in believing that the freedom from the constraints of nature is an absolute value, when it really constitutes a negative view of freedom. Freedom from the constraints of nature is a positive value in the sense that it allows freedom for human fulfillment. If human are to have any possibility of being at least part authors of their lives, of having a range of life choices, uncoerced by others or nature and of possessing the necessary capacities and resources for their self chosen paths, then individual development depends very much on ecologically responsible behavior. It depends upon human development strategies which enhance the mutuality of ecological and social goals.

The question to be asked is whether sustainable development as economic strategy can reconcile personal autonomy with freedom of nature and interdependence of life forms. The capacity to achieve this varies with the degree to which human embeddedness in nature is acknowledged. Thus, the conservative approach retains the modernistic attitude of a society-nature divide, wherein sustainability is achieved by the management of resources through more efficient energy and resources use and new ecologically benign technologies. By contract, the radical approach, in accepting human embeddedness in nature recognizes that it is human activities which have to be managed in order to achieve ecosystamatic and social viability. In policy terms, this distinction, between interpreting sustainability as a problem of human activity rather than as a problem of resource management allows consumption patterns and values which underpin them as well as structured rigidities which militate against the assumption of environmentally sustainable practices to come into focus. It then becomes clear that the transition to an ecologically sustainable society requires more integrated policy approach, in which a range of policy modes is utilizes, including standard selling, regulatory intervention, institutional reform, markets, economic instruments and technological innovations. Important elements of any policy mix will include an educative function and incentives for environmentally sound practices in order to stimulate the assumption of ecologically sympathetic attitudes and values.

Another negative manifestation of market economics has been the break down of community and other binding ties and the loss of tradition. The success of a market society is measured by its GNP and by its rate of economic growth the total aggregation of goods and services and the speed at which they are produced, not in how well it fosters and supports the personal and communal relationship, which make up the community, not in how well it cares for ecosystems on which the community depends for life support. Hence there is need for an economic order that supports the pattern of personal relationship that make up the community. Moreover, since we have also extended the field of relationship to the non-human community, the economic order should support not only communal relationship but human / nature connections.

In the conservative approach, government solely relies on experts and sees environmental problems as questions of appropriate management. These experts focus only on remedial measures, environments continue to degrade. The top down management structures limit public participation and view it as having only instrumental value in implications of projects initiated by aforesaid experts. They fail to support and build communal relationship. On the other hand, the radical approach to radical sustainability uses ecological crisis to reflects on practices, values institutions of industrial society and therefore to rethink social relationships. Encouraging participations as a valuable learning process in negotiating their responsibilities to each other and to environmental protection if builds new solidarities and understanding of well being. Such process also produce long term commitment that having environmental problems produces, which top down management system fails to generate.

Our forgoing discussion leads to the following conclusion: First, only a technical solution in the form of simple economic restructuring in order to contain economic growth with in environmental limits is an insufficient attempt at a reformulation of economic problem.

Second, any economic strategy which attempts to match human needs and demand of nature and to guide human development must foster respect for the non-human environment as well as a sense of the mutuality of social and ecological values.

Third, sustainable development must ensure sound human flourishing, by furnishing those goods which ensure human autonomy (survival, opportunity) for participation, and a good life.

Fourth, SD must preserve and foster forms of community well being which insure connection with past and future.

Fifth, SD must also preserve and foster ecosystem viability. Sound human development consistent with ecosystem is really only possible with the radical interpretation of sustainable development.

Sixth, sustainability as ethical ideal challenges the view of the liberal state as neutral umpire between different conceptions of the good. Radical approach to SD demand a conception of human flourishing that recognizes the intrinsic value of other nature, whose own flourishing is constitutive of a good human life.

Seventh, not only the concepts of human well-being but also of individual autonomy, solidarity and collective interest are to be rethought for the purpose of societal transformation according to SD.

Eight, sustainability is but an interim phase in the pursuit of a livable society. An essential precondition for such transition is to overcome the structural rigidities of capitalist market economics. This means to replace the imperative of ever increasing quantitative growth and individual consumption with an imperative that furnishes qualitative social development and improved communal and ecological well-being. But, who will do it?

Books Consulted

1. Julie Davidson, Sustainable Development : Business as usual or a New Way of living, Environmental Ethics, Vol. 22, No. 1, pp. 25- 42.
2. Rudi M. Vervurg and Vicent Wiegel, On the Compatibility of Sustainability and Economic Growth, Environmental Ethics, Vol. 19, No. 3, pp. 247-265.

24

AHIMSA: THE JAIN'S STRATEGY FOR THE CONSERVATION OF BIO-DIVERSITY

Ms. Kavita Bhatt

Mahatma Gandhi said that the nature has sufficient to fulfill the need of everybody, but not the greed of any body. The present crisis of environmental degradation is the result of greedy nature of Man and consequently high level of exploitation of nature. The greedy tendency of human being leads towards undue damage to the natural entities and the degradation of the biodiversity-created by the extinguishing of various species. Our anarchist activities and high consumption of nature are the root causes of the imbalance of eco-system, and it is resulted as the destruction of whole organism. Obviously we depend on other creatures of earth for our survival. We are consuming and spoiling several types of species not for fulfilling our basic requirement but more than that for greed. And this human tendency for greed is prompting him to exploit nature up to the extent of extinguishing of many species of our biodiversity. The eco-system imbalance has reached up to the point that we should be careful not only for us but our whole bio-diversity to maintain eco-system for universal balance of environment.

The present paper is an attempt to review the fundamental cause of the degradation of biodiversity with reference to human greed which leads him towards the exploitation of Nature and creating violence to the species other than human being. Violence could be countered only by inculcation of moral values based on the theory of non-violence. Almost all the religion and moral traditions argue for the practice of non-violence and accepted it as the core value. In India, from the ancient period, *Ahimsa* has been taken as the supreme religion or duty and coined statement like "*Ahimsa Paramo Dharmah*" has been the basis for many moral ideals. Out of ample systems reflecting the importance of Non-violence, we here for the purpose of conservation of bio diversity, shall reflect upon the notion and ideal of Jain's view of Non-violence, because the Jain notion of *Ahimsa* is against the Vedic notion of *Ahimsa* which thinks "*Vaidiki himsa himsa na Bhawati*" i.e. the sacrifice of various animals is not dreadful for the purpose of Yajyan or religious functions. If the concept and ideals, modes of *Ahimsa* as described in Vedic texts are taken to be model it will further favor human beings to perform violence in the name of Vedic violence to favor human being desire. In the present scenario we need a model based on the morality of Non-violence to protect the interest of all and conserve the rich treasure of biodiversity. From this point of view Jain Model of *Ahimsa* is the most ideal model and thus we shall focus our attention on describing the importance of *Ahimsa* with reference to the conservation of biodiversity.

Here, *Ahimsa* initially refers to "non-injury" without a moral concern, but later on to the concept of "non-violence" to animals and then, to all beings. So we can say that the thought of *Ahimsa* is most prominent in the ethics of Jainism. Therefore, in order to develop a right and appropriate kind of ethical strategy, we should focus our attention towards ethics of Jainism for the conservation of species.

But, before we take up the strategy to protect bio-diversity, it is necessary to know the concept of bio-diversity in its technical sense and then, understand the concept of *Ahimsa* for the conservation of it. Since Jain Philosophy has strong ethical appeal of *Ahimsa*, firstly we shall make an attempt to know how far it is useful for the purpose of eco-balance through conservation of biodiversity. Secondly, we shall try to see and examine that up to what extent *Jain* strategies are capable of addressing the present crisis of degrading bio-diversity. For the above purpose we will divide the present paper in to three parts. To know the role of Ahimsa in field of the conservation of bio-diversity it is essential to know what bio-diversity is, and what are the root causes of degradation? We shall try to answer the above questions in the first part of the present paper. After that we shall try to examine the *Ahimsa* (non-violence) according to Jainism, in the second part of the paper. Then, it will be easy to ascertain a strategy for the conservation of bio-diversity; finally we shall try to do it in the third and conclusive part of the paper. Let us move to identify the term biodiversity in the first part of present paper.

Part I

As we have stated that in order to see the relevance of *Ahimsa* with reference to conservation of Biodiversity, it is required to identify the root causes of degradation but before that we need to be clear on what biodiversity is, how it is beneficial to human being and what are the activities of human being that damage and threat to the existence of the different species of biodiversity. We shall try to reflect upon the above points in this section but before that let us know the meaning of biodiversity in its techno-scientific sense and popular use of the term.

Bio-diversity is a word which is the accumulation of biology and diversity, originating from and used with 'biological diversity.' "This term was used first by wildlife scientist and conservationist Raymond F. Dasmann in a book advocating nature conservation. It was not widely adopted for more than a decade, when in the 1980s it and "biodiversity" came into common usage in science and environmental policy. Use of the term by Thomas Lovejoy in the Forward to the book credited with launching the field of 'conservation biology' introduced the term along with conservation biology to the scientific community. Until then the term "natural diversity" was used in conservation science circles, including by The Science Division of The Nature Conservancy in an important 1975 study, "The Preservation of Natural Diversity." By the early 1980s TNC's Science program and its head Robert E. Jenkins, Lovejoy, and other leading conservation scientists at the time in America advocated the use of "biological diversity" to embrace the object of biological conservation."[1]

The meaning of above term is the variation of life forms within a given as a heritage for the balancing of eco-system gifted by nature. Bio-diversity is frequently used as a measure of the health of biological system. The biodiversity found on Earth today consists of many millions of distinct biological variety of species, which is the product of virtual evolution. Currently both terms and the perception have accomplished prevalent use among biologists, environmentalists, political leaders, and concerned citizens worldwide. It is generally used to equate to a concern for the natural environment and nature conservation.

After the brief sketch of the term biodiversity, let us try to know its definition. According to biologist, "Biological diversity is the totality of genes, species, and ecosystems of a region, variety of life forms...at all levels of biological systems (i.e., molecular, organism, population, species and ecosystem)..."[2] An improvement of this definition is that it seems to describe most circumstances and present a unified view of the traditional three levels at which biological variety has been identified: those are genetic, species and ecosystem diversity.

Bio-diversity is usually conspired as taxonomic richness of a geographic area. Now the question is that why we should conserve species? To know the answer, we must know its foremost benefits to mankind.

Benefits of Bio-diversity to Mankind

1. Benefits for Natural Eco-System- It provides qualitative air, water, climate purification, disease control, pollination and prevention of decomposition and making of the stability in eco-system etc. are the natural benefits of bio-diversity.

2. Beneficial to Agriculture- There is a range of species which are beneficial to control the disease in lots of crops.

3. Benefits in Basic needs- Due to most of species we are able to acquire our basic needs like- a range of food production, clothing, residential facilities and shelter etc.

4. Health of Human Being- Our physical, mental, psychological and spiritual health depends on bio-diversity by food, nutrition and drugs. Primary health also depends on fresh food, water, air and all over wholesome environment.

5. In Business and Industry- We also obtain the rubber, oil, building material, water, paper, timber and fiber etc. for industrial purpose.

6. Cultural, Creative and Artistic Benefits- The different features of nature and environment inspires the artists of different fields to create the high quality paintings, classics, songs and music etc.

7. Different Hobbies and Aesthetic Morals on Basis of Bio-diversity- Various hobbies like gardening, caring of aquariums, collecting of butterflies, animals collections in zoo and plants in garden center depends directly on the assortment of species.

In this reference it has been disputed that the present rate of extinction is sufficient to eliminate most species on the Earth within 100 years. Most of species are being used by human being not for primary needs, but for greed. So it is necessary to identify the root causes of disappearance of several species, because if any one species disappeared from the circle of eco-system that will be hazardous to all over creation with humanity and his environment. Overpopulation, deforestation, pollution and global warming or climate change are the major factor to decrease biodiversity, but there are some other causes for above loss; those are given bellow:

1. Hunting for non-vegetarian food.
2. Hunting only for hobby.
3. Smuggling of rare organs of several species.
4. The uses of many plants and herbs in medicine and drugs.
5. Fishing rule of numerous nation which depend on these for food.
6. Illegal consumption without any government policy for individual benefits.
7. High consumption for industries and everlasting desire of mankind.

8. Another main imperative cause to diverse the bio-diversity is the spontaneous consumption of various species without any conservation policy.

After identifying the focal roots of spoiling biodiversity, we must know that this is the conflict between scientist, environmentalist, and sociologist etc. to protect bio-diversity in recent scenario; for the safe future of human race. Thus after the meaning, definition, a brief idea of bio-diversity and its benefits to mankind and causes to diverse it; we must know the techniques to defend this vital part of environment; let us concentrate on that.

There are two principles to protect anything;

1. Preservation
2. Conservation

The first one is not appropriate to defend species. But another one is the best policy to make a circle of eco-system. Most of scientist, environmentalist, sociologist and intellectual agree on this point that, conservation is the best ethical strategy to protect bio-diversity. But the question is that; how could we be successful in such policies without developing any ethical strategy in human behavior?

Consequently, there is a need to move on the ethics and to point out the strong philosophical strategy to conserve bio-diversity for healthy eco-system and environment. We may opt to develop a view of non-injuring of living beings, that is called *Ahimsa* (non-violence). It is an important ethical instruction of the Jainism; which originated in ancient India.

Part II

As stated earlier, Ahimsa primarily refers to "non-injury" without a moral implication, but later to non-violence to animals and then, to all beings. The idea emerges in the Hindu texts *Manu Smriti*, *Patnjal Yogasutra* and *Mahabharat* where *Ahimsa* is said to be valued by good conduct (*Karma*).Though meat-eating and slaughter of animals are criticized by some Hindu texts. Prominent figures of Indian spirituality such as Swami Vivekananda, Ramana Maharishi, and Swami Sivananda emphasized the importance of *Ahimsa.*

Mohandas Karamchand Gandhi applied ***Ahimsa*** to politics, by his non-violent ***Satyagrahas.***

Ahimsa is a rule of conduct that bars the killing or injuring of living beings. It is closely connected with the notion that all kinds of violence entail negative consequences. The thought of Ahimsa is applicable in Jainism for the conservation of species. So it is necessary to explore the ethical strategy of Ahimsa in Jainism. So let us focus our attention on it in the next part of the paper.

"***Ahimsa*** is Sanskrit term meaning to do no harm (to avoid the violence - *Ahimsa*). The beginning of the concept of Ahimsa is unknown, the earliest references to Ahimsa are found in the texts of Historical Vedic religion dated to 8th century B.C."[3]

Jainism defined the *Ahimsa* in the following words, "*Ahimsa nianam dintha swawabhuesu sanjamo*" i.e. Ahimsa is to restraint for every creature. *Ahimsa* is fully scientific, logical and intellectuality. *Ahimsa* is the basic need of good conduct of humanity."[4]

Thus, we can say that the thought of Ahimsa is the richest heritage of Jainism in comparison to all over religions and branches of Philosophy. Let us know the Ahimsa as the pertinent part of Jainism.

Non-violence: the Core Moral Ideal of *Jainism*

In Jainism, non-violence is not limited to refraining from mental, verbal and physical injury to human beings. It encompasses abstaining from injury to all living beings - all animals and plants. "The ancient Jain scripture, Acharang Sutra (about 4th century B.C.) presents a highly sophisticated discussion on non-violence. It states that one should not cause injury to any living being, including the tiniest creatures and plants. All life depends on nature for survival. Thus disturbing the ecological balance by wasting natural resources and polluting water and air also constitutes violence. Acharya Umaswati, in his celebrated work, Tattvarth Sutra, defines violence as the obstruction of life processes through activities of body, speech and mind tainted with negligence."[5]

There are two types of violence: physical violence and mental violence. Obstruction of or injury to physical life processes is physical violence and bringing about untoward thoughts and feelings constitutes mental violence. According to the ancient literature of Jainism, violence has been classified as follows:

The First one is projected violence ***(Sankalpi Himsa)***, which is intentional killing or hurting of self and of others. Second is subsistence-related violence ***(Aarambhi Himsa)***, which is the violence, involved in cooking, cleaning, etc. Third is occupational violence (***Udyogi Himsa***), which is the violence, involved in pursuing agriculture, industry, business or profession. The fourth and last type of violence is unfavorable- violence (***Virodhi Himsa***), which is involved in dealing with undesirable elements of society. It is the violence for one's protection from one's adversary.

Dr. S. Radhakrishnan describes the Ahimsa in Jain religion in the following words, "The chief feature of Jainism is Ahimsa, or respect for and abstinence from everything that has life. The scrupulous enforcement of this rule has let too many practices which come in for chief sneering at the hands of unsympathetic students. Lest any life be destroyed some Jains sweep the ground as they go. Walk veiled for fear of inhaling a living organism, strain water and reject even honey."[6]

Jainism advocates that injury to others regularly involves injury to the life processes of self. When we aim to destruct or harm others, we have passions such as anger, pride, deception and greed. Thus we always commit violence of the self in the process. "It is true that Ahimsa in the strict sense can not be practiced. The Mahabharat says that the world is filled with creatures which can not be seen by the eye, though inferred by logic. When we move our eyelids, there limbs break and fall. The Bhagwat Purana declares that the life is the life of life. When these simple truths are forgotten life becomes well-nigh impossible. A morbid fear or injuring perchance any life anywhere governs the conduct of the orthodox Jains."[7]

In this reference Jain thinkers also felt that it is not possible to avoid violence completely. No matter how conscientious we are, we commit some violence in our daily activities. We must avoid willful, intentional violence and minimize other kinds of violence as much as possible. There are some interesting essentials in the ethics of Jainism which could play an important role in field of conservation of bio-diversity, here we should point out those favorable point.

Contrasting factor is that, Jains agree with Hindus that violence in self-defense can be justified and they agree that a soldier who kills enemies in war is doing a rightful duty. Jain communities accepted the use of military power for their defense, and there were Jain monarchs, military commanders, and soldiers. Some Jains withdraw from farming because it inescapably entails unintentional killing or injuring of many small animals, such as worms and insects, but agriculture is not forbidden in general and there are Jain farmers. Jainism emphasizes vegetarianism and bans hunting and ritual sacrifice. Jains go out of their way so as not to hurt even small insects and other minuscule animals and make considerable efforts not to injure plants in everyday life as far as possible. In accordance to this policy, eating of some foods, whose cultivation harms small insects and worms as well as agriculture itself, is to be abstained from.

After the discussion of bio-diversity and the ethics of Ahimsa in Jainism, now we are in position that we can examine how ahimsa can play an important role in field of the conservation of species, for maintaining of bio-diversity, for perfect eco-system. So, now as a conclusion, we shall try to examine that how Ahimsa could be established as a maintaining and balancing strategy for flourished bio-diversity and prosperous eco-system, to control the degradation of environment.

III Part

The rapid development of science and technology with everlasting desires is responsible for the luxurious and prosperous worldly life, but we know well that it is also the key factor to diverse the environment. And in the present condition of the major degradation of environment is so critical that we are struggling for our own existence. Usually all the religions and branches of Philosophy guide for a disciplined life to man, but the selfishness and greedy temperament of man threat himself. Consequently there is a need to search and turn towards ethical strategy for the protection of environmental component, not only for other species but ourselves too. Here it is necessary to know that the present ethical strategy of Jainism is more rich and helpful for the prosperous bio-diversity. We should know that how the cherished ethics of Jainism afford a perfect way to develop the discipline in our life for the conservation of species for prosperous biodiversity in term of eco-system. Consequently now we are trying to present point wise strategy of Ahimsa, for better biodiversity.

1. *Ahimsa* as a controlling tool for the selfish and greedy attitude of man—The pertinent part of the ethics of Jainism is Ahimsa (non-violence), which is most applicable in field of environment for biodiversity. We know very well that we are devastating several species not for our basic needs, but only for our greed or pursuit.

The variety of plants and animals based foods, cloths, various hobbies, smuggling of several organs of rare species are the example of our greed in contemporary scenario. We kill the animals or plants cruelly, only for our baseless desire. As a result we disturb the chain of nature, even if it is necessary to maintain the balance. The ethics of Jainism guides us to discipline our food, other requirements, conduct and vision towards life. The Jain Thirthnkaras permit the food, other requirements and basic needs to make us live only, but not for our nonsense worldly desires. While we know well that bio-diversity is an essential part of eco-system, for healthy environment. One thing, which is peculiar in Jainism, that is to guide a proper way for every type of person, either that is domestics or monks. The *Jainism* makes a perfect guideline to make the disciplined lifestyle of person that is called *vrata.* Jains have described two types-*Anuvrata* for domestic person and *Mahavrata* for monks. In the practice of *Ahimsa,* the necessities are less rigorous for the lay persons who have undertaken *Anuvrata* (Lesser pledges) than for the monks and nuns who are bound by *Mahavrata* (Great pledges).

Hence, we should develop a policy to conserve bio-diversity by applying the Ahimsa in our realistic life to persist with *Vrata* of Jainism.

2. Way of disciplined life for conservation of species - We see that there is a deep understanding of the conservation oriented thought and disciplined life style in Jainism for the conservation of bio-diversity in term of healthy and balanced environment. According to the Jain philosophers, "The visualization, character, conduct and food etc. should be right (*samyak*) and non-violent. The *Jain Tirthnkaras* have began their spiritual practice (*sadhna*) from conservation of environment. *Rishabhdeva* taught the art of living for the protection of agriculture and forest. *Neminath* proved the luxurious life of man as nonsense in comparison to lives of animals and birds. He saved the liberty of creature by his sacrifice. *Parshvanath* did not permit the ritual sacrifice. *Mahaveer* leads the life at five level, where the violence and desire would be finished"[8]

3. All life forms are said to deserve full protection - However, hypothetically, all life forms are said to deserve full protection from all kinds of injury, *Jains* confess that this ideal cannot be completely applied in practice. Thus, they distinguish a ranking of life. For the vital beings has one sense to five senses. The creature with more senses cares about its protection more then one to four senses. Among the five-sensed beings, the rational ones (humans) are most strongly protected by Jain *Ahimsa*.

4. Scheme of conservation - There is an excellent scheme of conservation in the thought of *Mahaveer*. He has tried to protect the earth, water, fire, air, plants, insects, animals, birds and man ; to declared religion in the protection of *Shatkaya (Jiva)*. Thus he said, *"Bhitti me savva bhuvesha, Varem majjam ma kenai"* i.e. I am friendly for all creatures and have not enemy for any creature. Restraint, practice of religion, protection of environment is not possible to avoid this sutra. How painful that the religious person spread pollution.[9]

The Jain concept of ahimsa is characterized by several aspects. It does not make any exception for ritual sacrifices and professional hunters. Killing of animals for food is absolutely ruled out. The above instruction of *Jainism* is applicable in present scenario, when we are facing the problem of the destruction of bio-diversity as the cause of disturbance of environment. We strongly ruled out from our desire full conduct and greedy consumption. This is so because if we do not get aware even now then we shall be responsible for our ruin, due to the destruction of bio-diversity with eco-system. Now we could point out some facts in favor of eating only vegetarian food as the *Ahimsa* of *Jainism.*

5. The scientific study does not permit the Non-vegetarian food which is the major feature of Jain's concept of *Ahimsa*- Hunting for non-vegetarian food and hobby should be strictly restricted. The basic reason, why the science restricts non-vegetarian is that the anatomy of human's gastro-intestinal track is not made as carnivores, which can digest non-vegetarian food with an ease. Another reason is that non-vegetarian food contains cholesterol in high quantity that causes heart diseases. Further more a study says when the victim animal is killed some distress hormones are produced in its body, which arrive and influence the consumers. Although there is a long list of reasons to restrict non-vegetarian food, but one more reason we should point out here. That is bio-amplification, in which the concentration of any pesticide is increased in order of increasing consumer level. If we be the consumer of second level i.e. vegetarian then we acquire lower amount of pesticide in comparison of non-vegetarian (third level consumer). Thus we can say that non-vegetarian food is not harmful for the destruction of species victim animal but also for ourselves.

6. The similarity of rules for plants - The rule of *Ahimsa* is similarly able to raring for all creatures. Except above, *Jains* also make considerable efforts not to injure plants in everyday life as far as possible. Though they admit that plants must be destroyed for the sake of food, they accept such violence only in as much as it is requisite for human survival, and there are special instructions for preventing unnecessary violence against plants. *Jains* go out of their way so as not to injure even small insects and other microscopic animals. In their view, injury caused by carelessness is like injury caused by deliberate action. Eating honey is strictly outlawed, as it would amount to violence against the bees.

As a conclusion we can say that, when we change our conduct, then even violent animals are also changed in their aggressive behavior. "Indeed, it is believed that even animals of prey loss their tendencies to kill there natural victims, when they are near search *Yogies* and saints. Pictures are seen where tigers and their natural prey deer as well as cows and other such animals, which also may serve as their food, are seen staying and even playing together in a very friendly manner. Such a depiction of *Mahavira*, the last, 24th *Tirthankara* of Jainas is popularly displayed and similar pictures of other saints."[8] So it is necessary to modify ourselves to non-violent conduct, to conserve the numerous species, which is the first condition of the healthy eco-system. So it should be developed in our daily routine to follow the strategy of *Ahimsa* according to *Jain* ethics, for the protection of every creature of universe and well being of mankind with the environmental arrangement.

References

1. Source–www.wikipedia.org, p. 3.
2. *Ibid.*, p. 4.
3. Source- www.wikipedia.org, p. 1.
4. Vinod Kumari, Issues in Applied Ethics, Satyam publishing house, N-3/25, Mohan Garden, New Delhi, 2009, p. 135.
5. Source- www.wikipedia.org., p. 5.
6. Dr. S. Radhakrishnan, Indian Philosophy Vol. I, Rajpal & Sons, Kashmiri gate, New Delhi, 2004, p. 327.
7. *Ibid.*
8. Vinod Kumari, Issues in Applied Ethics, Satyam publishing house, N-3/25, Mohan Garden, New Delhi, 2009, p. 136.
9. *Ibid.*
10. Dr. P.V. Karmbelkar, Patnjal Yoga Sutras, Kaivalyadham, Lonavala, Maharastra, 2002, p. 264.

CONCLUSIONS

Two Alternatives for Human Freedom and Environmental Concerns

In the concluding part of this book, I would like to reflect upon the two strategies to maintain a balance between individual freedom and environmental concerns i.e. spiritually inclined moral instruction and pragmatic assessment of human nature and environmental concern, and practical strategies formulated on the basis of experience of day to day life.

All thc moral instructions and spiritual deliberations suggest the enhancement of individual consciousness and accept the equality in terms of right to live and enjoy the freedom to live life in a secured manner with dignity. Prof. JP Shukla, the ex-vice-chancellor of RDVV, Jabalpur M.P., suggested the question of human freedom and environmental concern involves multi-dimensional problems and multi-layered remedies. The enhancement of individual consciousness will enable human beings to address this complex problem in holistic manner. A person with enhanced level of consciousness always acknowledges his responsibilities. He accepts his duties prior to his right. It is equally true to his approach and attitude towards environment, be it conservation or protection of natural entities for the interest of human being, or be it for the respect of nature as such. In both the cases, a person with enhanced consciousness will never cause damage to environment. At the sametime, he visualizes his freedom with reference to the care and concern he has for other human beings and non-human beings. Human being possesses both divine and demon attitude. He should overcome the demon's longing for the worldly acquisition. Rather he should opt for the divine desire of love, care and concern. For this purpose, the de-conditioning of negative temperament and attitude is required and this requirement could be fulfilled through practicing the path of any of spiritual sects or constant self introspection of behavior and wider implications. For a wider interest of human beings and other cosmic entities the flexibility of interest and attitude is the first condition. This is so because, unless and until we do overcome our temporarily temptations, it would be almost impossible to realize the self and enhance its level of consciousness through which the wider interest of freedom and environmental concerns could be persuaded. Professor Shukla suggested that the stage of Nirvan is meant to acquire the level of consciousness to see the all human and non-human beings at the equal footing and be careful to all. And, that is the best way to address the question of human freedom and care for the environment.

Another approach reflects the pragmatic way for common people to address both the aspects of development and environment. Adhering to this opinion, Prof. SK Singh, acclaimed scholar of Physics and at present the Vice chancellor of HNB Garhwal University, holds that Freedom in the absolute sense is nothing except a kind of idealism. In fact, human nature is complex one. To understand this complex notion of human beings, we should focus our attention on the process of the freedom of thinking and knowledge. The observation of the surroundings exposes two extremely contradictory subjective and objective states of freedom. In such scenario revised thinking to have objective approach to strike a balance is required. For example the particles in box and outside of box have changed notion of freedom of that particular particles. Barriers or boundaries change the scenario and meaning of freedom and balance. For the purpose of saving environment, the barriers made by religion, society and nature should be adhered and respected. Crossing the barriers is neither good for human beings nor environment. Thus one should be within the limits and introspective of his own behavior. The best way to live with nature could be the way a bee lives which extracts the needful elements from the flowers without damaging a single aspect of it. Thus we may learn from nature the ways to save the nature. This could be most practical approach.

A review of both the approaches reveals the fact that they are different only in approach, but they are not contradictory. Rather they are complimentary to each-other in the sense that both are trying to address the question how to modify the human behavior in favor of environment and nature. One is addressing the problem from the higher level of consciousness and traveling to grass root levels of problems. The other one is trying to address the problem from root level and trying to reach to the higher level of consciousness to modify the human behavior. Both the way objective is to save environment with its dignity and address the notion of human freedom with reference to genuine need, but never promote the greed of particular at the cost of general damage of the nature and environment and disturb the balance of nature.

INDEX

D

E

K

L

M

N